Raven Blair Davis
presents

Careers *from the*

Kitchen Table

BONUS
INCLUDES OVER
8 HOURS WORTH
OF DOWNLOADABLE
AUDIOS!

2nd Edition
NATIONAL
HOME BUSINESS
DIRECTORY

Insider Secrets to Starting & Running a Successful
Home-Based Business, Even During a Recession

Featuring Interviews With:

Kim Kiyosaki, Michael Senoff, Khaliq Glover,
Diana Nightingale, Brian Tracy, and Fran Harris

PLUS Over 50 Inspiring Business Success Stories!

Careers from the Kitchen Table National Home Business Directory 2nd Edition

Interior formatting and design: Peggy Knudson
Cover Graphic Design: Darnell Brown

First Printing January 2012

ISBM 978-1-61364-908-4

Library of Congress Cataloguing-in-Publication Data
Blair Davis, Raven

Careers from the Kitchen Table National Home Business Directory 2nd Edition

Table of Contents

Dedication

Our second edition is again dedicated to all those who purchased this book having lost their jobs but not their hope or desire for a better tomorrow. Those who still believe in their dreams and are determined to create a better lifestyle for them and their family despite setbacks or challenges they face. For the entrepreneurs and business professionals who are choosing to not settle for survival during these difficult economic times but instead are determined to "thrive."

I also want to dedicate this book to the many contributing authors who helped make this book possible with their amazing stories they shared from their hearts. I especially want to thank the incredible featured experts I was blessed to interview on my show that gave up time from their busy schedule to come on *Careers From The Kitchen Table* radio show and share their insider secrets, strategies and formulas for success freely with the listeners. Their selflessness has assisted hundreds of thousands worldwide who have tuned into the show the past three years. Thank you so much for being a blessing to us all.

Thanks to my family and close friends who always encouraged me along the way and especially to my DYNAMIC and Talented team Peggy and Darnell. Thank you for all the support, long hours and hard work you contributed to the creation and success of this book. I am very proud of the outcome and have no doubt *Careers From The Kitchen Table Home Business Directory* will be responsible for changing many lives, giving those who lost hope the will and desire to hope again; and assist those struggling in their business with tips and strategies to grow their business more effectively from the stories and insider secrets they read along the way. Thank you all so much. This book could not have been possible without you.

Sincerely,

Raven

Introduction

What Started as an Idea Turned Into a Dream Come True with Only the Sky as the Limit: *The Life & Future of Careers from the Kitchen Table*

It's hard to believe another year has passed. Our first edition of *Careers from the Kitchen Table Home Business Directory* was well received and we heard from so many on how it gave them the courage to pursue their dreams of starting their own business.

For those of you just learning about this publication, we congratulate you on taking a step to make a difference in your life. By purchasing Careers from the Kitchen Table Home Business Directory, you've just proven to yourself that you can do exactly what this book was written to help people do.

Remember your work has just begun. Being an entrepreneur requires much more than buying a book and reading it. Be sure to apply what you are reading and get ready to work hard.

For those of you looking for connections or solutions; be sure to turn to our contributors for both. Our contributors have many services and products to meet your needs.

You've made a great move in purchasing this book!

The mission of Careers from the Kitchen Table Radio Show and this Home Business Directory has and will always be to let people just like you know:

- Whatever you do now in your job, or have a passion to do – it can be turned into a profitable and fulfilling business and do it without hype and empty promises.

- There is a ton of information out there to motivate and inspire you, and while we do that too we don't just stop there. Careers from the Kitchen Table offers you the missing link by also telling you what you NEED to be successful and giving you the opportunity to shine just like the big dogs do.

- We only put authentic people in front of you who can keep it fresh, have a customer service oriented business and base not only their business, but their lives on ethical choices. This is something that will never change at Careers from the Kitchen Table – not even when the economy has bounced back and is up and running again (and it will be).

- We are here to help you WAKE UP and create your own Plan B, instead of hoping, praying and relying on someone else to create it for you. As much as we may not want to think about it, the reality is thousands of people's Plan A, which they were certain, would always be there for them, and has been taken away in this downturned economy. So, let's get proactive and create a Plan B that can easily be turned into your first choice should it become necessary.

The truth of the matter is, owning your own business isn't a free or easy ride full of roses and sunny skies all the time. It takes hard work, determination and dedication among other things, but hopefully with the help of the excerpts of guru interviews and stories included in this book, you'll see that not only is it possible to create the life and business you've always dreamed of, but others have been there before you and are willing to help you along the way and make your journey a little bit easier. The key is not just reading this book – you must TAKE ACTION and APPLY the things you learn to your own business, which is why we've included sections throughout the book for notes. Jot down the steps you want to take as you're reading through the interview excerpts and stories.

We trust you will enjoy the many transcripts, stories and incredible recipes that await you!

Enjoy!

ARE YOU READY TO GET STARTED? GREAT! LET'S GET COOKIN! MEET OUR GROUP OF INSPIRING MENTORS, MASTERS AND AUTHORS!

Brian Tracy

Diana Nightingale

Fran Harris

Khaliq Glover

Kim Kiyosaki

Mark Thompson

Michael Senoff

Alanna Levenson

Anita P. Kirkman

Anne Duffy

Anne Gordon

Annie Kirschenmann

Arris Charles

Ashley Dias

Bonnie Terry

Carmen Chandler

Carol Mazur

Chris Barnett

Christal Mercier

Christina Suter

Deb Scott

Deborah Bishop

Fred Simkovsky

JJ Frederickson

Jean Jones

Jeff Tollefson

Joan Day-Gilbert

Judy Winslow

Kathryn Reeves

Keiko Hsu

Kelly Poelker

Khatira Aboulfatova

Kim L. Miles

Kimberley Borgens

Kristen L. Baker

Kristi Pavlik

LaTricia Smith

Leslie Cunningham

Linda Adams

Lisabeth Saunders Medlock

Lorraine Edey

Lynn Doxon

Lynn Hidy

Martha Lask

Melanie McGhee

Michelle Peavy

Misa Leonessa Garavaglia

Nancy Alert

Patricia Clason

Rayna Bergerman

Sandra Tucker Jones

Saskia Jennings-de Quaasteniet

Sheila McClain

Sherry Prindle

Susan Bock

Tami Gulland

Tanya Jones MD

Timi Gleason

Tina Forsyth

Tom 2 tall Cunningham

Dr. Venus Opal Reese

Vicki Garcia

Yvonne Silver

Careers from the Kitchen Table Home Business Directory Second Edition

Raven
INTERNATIONAL

World's leading 24/7 positive programming network
listenwhile you work http://www.amazingwomenofpower.com

Enjoy these excerpts and audios from previous interviews heard on
CNN 650, CBS Talk 650, 1320 WRAL, 1270 KLAV

Be sure to also visit
www.careersfromthekitchentable.com/audios
to get more downloadable audio interviews!

And now….

Raven Grills
The Gurus

Brian Tracy

Speaker, Author, Coach and Consultant

and Mark Thompson

Coach, Speaker, Author and Angel Investor

For the last 3 decades Brian Tracy has devoted his life to helping people just like you (business owners) attain personal and business success.

Not just success, but the success key itself. Once you insert this key into your business you will unlock a whole world of profitability missed by many.

Together, with my good friend Mark Thompson, we have put together, what I think you will find, a most compelling guide to your future business success.

I have consulted for more than 1,000 companies and addressed more than 5,000,000 people in 5,000 talks and seminars throughout the US, Canada and 53 other countries worldwide.

Prior to founding my company, Brian Tracy International, I was the Chief Operating Officer of a $265 million dollar development company. I've ranged successful careers in sales and marketing, investments, real estate development and syndication, importation, distribution and management consulting.

I don't tell you all of this to brag, I want you to know that I am in a qualified position to teach you about building a successful business.

Mark Thompson is a world-renowned executive coach and an expert on innovation and customer engagement. He is an active angel investor in over 20 industries and author of the best-selling business book, Success Built to Last.

Former Chief Communications Officer for Charles Schwab & Co with five million client accounts with over $800 billion in client assets, he also served as Senior Vice President of the Schwab Client Experience.

Later, as Executive Producer of Schwab.com, he created and hosted the Charles Schwab Leadership Series with dozens of great innovators, from Warren Buffett to Steve Jobs.

Mark is a rare speaker who has been a senior corporate executive, entrepreneur, business school coach, board member of a dozen Fortune 500 firms and Forbes called him "a venture investor with the 'Midas' touch."

Raven Blair Davis: Welcome to America's hottest home business show that everyone's talking about, Careers from the Kitchen Table. The show that teaches how to cook without the cooking, giving you my friends some good old home recipes for success. Again we appreciate you coming by and wow look at this, you brought a friend this time and it's a good thing you did because of the guest we have on today.

My name is Raven Blair Davis, aka, Raven The Talk Show Maven and you're looking to go from that hectic highway to the – oh so dreaded nice, nice commuted hallways. That's the way you want to grow your business. You want to go from your bedroom to the shower and from the shower to your office or if you like to do like I do, from your kitchen table, that's what this show is all about. But you know it doesn't do you any good if you just listen and you don't take action so I'm gonna encourage you, if you haven't got anything to write with, go right now and grab something to write with so you can take some notes. Remember, our show is brought to you each week by sipping healthy coffee is simple, is easy, is oh so healthy and Coffeelicious how about that?

If you're standing, sit down, if you're sitting, stand up because the two gentlemen that I am bringing on have just released a book. It's called "Now Build Great a Business," seven ways to maximize your profits in any market. These gentlemen are extraordinary authors. They're legendary experts and exceptional leaders, their names, Mark Thompson and Brian Tracy. Didn't I tell you this was an amazing show? I'm going to share just a couple of the quotes that thought leaders like Tony Robbins gave these two on this magnificent book. They poured their love, passion and heart lessons into Now Build a Great Business. It is a book that will challenge your assumptions and transform your work.

This is your call to action to build a great business. Perfectly in line with what we share with you every week. It's time for you to move your business despite the economic times that we're having. Jack Canfield goes on to say "do you want to know the secret to building that great business? This is the most important book you can read." Brian Tracy and Mark Thompson go straight to the heart of what it takes and how to do it and then there's so many but I want to share one more by Harvey Mackay and it says "Entrepreneurs alert: now build a great business is the book you've been waiting for." Mark Thompson and Brian Tracy explained the seven keys to business success with inspiring examples and solid advice. We've got them here. They're live and they're here to talk about their seven principles for sustaining business success. Become a great leader, develop a great business plan, surround yourself with great people, offer great product or service, design a great marketing plan – wow, let's bring them on.

First let me tell you a little bit about Mark Thompson. He's an executive coach, leadership adviser and investor in growing businesses; he's the co-author of the international best seller "Success Built to Last" based on his broadcast interviews with hundreds of world leaders from Warren Buffet to the Dalai Lama.

This man is incredible Brian Tracy, a top business and motivational speaker, consultant and bestselling author, he's the chairman and CEO of Brian Tracy International, a company specializing in individual career and organizational development as well as the president of Business Growth Strategies, I know you've heard of this man. I could go on and on. This is a dream come true interview. Mark Thompson, Brian Tracy welcome to Careers from the Kitchen Table. I'm so thrilled to have you on the show.

Brian: Well thank you, it's a delight and what everybody should realize is it takes just as much time to have a mediocre business, to fail and to worry about money all your life as it does to be successful and just a matter of how you use your time in which you're doing it.

Raven Blair Davis: Absolutely, I agree with that. We've got to give it all we can give. Let me start off by asking you how did you two – the world's foremost authorities on success come together as co-authors? What glued you together?

Brian: Go ahead Mark.

Mark: We've had the great pleasure working with each other for the last two years on this book. We'd been introduced by mutual friends in the circles that we're in and we were so excited because of the great experience that Brian had and the experience I've had as entrepreneur, wanting now to really give back. We want to find seven ways that you can build a profitable business, make your dream happen and so we decided we'd create Now Build a Great Business because this is a time when people can take advantage of this economic cycle and start to realize their dreams and we wanted to give you a tactical plan, a strategy so that you could actually build a great business today.

Raven Blair Davis: I love the word strategy Mark, that's what it's about. You can read and you can be motivated and empowered but now that we need some specific strategies, we need a system, something that's gonna take us to our goal.

Brian: Absolutely. The three words that every business owner has to think about everyday are *competition, competition, competition*. The first job of the business owner is to get a customer. The second job is to get a customer. The third job is to get a customer. And business owners have to be really, really focused on that primary result. Our studies show that business owners will say that sales and marketing is the most important part of their business and on average they spend about 11% of their time on sales and marketing and all the rest is playing with the computer and phoning people and talking to their friends and having coffee and they don't even realize it. It's called invisible time wastage. The reason people do not succeed in their business is because they're not spending 80% of their time getting customers.

Raven Blair Davis: How much % of the time?

Brian: About 11% of the time is actually getting customers.

Raven Blair Davis: Wow.

Brian: Now, what I say to business owners is that your job is to ask people for money. When you get up in the morning, the first thing you do is say 'who am I gonna ask for money today?' and you get there as fast as you possibly can and start asking for money at 8 o'clock. If you're not asking for money, you're not working. You're officially unemployed. You're a member of the statistics and you have no future in your business.

Raven Blair Davis: We're just twiddling and doing all this non income producing stuff.

Brian: That's right and it's very easy to slip into it. So what do we say, it's chapter one, become a great leader and a leader is a person who clearly defines what the individual and other people have to do right now today to drive business, to make sales and generate revenues and then focus on that result all day long. And in every single business there's a key result that the leader is responsible for and the leader's job is to pick that and do only that until it's done well.

Mark: That's being clear about how to serve a customer and solve their problem. I mean this is exactly what you did Raven with your business. You came out of the kitchen and you created a forum for people to talk about how they can realize the dreams that they have and turn those into businesses and we really wanted to give you seven clear steps. A road map that would allow a person to be able to become a better leader, make that plan happen and find solutions for customers and it's perhaps the most critical thing you can do right now.

Raven Blair Davis: Absolutely and I received your book a few days ago and I'd been looking at it, reviewing, and I love it because you guys are so detailed in what you do. Again it's not a fluff book. This is an action taking book so I applaud you and thank you so much for bringing this to use because we need this. Now, Brian I like when you said we have to ask for the money and go for the fastest way to cash and I want our listeners to realize that if you don't ask, you're certainly not gonna get.

Brian: Right.

Raven Blair Davis: Mark, let's get into a little bit more about why you feel that this is a great time to build your business?

Mark: Well you know it's amazing. You think about the economy in the US right now and when we look back over the history of the greatest companies, almost all of them and including the businesses that Brian and I personally have been engaged with, started in the worst possible times. What appeared to be the stagflation of the 70's or difficult cycles and what really is going on there is it's during those times that customers are abandoned. They really need your attention. They need your TLC. They need your love and support and if you could find out how to serve them when they're being abandoned by your competitors, you can really differentiate yourself. You can really come to the party with the better – what we hope they say is a great service or a great product. It's also a time when there's less noise in terms of competition in the air waves if you want to buy advertising and marketing, if you want to be able to recruit people to your dream and find people who might be available, this would be the time when you can recruit the best and the brightest to come see you shoulder to shoulder and help you build this dream. It's a time when you can really carve out the resources that you need to build that plan and listen carefully and it gets appreciated more by the customer because it's used to not getting this kind of attention what they got in the past. It's really remarkable when you look at whether its Google or ESPN or you talk about companies that have been created and lasted year in and year out. These are the ones that often started when the market seemed to be the least likely to accept a new business.

Raven Blair Davis: A lot of that I would imagine Brian is what we believe in. Napoleon Hill said what a mind of a man can conceive and believe, they will achieve, so mindset is important and it does play a part in this.

Brian: Yes absolutely.

Raven Blair Davis: Before we get into the nuts and bolts of building one, how do you define a great business and either one of you can take a stab at this one.

Brian: Go ahead Mark.

Mark: A great business in my belief system is one in fact – and this is really the premise that we started with. We thought "what does it take" for a person who's a customer to step out of your office or out of your establishment or to receive your product and say "this is a great product." It's actually providing the kind of quality that I was looking for. It's solving the problem that I had. It's making it possible for me to be able to save money or do better or perform at a higher rate' or as Brian would say in a sense it's free because you've been able to cover your cost and it's something that's going to be producing a valuable result in excess of what you paid for it. So, that's what a great business is.

Raven Blair Davis: I like that. So how big of a part Brian is it for us to get creative and step out of the box now? Is that something we should be doing or staying away from?

Brian: Well, remember you have to love your product or service or you'll never be able to sell it effectively. You have to use it yourself. Everybody in your company has to use it. You have to have sell it to your mother and father and brother and best friend so that's the starting point. Second of all, you have to compare yourself. Everything is comparison against competitors. What do you have to do to make your product better? I'll give you a very simple example. A poor boy, orphan going to college found that when he delivered pizzas, he was trying to make money deliver pizzas, the people complained because it took so long. It took an hour after they place the order for the pizza to be delivered and he came up with an insight. The insight was that when people order a pizza, they're already hungry therefore they value speed over quality and he went on to start Domino's pizza, sold 8,000 units and became one of the richest man in the world with one insight which is that when people order something, speed is more important than anything else in some cases. Zippos.com has done the same thing. When people order shoes, they want them as soon as possible. They look forward to wearing them so they deliver them overnight and went from zero to a billion dollars in nine years.

Raven Blair Davis: They've given them that speedy service and a lot of people nowadays – I'm sure you two would agree, they're flipping on the customer service end and that's the main thing we shouldn't be dropping the ball on.

Brian: Yup, very important.

Raven Blair Davis: Is becoming a great business leader really within reach of anyone and if so, what are of the other qualities that are most critical for aspiring business leaders that are listening to the show right now to learn and develop?

Mark: Well leadership we think is something that you do and choose to do. It maybe that you're born a leader but if so few people are, it may not make a difference. The truth is we all have to step up and choose to lead and the way we do that is we have to be a person of integrity who Brian says wants to use this product or this service and solve a problem for a customer or community or a cause that you have to be a person that is willing to learn. It's interesting, one thing that distinguished all the best practices we saw, the great leaders that Brian and I spoke with, was the fact that the best always wanted to get better. They're always willing to learn. They're always willing to ask why are we doing this, am I doing the work that the leader needs to be doing, how can I empower others and make sure that they're more effective, how can I make sure that I can second guess what I've been doing in such a way that's constructive and I could say 'hey if I shut everything down today, what would I pick up and do tomorrow' and be able to be more effective in serving customers. So it's a constant process. It's a process that's learned – I think a lot of people, when they realized that the purpose of their business is to serve customers or a community or a cause or all of the above, it's the cause that has the charisma. They don't have to necessarily worry about being a leader themselves.

What they have to do is take the responsibility of being a leader and serve that market or serve those customers in a way that's responsible, valued in integrity.

Raven Blair Davis: I like that; it's the cause that's the charisma.

Mark: Yeah, indeed. Just the cause because sometimes some people when they're starting out saying 'I'm not sure but I'm ready to call myself a leader' I found that there were a number of people who said that but the truth of the matter is you are a leader by the way you behave and the way you decide to grow and the way you decide to serve and contribute.

Raven Blair Davis: Good point. Let's take a break now.

Raven Blair Davis: Welcome back everyone to Careers from the Kitchen Table, we are visiting with Mark Thompson and Brian Tracy. Mark had to go but we still have Brian Tracy here and if you don't know Brian Tracy I don't know what world you've been on. Again he's a top business and motivational speaker, consultant and bestselling author. He and Mark collaborated on this really fantastic book. It's called "Now Build a Great Business, Seven Ways to Maximize Your Profits in Any Market." Welcome back Brian, we are so thrilled to have you.

Brian: Well, thank you.

Raven Blair Davis: Now, let's go ahead and talk about your book "Now Build a Great Business, Seven Ways to Maximize Your Profits in Any Market" because you place high priority on developing a great business plan. How can the process of planning help make a business stronger even if business doesn't always go according to plan? As far as you know, it doesn't always go according to plan.

Brian: Well, if we were to ask "what is the most important work that a business owner does," the answer is thinking and thinking clearly about your business is the determining factor between success and failure. Every mistake you'll ever make, you'll say 'if I only thought about that or gotten a little bit more information I wouldn't have made that mistake' planning on paper. I say think on paper. When you think it, ink it. Write it down. There's a connection between the head and the hand that is absolutely miraculous so write it down and planning, we provide an outline or structure for this with – when you purchase the book, there are several thousand dollars' worth of forms, videos, advise, guidance and surveys that you can use that are on a special website that you have access to when you buy the book so it's a fabulous deal.

You have to think through who is my customer, why does my customer buy, what does my customer consider value, when do they buy, where do they buy, who else do they buy from, what is my competitive advantage and so on so that's the starting point before your start the business. I worked with a very successful business man – started from nothing and now is very wealthy and he spent six months evaluating the new business, he was determined to get into –

at the end of six months after he'd done his planning, he concluded that this was not a good business to go into and he didn't go into it and he saved himself an enormous amount of money because he did the planning. The second thing is where are my customers going to come from? How am I going to reach them? What appeals will I use? Why would people buy my product rather than somebody else's and how am I going to get to my customers and get them to buy? How am I going to produce my product or service and get it to them in a time effective way? What are my costs going to be at every stage of the deal? How much am I going to make at the end of the day? These are all things – what technology I need, what people I need, what finances I need, packaging, resources, offices, you need to think this things through and write them down because if you don't think them through, they will come up and bite you in the bum. Later you'll say 'I didn't even think about that.' I knew a company that went broke because they did not calculate into their business deliver charges. From the manufacturer to their place and from their place to the customer – very competitive business, they went broke because the delivery charges bankrupted them and they hadn't even thought about that because they didn't write down the plan.

Raven Blair Davis: You're saying write down even the smallest things.

Brian: You have to think it through. Now, here's the wonderful thing. Every minute you spend, every minute every dollar you spend in planning will save you 10 minutes and 10 dollars when you implement the plan.

Raven Blair Davis: Wow.

Brian: Save you a fortune. All big businesses get big because they plan. All little businesses go broke because they don't plan so that's chapter number two, develop a good business plan. It's like planning a vacation or a party or a trip. Sit down and plan it out. You just don't do it by random. You wouldn't even have a barbecue at your home on Saturday without thinking through who's going to be there, how much food will you need, how many plates, chairs – you'll plan a party but people will not plan their business.

Raven Blair Davis: That is so true. We plan for summer vacations, football parties but like you said, we sometimes will just sit down and we'll start going at it without a plan and if we don't have a plan, we don't have a roadmap and that's why we're all over the place.

Brian: Yes, exactly.

Raven Blair Davis: Would you share a few tips on techniques that will ease the challenges – because you spoke about finding people. So, finding those great people and keeping them motivated. What kinds of techniques can you gives us or offer us that will assist us in that area?

Brian: Well first of all unless you're going to be poor and just barely making a little living all your life, you cannot grow unless you can attract good people. Here's the rule. Good people are free. Poor people are very expensive. Good people are free and they are free plus the profit. The only time you hire a person is when they contribute more in profit bottom line than they cost, if they don't, you don't hire them. So if have a good person, they'll not only pay for themselves but they'll contribute a profit so they'll actually earn more than they cost so that's why big companies can hire thousands of people because they do it properly and every additional person adds profit to the company. Now, when the tide goes out and the economy goes down, they have to lay off people until they reach the point where every person is still contributing more than they cost. That's the basic understanding of the job.

Second thing is you take a piece of paper and you think for this job, who would be the perfect person? If there was a perfect person factory and you could send an order to the factory and they would send you back the perfect person to walk in the door, how would you describe that perfect person on paper and fill out your order. Then, you review that, every time you talk to a person, to make sure that this person has the most important qualities on your list. Proven experience, small companies never hire a person that expects to train them. They hire people who are already trained and ready to start day one. That's very important. So when a person comes in, the first thing you ask is where and when have you done this job successfully in the past? That's about 80% of the hiring. Then what is your education, background, experience and so on but the most important thing is can they do the job? Do they have proven experience, verifiable that they have done this job well in the past, if they haven't, don't hire them. You're just pointing to quicksand. And once you hire the wrong person, getting rid of them could lead to lawsuits and frustration, stress and all kinds of things.

Raven Blair Davis: That's where the real hitting comes in for sure.

Brian: Yeah.

Raven Blair Davis: I want to take a moment Brian if you don't mind and give our listeners the website where they can go get a copy of now build a great business.

Brian: The website is actually called www.nowbuildagreatbusiness.com. If you go there and order it now its $24.95 and when you order the book, you have access to several thousand dollars' worth of resources that can help your business immediately from some of the best business experts in America that we have partnered with and they're all free.

Raven Blair Davis: Yeah. I actually got a copy of the book and I went to the website, there is lots and lots of great resources and you can't get this website address until you buy the book. So go to www.nowbuildagreatbusiness.com and pick up a copy.

This is Raven a.k.a The Talk Show Maven and we're here speaking with Brian Tracy. Mark had to go but he gave us some great information before he did and we look forward to having both

Brian and Mark on our show again because what a delight this is. Now, I want to jump back into our questions Brian. I know you know that in your book "Now Build A Great Business" that a great product or service is the key to business success. What can every entrepreneur learn about quality from Akio Toyota?

Brian: Yes well the great lessons from those companies is they usually start when the product is not very good and then they dedicate themselves to continually making the product better and better until finally people say 'this is a great product' so the critical measure, the jelly in the jelly donut of your business success is the number of times, the percentage of customers who after using your product or service say 'this is a great product' and tell other people. In fact one of the most important parts of customer service and your product is to ask the question of your customer 'would you recommend us to others?' this is the ultimate question – based on your experience with me, with us, would you buy again and recommend us to others? And the percentage of people who say yes will largely determine your future.

Raven Blair Davis: I like that. That's a very important key. One of the things that caught my attention is you said that if they value something or produce something that they can go back and make it better so we don't have to be afraid that maybe it didn't work that first time. We don't have to scratch and say it's no good. We need to look at how we can make it better and approve it.

Brian: Yes, exactly. There was an article in INC magazine last month about several people who had built large businesses and the one thing they had in common is when they started, the product was not very good. Service was not very good and they had to continually improve it including Akio Morita who founded Sony. His first product was a rice cooker and the rice cooker turned the rice into a clump in the bottom of the pot and he had to go back and rework it until he could actually produce right. So if your product is not terrific right now, that's okay, just go to work on it, make it terrific. Ask your customers what could we do to make this product or service better and your customers will quite candidly tell you 'do more of this, do less of that' and you say 'okay' and if you do it, your customers will become loyal and they'll buy and they'll buy again and tell their friends.

Raven Blair Davis: Love that. Again, we can't be afraid to ask and we can't have that attitude that we got all the right answers because our listeners, our clients, our customers, they're the true key to our success.

Brian: Yes. Now, the other thing that your listeners have to understand is what is called the power of 'no' the fact is when we go into business, we go into business seeking yes. We want as many yes as possible – yes I will, yes I'll do the job especially yes I'll buy.

Raven Blair Davis: Yeah, really.

Brian: So we do everything possible to avoid no and we consider that the more yes we get, the more successful we are. The more no's we get, the more we fail. What you have to do is you have to rewire that like pulling up plugs in an old switch board and reverse the plugs.

Raven Blair Davis: Okay.

Brian: And say my job is to get no's. The more no's I can get, by the law of probability, the more yes I will get, your job is to fail as often as possible to get as many people saying no as possible, start in the morning and go for no. All day long, keep asking people to buy your product or service and the more people, who say no, the more successful you'll be.

Raven Blair Davis: I love that. You know what, that brought back a memory. I come from 25 years of telemarketing. That's where I was first introduced to you Brian and what I learned was every time we got a no, pays up the money.

Brian: Absolutely. I used to teach that. Take every single sale that you do get and divide it by the number of people you have to talk to, to get that sale and that's the amount you get. If you make $100 of sale and you have to get 9 no's to get 1 yes then you get $10 for every no or you collect it on the last one. With that attitude, then what you do is you speed up your tempo. In starting a small business, remember the key to success is to fail more often.

Raven Blair Davis: The key to success is to fail more often.

Brian: Fail more often, fail repeatedly. As a matter of fact, every time you get a no, you should say thank you because you get closer to somebody who will buy.

Raven Blair Davis: Wow. That's huge. That's a little thing but a big thing Brian.

Brian: Yes.

Raven Blair Davis: Listen, when it comes to breakthrough success, why do small startups routinely beat big businesses? How can corporate executives and managers apply your principles starting today?

Listen to the rest of this great interview via audio!

To listen to the full audio of this interview visit:
http://www.careersfromthekitchentable.com/2ndEditionaudios

Plus be sure to visit http://amazingwomenofpower.com/radio and grab your free copy of *"Talk Your Way to Success – Unleash Your Dynamic Voice"* by Raven!

Diana Nightingale

Speaker, Author, Coach, and Radio Host

An author, an internationally known speaker, a life coach and mentor to people around the world. Through her writing, coaching, speaking and private retreats, Diana is dedicated to the memory, the works of her husband, Earl Nightingale, to "carry the torch" and light the path of those who follow.

During his lifetime, Earl Nightingale wrote and recorded over 7,000 radio programs, 250 audio programs as well as television programs and videos.

People were always amazed that they could pick up the phone and call Earl. They were pleased and delighted that he personally answered each and every letter written to him. In his absence, and through the web site, are you able to contact his closest confidant – his wife, and partner

Raven Blair Davis: Today, I am just delighted to introduce to you this next guest. I am talking about none other than Diana Nightingale. Diana Nightingale is the widow of Earl Nightingale and boy, these two are a legend. It is truly a dream come true to have her on my show and to have her now as a friend I tell you, that's why we always tell people believe in your dreams and go for it because if you are committed to your dreams, it can happen. But that's not what we're gonna talk about today. Diana is gonna share with us some of her insider secrets and tips on mastering the mindset to succeed. Let me tell you a little bit about Diana before I bring her on. She is an author, an internationally known speaker, a life coach and a mentor to people around the world through her writing, coaching, speaking and private retreats. She is dedicated to the memory, the works and carrying the torch of her husband Earl Nightingale to light the path of those who follow. Now, during his lifetime, Earl Nightingale wrote and recorded over 7,000 video programs, 250 audio programs as well as television programs and videos. You might remember his work being part of the Nightingale and Conant series. In 1966 he wrote and recorded the strangest secret, remember that? That recording earned him a gold record and from which the personal development industry grew. I am so excited to have Diana here and the subject she's gonna be talking about tonight, mindset to succeed is really important to all of us as home business owners. Without further ado Diana, are you there?

Diana Nightingale: I am here Raven. Good evening.

Raven Blair Davis: Welcome.

Diana Nightingale: Thank you.

Raven Blair Davis: I'm so excited my friend. It is great to have you here and I know our time is short, these 25 minutes Diana, they go quick so we're gonna dive right in there but before we start with the questions, for those people that may not be familiar with you because we have a lot of people in the younger set that are wanting to be entrepreneurs as well and they might not be familiar with you and your husband so can you share a little bit of your story as far as how you got into the business and building and continuing this legacy?

Diana Nightingale: Yes. Before I met Earl – we met later on in life, I had been busy with my own life of course. I have been a successful real estate realtor and I had my own office so I certainly knew how to run a business and I had also worked extensively with teenagers in the intercity and working at state level with education situations and the mental health associations and so when I hooked up with Earl, one of the things that concerned me even though his company was highly successful, they were the number one leader in the world as far as personal development, programs for people that wanted to move ahead, most of the programs had been created by successful men for successful men which left the whole rest of the world trying to figure it out for themselves. So it has been a desire of mine to make that kind of information available to everyone and of course his daily radio program "Our Changing Worlds" have been heard all around the world and so younger people, men and women of all walks of life were able to get those messages but there were no real success programs set up for them.

At that point in time, Earl was getting ready to retire from the company that he had founded many years before and we decided that we were going to create our own publishing company. We were going to call it Keys Publishing with a mission statement on unlocking doors through education therefore you would have a pocket full of keys that would help you to walk through doors and find the information that you need to be successful in life and we did form that company. We formed it in 1987 and we were determined we were going to take his work and the work that I have been doing, combine them together and move forward with that situation. We were all set to do that, we did quite a few programs that– as they stay are still in the tins. They had not been released so they were still in the tins back in the days when we used reel to reel and then he passed away two years later. So, we had already started our home based business just because we worked out of our home. We did our recording at home, he did his writing at home. We made all of our plans for travel and everything that we did, we had a home office. It started out more as a convenience. I don't think we really realized that we were going to end up with a home based business at that point in time because people didn't know that back then.

Raven Blair Davis: Right, I can imagine. Well you guys, I mean your late husband obviously is a legend and to me you are too because you are definitely carrying on the torch and I just so appreciate you coming here and agreeing to donate your time today to come and share with all these new home business owners because the mindset to succeed is important. Before I have you really elaborate on why you feel it's important, I want to ask you this Diana. How difficult was it for you to make the transition from being a supportive wife – with other things you did but then after your husband's death, you had to really step in there and be the woman in charge and carry on this legacy. How difficult was that task?

Diana Nightingale: It was extremely difficult back then because we only had the old traditional methods of getting materials out. In other words, if we wanted to create and audio program, it meant that you had to invest a great sum of money into your studio time and to the creation of the product you'd have to pay massive amounts, you'd have to warehouse it, you'd have to fulfill it and that was very, very difficult and in that point in time, I was still trying to unscramble my mind as far as having lost Earl and the direction that I was gonna be taking. So, for a number of years, things really stalled out for me until the internet came along and the capabilities of having a website which I think to younger people today, just take this all for granted and I think the older generation sees it as just an absolute miracle. I mean even what we're doing right now. You are in Texas, I'm in Arizona and this is going to a radio station on the East Coast and you never used to be able to do that. We all had to be sitting together in the same studio and so the miracle of the internet is just amazing for me today.

Raven Blair Davis: Yes, technology, you are so right. Technology, wow it has truly, truly changed all of our lives. I always tell people having the internet and Google and all of that, we actually have something better than the library right here in our homes. How you used to have to get out and do your research, you can do it with just your fingertips in your computer and the way you go and like you said, being able to have several different people in different places talking on the phone so yes, I think the younger generation does take this for granted but us oldies, we love it don't we?

Diana Nightingale: We do. The great thing too is we don't have to depend on just a few people feeding us information. It used to be that if you wanted to become an expert on something, you would have to have a teacher. You would have to go under classroom situation and pretty much you'd get the information that organization would prepare for you and today, with the computer if you have an open mind, you can just fill it 24 hours a day from every place in the world literally and get a really well-rounded education just being inquisitive.

Raven Blair Davis: Absolutely. Diana, in your opinion, why is having a right mindset so important to building a successful business?

Diana Nightingale: Well it's important to have a mindset when you're going in to business as it is to have a destination when you get in your car. You really have to determine where it is you want to go and how determined you are to get there. I often say that this journey of life is lived out basically in our minds and the physical aspect comes along afterwards but if you get in a car and you're going someplace and there's a detour, you don't say 'oh well, that's it, we'll just go back home and we can't ever go anywhere again because down the road we have a detour' we don't do that.   We do whatever we need to do to get to where we want to go and we arrive hopefully safely but you just have to be determined to achieve your goals.

Raven Blair Davis: You are so right. Now, real quickly, speaking of goals, can you share with us what a couple of your goals were starting out?

Diana Nightingale: Basically making all of the great positive information available to everybody and I think that is made possible through our website and it is certainly made possible through radios because when I post the questions to my husband's partner many years ago about why all these great programs weren't marketed to everybody his answer had been that those people don't have money. And that's really sad that's the way that world looks at things. If you are in a position to buy something most people are not gonna create it for you and I think that it's important for people everywhere in the world, young and old, no matter what your past situation has been, no matter where you are born into the economy or what your situation is, I think you need to have all the positive information that you can get to know that you are not out of control. You are in control of your life and that you can change the direction and you have what it takes that doesn't take money, it doesn't take things outside of yourself, it takes what you have on the inside just to be sparked and to be opened and to be cultivated.

Raven Blair Davis: You're 100% right. We have to protect our mind don't we?

Diana Nightingale: We do.

Raven Blair Davis: And feed it the right things. What do you attribute to being able to develop the right mindset, the winning mindset that we need?

Diana Nightingale: I think some of us are born with it because as children, we were the stubborn ones that didn't believe it couldn't be done. We'd have to try it just to make sure and to think also at an early age, I was disorganized and that bothered me and I realized that I wasn't able to get a lot done and so basically I trained myself to be more focused and to realize – I think you go through a moment where somebody turns and says 'I only have two hands' and it's great because if you only have two hands, there's only so much you can do with them. Well, each of us only has so many hours in the day. We only have so much energy and we only can be attentive to those things. So, to have too many expectations of yourself and what you can accomplish is very debilitating. You're just going to get stressed and you're going to get tired out and you're going to find that you're very discouraged because you feel like 'I just can't do this' but if you can really be focused and you learn to prioritize, that's the key.

Raven Blair Davis: You're so right and another thing I'm finding out Diana is you have to learn how to discipline your disappointments.

Diana Nightingale: Sure.

Raven Blair Davis: And not get so frustrated and so overwhelmed with everything that's going on that you throw your hands up or you just get down and you don't move forward because that's definitely not good. For the benefit of the listening audience, could you share three tips that you feel will assist them on a day to day basis – putting together their business or building their business, how can they go about this and what three tips do you feel are important?

Diana Nightingale: Well I think it's important to not just say 'I think I'll start a business' and leave it open. I think you need to have an objective. There's something that you are going to strive for. You need to put some time zones in there. I'd like to be at this point in time, in six months, a year from now this is where I'd like to be so that you have a visual – the progress that you would like to make. I think the other thing that you need to do is you need to – going back to what I said before, there's only so many hours in the day so you need to prioritize. You need to sit down. You need to write down the things that you want to accomplish say this week and then put down what you want to accomplish this month but what you want to do is you want to see "what do I need to accomplish tomorrow" and only pick three things because chances are you're not going to have time to do anything else. Now, if you get those three things done, you're going to be very encouraged because you're going to say 'wow I got that all done and I've got time left over' because nothing else has been out before you that day. Then the next day, the next three things on the list get moved up and eventually when other things come along, you put them to the bottom of the list and the other part is I think when you have a home based business, what you have to do is you have to run it the same way you would if you were in an office because you are. You are the chief executive – CEO, financial person, you are everything so there you are, you are in your office, you're doing your job and you have to put your phone on answer because you would not be answering the phone all day long if you were in an office.

Raven Blair Davis: Good point at that.

Diana Nightingale: So, let the phones take the messages and don't be checking your email every two minutes. You have to stay focused on what you're doing and just pretend that you have that invisible person out there that's taking your messages and everyone will have to wait until it's convenient for you.

Raven Blair Davis: So you almost have to act like you have that invisible boss.

Diana Nightingale: Absolutely.

Raven Blair Davis: Yeah you wouldn't be eating at your desk and sitting back and talking on the phone all day and checking emails all day. You would be in action mode.

Diana Nightingale: Yeah that's not running a home based business, that's compromising really – I think it's compromising your integrity quite honestly. I think you have to be as dedicated to yourself and your goals as you would be to someone else because I chuckle at people that think that they can go out and take a course in self-esteem because self-esteem is something that we earn for ourselves and it's what we do when no one is looking. That's the mark of real integrity so you can get away with stuff but you're not gonna feel good about you so I think that you really have to run your home based business just as though you were in some tall sky scraper in some large city some place and you were – I guess in today's world wearing Prada or something and accountable to other people. Just because you have the luxury of being at home, you really do have to have the discipline of a good business person.

Raven Blair Davis: Be committed to your success and what it takes. You know what, I get the feeling Diana that people are saying right about now 'boy she's fabulous and this is some great, great information that she's giving' but what about those times you were truly struggling and you're having overwhelming challenges, how do you keep your head up Diana? How do you keep going on?

Diana Nightingale: In a book interview form or in the real world?

Raven Blair Davis: In the real world. Just keep it real here.

Diana Nightingale: In the real world I know that's part of life and I know that that comes and I know that if you're a high powered person that you are subject to burn out and so what I do when I have those days is I give in to it. I cry when I need to cry and I get in my car and I go for a drive or you take a walk or you do something else because you're not going to be effective that day anyway and so what your body, what your emotions are telling you is 'hey you need a break.' I have a little dog and he's the joy of my life because I'll be sitting at my computer for hours and all the sudden he'll tap me and I'll look and he would've brought all of his toys into me and I think he's right. He is absolutely right. It's time to play and you have to be kind to yourself. You need to realize that you're a human, you have to realize that there are gonna be days when you're just gonna absolutely run into that brick wall and you're gonna have really not feeling good days and the great thing about it is if you have to take off Wednesday and Thursday because you're having a really rough time coping, that's okay because you could work Saturday and Sunday if you want to because you're running a home based business.

Announcer: Excuse me Raven.

Raven Blair Davis: You are so right. Yes?

Announcer: I was just wondering. Greg Norman's online. He wants to know if you'd take a call…

Raven Blair Davis: Oh my goodness Greg is here. Diana, Greg is a huge fan of you and your husband. Yes, put Greg on.

Announcer: Alright and here is Greg Norman.

Raven Blair Davis: Hi Greg.

Greg Norman: I just want to say quickly I really enjoy this show Raven and I really honor what you're doing with Diana and with the information you're sharing but it's a great, great show so I just want to say good job.

Raven Blair Davis: Thank you, thank you. Diana, you have a fan.

Greg Norman: Thank you very much.

Diana Nightingale: Thank you Greg, my pleasure.

Raven Blair Davis: Yeah, he has your husband's picture in his office. Big, big, fan I'm glad he got a chance to call in. He's a great guy.

Diana Nightingale: That made my day.

Raven Blair Davis: Wonderful. Wow, this time is going really quick and I know we've got some exciting news we want to share with everyone so I guess I'm gonna ask you, is there any final tips that you want to share with our listeners before we announce your new news?

Diana Nightingale: I'm gonna share a tip with you that Earl always used to be really be fond of telling his audiences and that is when you have a really great idea, when this is something that you are truly passionate about, I'm not talking about the excitement of the day but I'm talking about something that is just welling up inside of you that you really want to do and you believe in yourself and you believe it can be done, only share it with people that will help you.

Raven Blair Davis: That's a good one.

Diana Nightingale: Because other people who have no dreams of their own are going to be very eager to destroy yours.

Raven Blair Davis: They will shut it down.

Diana Nightingale: All the reasons why it's not going to work, it can't possibly work. What do you know about it, you've never done that before, I knew somebody and they failed and they lost everything and so basically he used to say if you want water to boil, you don't keep taking the lid off of it and letting steam out? So, you want to keep that excitement inside of you, share it only with people – if you need financial advisers or legal advisers or someone that's going to assist you in achieving your goals but don't just share it with anybody especially people in your family because they're going to give you 100 reasons why it's not gonna work. So, be faithful to yourself and be committed.

Raven Blair Davis: That's wonderful and you brought up a really good point. We don't like to think about this sometimes but you're right. Surround yourself with positive, encouraging, empowering people and empower and inspire each along the journey for sure. Now, we've got just a few minutes left and I don't want to end this show without two things. Number one, we want to make sure that they know about your book, "Learning to Fly as a Nightingale" and how they can get it and also we want to share your news about this added addition to your business so I'm gonna let you share.

Diana Nightingale: I did write a book some years ago and it's called "Learning to Fly As a Nightingale" and it along with all of Earl's classic works are available on my website which is www.earlnightingale.com and I am presently writing another book and it's called "The Spiritual Flight of the Nightingale" and it's Christian based and it's full of my life story experiences and how they've taught me lessons about the lord's constant love and guidance for us.

Raven Blair Davis: Fabulous.

Diana Nightingale: The other news is after 25 years, one of the things that Earl really wanted more than anything after having one of the most highly syndicated radio programs in the entire world, he always wanted us to have a program together and so I'm going to start broadcasting a radio show thanks to someone named Raven which started out as a request for me to be her guest that ended up with me really getting involved with her radio course and I'm so excited because I will at last be able to share a lot of messages that Earl created in his lifetime, some that we created together and hopefully I have lots of good friends that are in the positive message business and hopefully some of them will come and join me from time to time and this is the most exciting thing that I think has come along in 25 years so getting back to what you had asked before, keeping your eye on the price, this is something that I had pursued so many times and finally it was just a dim little memory of something that I had once desperately wanted to do and then it showed up so I'm really excited. Thank you so much Raven.

Raven Blair Davis: Oh, you're welcome. I'm just honored that you wanted to take the course so thank you and I'm excited and we're not quite sure yet but we're thinking maybe in a couple weeks the show may launch.

Diana Nightingale: I think that it will.

Raven Blair Davis: Oh, good.

Diana Nightingale: My birthday's next month so I'd like to give that to me for my birthday.

Raven Blair Davis: There you go and the name of your show...

Diana Nightingale: Nightingale radio.

Raven Blair Davis: Nightingale radio with the voice of Diana Nightingale

Diana Nightingale: Right.

Raven Blair Davis: Absolutely wonderful, well this has been just a true delight and a dream come true. Thank you so much for coming and sharing with us, we didn't have a whole lot of time so you know what that means. That means we're gonna have to bring you back.

Diana Nightingale: Well sometimes you just have to what you have to do.

Raven Blair Davis: There you go and again her current book is "Learning to Fly as a Nightingale" is a true motivational love story, thank you for sending me my autograph copy. I keep it by my night stand and it is truly a motivational love story. It's great. Absolutely wonderful, give me your website one more time Diana before we go to commercial.

Diana Nightingale: www.earlnightingale.com

Raven Blair Davis: www.earlnightingale.com it's as simple as that. We've been speaking with Diana Nightingale and this has been a true pleasure.

To listen to the full audio of this interview visit:

http://www.careersfromthekitchentable.com/2ndEditionaudios

Plus be sure to visit http://amazingwomenofpower.com/radio and grab your free copy of *"Talk Your Way to Success – Unleash Your Dynamic Voice"* by Raven!

Fran Harris

Coach, Speaker and Athlete

Fran Harris, Ph.D. is a WNBA champion, international speaker, coach, business and Internet Marketing expert.

A former Fortune 100 sales executive and former ESPN & Lifetime Television announcer, she's the CIO of Fran Harris Enterprises, LLC, a multimedia company that specializes in television, film, publishing, Internet and video games properties.

A member of the Houston Comets' first WNBA championship in 1997, Fran is a popular speaker on the college, youth, inspirational, faith-based, corporate and sports circuit.

Raven Blair Davis: Well, good evening and welcome to Careers from the Kitchen Table, you know that show that teaches you how to cook without the cooking. This is Raven Blair Davis. I'm the host of this show we are back again and more excited than ever because guess what, tonight is another dream come true interview from me and I'm bringing you some great stuff to help you get going in your business. Each week we bring you lots of good old home recipes of success to assist you in finding that ideal work from home job or the perfect home business opportunity, the choice is yours my friend and we love to bring you the experts right here so you won't have to worry about how do I figure this thing out, you got the gurus and the experts to help you figure it out. They're gonna assist you along your journey of being an entrepreneur, a home business enthusiast; this is the place to be so again, thank you for joining us.

I've got a question for you. Have you ever thought of writing a book but was worried about finding a publisher or thought you did not have the money to publish yourself or it's just gonna take four or five years if you just don't act, well if that sounds like you then you are going to absolutely positively love my next guest, Dr. Fran Harris. Let me tell you a little bit about Dr. Fran Harris, she's a WNBA champion, international speaker, coach, business and internet marketing expert; she's a former fortune 100 sales executive and former ESPN and lifetime television announcer. She's the CIO of Fran Harris enterprises LLC a multimedia company, specializes in television film publishing, internet and video game properties and she's also a member of the Houston comets first WNBA championship in 1997. I'm in Houston and I was like 'wow, go' yes, Fran is a popular speaker on the college, she use inspirational face based corporate and sports circuit. She is all that and a bag of chips with some m&ms on the side as you can see, she is my guest and we're gonna be speaking with her briefly on how to write, publish and sell your very own e-book and get this in five days or less and she has a product that's gonna assist you in that.

Welcome Fran to Careers from the Kitchen Table. I am truly delighted.

Fran Harris: Well it is great to be here on Careers from the Kitchen Table. I love that title by the way, good one.

Raven Blair Davis: Thank you so much. I had an opportunity to meet you and spend a little time with you at the direct selling women's alliance with Nicki Keohohou and her team and boy, you are some lady for sure and I appreciate all the assistance when you helped me with my camera so thank you, thank you. A lot of people have heard Dr. Fran Harris – have heard that name, they may have seen you on – the big idea with Donny Deutsch – had that totally wrong and you were fabulous on there. We had Genevieve who was also there with you on the show a few weeks ago so just real quickly can you share with us how you went from playing basketball to being this extraordinary entrepreneur or I guess you could say megapreneur really because you got so many businesses, share your story with us.

Fran Harris: Well I started my first business when I was nine years old. It was a snow cone stand in Dallas and the people said 'you have the entrepreneurial flame burning that early' well not really, it was about – I started that first business out of necessity because my mom wouldn't buy something for me and she was like 'you're a genius, go figure out how to get the money yourself' and after I've had it for a while, I started thinking of ways I could make money and I didn't want to do a lemonade stand because that was so 19 – whatever so it was 1970's let's do a snow cone stand. I'm living in Dallas and if any of you've been to Dallas, on a cool day it's like 130 degrees outside so it was a great product, service and offering for where I was living and there were tons of kids in my neighborhood and I made $1500 that summer and then an entrepreneur was born because I understood Raven in that moment that I did have the power to write my own ticket. I didn't have to depend on Mom and that's what kids grow up doing unless your parents drive you in a different direction – you always have your hand out, always asking for Mom and Dad, depending on them for your livelihood but that summer I realized I didn't need to that. It was a powerful lesson I got at age nine.

Raven Blair Davis: That's where you came out with your famous slogan, you got the power. It started at an early age, you go girl.

Fran Harris: Yeah and it really just took off from there and basketball came into my life as a teenager and I started speaking in church when I was six or seven years old I just loved being in front of audiences but didn't really realized that you could paid to go to junior high school and somebody gave me $500 after I spoke and I was like 'What is this for' and they were like 'well that's what we pay speakers' but it still didn't click that you can really make money as a speaker until I got to college at the University of Texas in Austin. The NCAA rules do not allow you to be paid as a scholarship athlete so you couldn't get paid during the school year. I could only get paid for summer jobs but that didn't stop me from wanting to speak and just getting out into the community and I've gone to speak at the fortune 100 company and of course they knew they couldn't pay me but after the thing they said 'man, you were fantastic' and I said 'let me ask you this, I know you can't pay me but if you could paid me, how much would you have paid me' and they said $10,000.

Raven Blair Davis: And you said...

Fran Harris: Okay well the next ones in trouble. I said 'oh yeah I'm in the right business.'

Raven Blair Davis: You're in the right one, right place baby.

Fran Harris: Exactly but Raven you know, that's the beginning of that introduction to – info-preneuring because I was selling my information. I was selling my expertise and that's what we're gonna talk about today.

Raven Blair Davis: Absolutely. In fact let me ask you this Fran. What do you feel are the important keys to being a successful home based business owners selling over the internet because it's not as easy as it sounds; there are some special keys there.

Fran Harris: Yeah there are some things. I mean you have to have a good product whether it's yours or not but even before you get to the product stage, you have to have a sincere belief in the fact that people are actually buying information over the internet. The thing that stops people from making money online is they don't believe that people are doing well which means that they don't believe that they can do it so it's all about the belief and people are so skeptical simply because they don't believe they can do it and it's the cheapest place to fail. I heard a lot of people say – I mean the internet, you can get online, see if something works – a day if it's gonna work or not. So, you have to have that belief, you have to have a great product that people want and that's really important. The second half of that, it can't be just a great product because you and your mother and your kids thinks it's a great product. If people don't want it and they are not buying it, it's not a great product.

Raven Blair Davis: Yeah.

Fran Harris: And so those are two things and then the last thing I would say is just persistence because you have to test and tweak and just figure out, get your sales page right, get the products right, get the price point right and you'll make money online.

Raven Blair Davis: Yeah and the good thing about it is you may not make it at the beginning but there's no rush. It will be there. Once it's found in the internet, it's there.

Fran Harris: Right.

Raven Blair Davis: So all of a sudden you might wake up one morning and just say 'wow where did this come from?'

Raven Blair Davis: Let's talk about eBook. Why write an eBook first of all Fran?

Fran Harris: Writing an electronic book is the fastest way to get to market. That's what I love about the internet. 10 years ago, if you wanted to write a book and unless you were John Grisham or some of these other writers that are just multimillion and billionaires…

Raven Blair Davis: Yeah.

Fran Harris: If you wanted to write a book 10 years ago, you had to wait at least a year. You get the idea, you get an agent, you send a proposal to a publishing house and they would say 'the book's will come out in about a year or 18 months but now with the internet you can bring the book to market tomorrow. When we get off the phone, I could write an eBook and be up and in business in the next hour so that's why people need to write an eBook and people always get intimated by the process of writing but an eBook can be anything from a five page list of resources or a report on how to quit smoking or a report on how to have better sex or report on how to start a business in 10 days, it can be anything, there are no rules about it and people are buying it. I have bought five page eBooks, I bought 500 page eBooks, and there are no rules. Again, that first to market, that quickness to market is what makes the internet so wonderful.

Raven Blair Davis: Now you make it sound easy. Let me ask you this, how difficult is it to get started if you never ever, ever wrote anything?

Fran Harris: And you still write a winning eBook…

Raven Blair Davis: And the sales.

Fran Harris: I made it sound easy Raven because it is. I made it sound really easy because if you can type or even if you don't type but let's say if you can just peck. If you can peck on your computer on your keyboard you can write an eBook because an eBook is nothing more than opening up your word processing program with a great idea and pecking, that's it. And you can get a free merchant account to sell it because you want to be able to sell it and take credit cards you can get a free one at PayPal.

Raven Blair Davis: Absolutely.

Fran Harris: You're in business

Raven Blair Davis: I love PayPal.

Fran Harris: You haven't spent any money.

Raven Blair Davis: It's my friend. I know you have a wonderful product there that's getting stellar reviews of Five Day eBook Solution, what insider secrets can you quickly share with us that will assist the beginner in getting started even if they – I don't see why they shouldn't but your eBook, we're gonna definitely lead them in that direction. They think okay I can take it from here, what are some quick tips you can throw out that whole system?

Fran Harris: Well the thing about The Five Day eBook Solution is – the reason I titled it that is because unless you have no desire to succeed there is no reason in the next five days you should have an eBook done and I actually walk you through, I hold your hand, its paint by colors.

Raven Blair Davis: I love that.

Fran Harris: Do this, do this then do this – that's what it is, some of the things I talk about in the book are how do you pick your topic, let's just start there. How do you pick your topic? And even when I'm coaching my clients when they want to say 'I don't know what I want to write about, I don't know what I want to speak about' I always take them through this process.

Everybody listen up, I say you have to think about it, you have to get your slice of the pie. You have to figure out what you're passionate about, that's the P, what you're interested in, that's the I and what your area of expertise is. So, you can write about any of those, you have to have expertise and if you're passionate about it just research and write about it. If you're interested in it, research and write about it. If you have expertise then you already got the content, just write about it so get your slice of the PIE meaning you're gonna get your passion, interest and expertise and that's gonna be the source of your eBook.

Raven Blair Davis: Okay, that's some golden nuggets you just threw out so I hope our listeners didn't take that lightly but run over real quickly one more time.

Fran Harris: Passion, interest and expertise that's what all eBooks have been written from. I've written a book because I'm already passionate about that topic. You see parents doing that a lot or you see the one who's been afflicted with some condition, all the sudden they are interested in breast cancer, all the sudden they're really passionate about getting the word out on domestic violence or incarceration or whatever. So, they're passionate about it, it's a great source of content. Then there's interest, I don't know a whole lot about gardening and if I ever come to your house Raven and start trying to tell you what to do with your petunias, you just start laughing and tell me that's not my domain. I don't know what's about that but I'm very interested in it. I'm very interested in how that works so I could write some – if I want people to hear that because I'm interested in gardening, I could actually write an eBook on gardening like the 10 top things you should never do if you want your plant to grow.

Raven Blair Davis: Absolutely, I can tell you that one.

Fran Harris: So don't think outside the box, think way outside the box so you're thinking about writing and that's interest. Expertise, my areas of expertise include how to build a six or seven figure speaking career, how to land your own television show, how to host your own radio show, how to write your first eBook so I can write from those places as well. Think about everything I just talked about in the last 60 seconds, all the content that's there, a lot of content.

Raven Blair Davis: Lots of content so somebody can actually take what they're doing now because a lot of people listening in to Careers from the Kitchen Table are still in the decision mode. They haven't left their job and they're trying to do something on the side until they make the big move so that's why they tune in each week so they can take whatever they've been doing for the past 20 years or even past year on their job, they're an expert now.

Fran Harris: That's right.

Raven Blair Davis: And they can take that, what they like or didn't like or find some kind of tips like you just threw out and write an eBook and that book can be selling while they're working that job and when they just can't take their boss no more like what happened to me, they walk.

Fran Harris: That's right and you bring up a great point. While you are waiting, you should be making money.

Raven Blair Davis: There you go.

Fran Harris: While you're waiting – think about whatever experience you're going through right now whether it's transitioning from corporate America to your own business, you can write about that and here's another tip, even if you're not gonna write an eBook just yet, how about blogging? Man, do you know how many people are in transition from working for someone to working for themselves. Setup a blog and just talk about it and invite people to come and contribute to the conversation and guess what, you can turn your post on your blog into an eBook.

Raven Blair Davis: Wonderful and you're building an audience right there.

Fran Harris: That's right, your potential buyers.

Raven Blair Davis: Offer them an article or something for free and have them go ahead and subscribe so they can hear your information or read your information all the time.

Fran Harris: Absolutely.

Raven Blair Davis: Let me ask you Fran, how does one discover what their niche is if they're just quite unsure, maybe they've been a housewife all their live or maybe they're just bored, and don't want to write about that. How do they find what they really are passionate about?

Fran Harris: I ask people, if I were to come to your place and spend a day with you and you didn't have any responsibility, you don't have to do the kids, the wife, the husband, the significant other – nothing, it's just gonna be me and you and I said 'I want the most awesome day you can create for us, what will we be doing?' that's a great indication of what people are passionate about, what their niche is.

Raven Blair Davis: Okay.

Fran Harris: Some people would take me to the spa and do a full day of beauty, some people would take me to the gym, we play golf, we play – you see what I'm saying?

Raven Blair Davis: Right.

Fran Harris: So that gives you some insights to what you really love.

Raven Blair Davis: Okay, that make sense, absolutely. Alright I have to ask you this, how are you gonna write a book in five days? How is it gonna happen girlfriend?

Fran Harris: Well I'll take you through those steps that are why it's called The Five Day eBook Solution because that's the question that people have and I got the solution.

Raven Blair Davis: They have to get it.

Fran Harris: Yeah you have to get it because every day we do something different. Generally like having me work with you for five days.

Raven Blair Davis: Okay, tell them how. I know they're on the edge of their seats.

Fran Harris: We have to figure out what you want to write about; we have to setup some systems meaning we have to figure out how to get you your payment.

Raven Blair Davis: Right.

Fran Harris: Get that taken care of so I'll walk you through all of that, we have to get you – do you want your book to be a Microsoft word document or do you want it to be a PDF – I share all these free resources and…

Raven Blair Davis: With most of your friends do you share it – what's the difference of…

Fran Harris: Yeah and I talk about why you even want a word document versus a PDF.

Raven Blair Davis: Okay.

Fran Harris: Yeah.

Raven Blair Davis: Good deal.

Fran Harris: So basically from pick up the book from day one to day five, no stones left unturned and you're in business.

Raven Blair Davis: What's the website again?

Fran Harris: The website is www.5dayebooksolution.com

Raven Blair Davis: www.5dayebooksolution.com has the answers and I strongly recommend if you ever thought about writing a book and you're major impatient, want to get it done and get the job done, get the tips from the guru herself – WBNA with the Comets are you ever impressed with any of them?

Fran Harris: Well, how funny, we are doing a WNBA legends weekend next weekend in Houston.

Raven Blair Davis: Oh my god not in Houston, are you serious?

Fran Harris: Yeah. It is going to be fantastic, it's gonna be so great. I can't wait to see everybody.

Raven Blair Davis: I know. Well if you see one, be sure and tell her Lily and I said hello.

Fran Harris: I will.

Raven Blair Davis: Yes and we've got more time for questions before the break so let's talk about some of the hot, hot categories of eBooks. What are they?

Fran Harris: Well a great place to research and I'm gonna give this old tool, a great place to research to find out what's hot is a place called click as if you were clicking your heels together, www.clickbank.com.

Raven Blair Davis: Okay.

Fran Harris: At clickbank.com you will find the hottest piece of info products that are selling but if you just look at the ads on television, if you pick up the New York Times or USA today you look at the best seller list, these are all great indicators for what's selling. You'll see weight loss, love or relationships, financial freedom, never going to be old and never going to be out of style, they will always be hot. How to get a better sex life, how to get a better relationship, how to lose weight, how to get a flat tummy, it's always going to be there so you can never go wrong with love and relationships, never go wrong with money and wealth and business, never go wrong with any of those because there are people always want to look and feel good and they want to be successful.

Raven Blair Davis: Now, let's say okay this is sounding good and I want to write this eBook, how important is an outline for your book and can you maybe throw out three real simple tips to creating a good outline?

Fran Harris: Outlining is very important and I always recommend when I'm working with writers that they do an outline because if you just figure out what you want to talk about, you've already written you book. So just put together an outline – what do people want to know about this topic then you delineate three or four 10 things the people need and want to know about this topic, you put an introduction at the beginning and you put a conclusion at the end so now you've got seven chapters. One is introduction, five and between the sandwich are things that people need to know and number seven is the conclusion.

Raven Blair Davis: Okay.

Fran Harris: And all you have to do is go fill it in, fill in the blanks.

Raven Blair Davis: I've often heard Fran that the hardest part of writing is coming up with that title, writing the first sentence and writing the last sentence. What are your thoughts on that?

Fran Harris: I think people have a knack for titles. I have a great knack for titles and if you just give me a couple of seconds I can come up with some really great titles if you ever just said "I'm writing a weight loss book" I gather information and I'll give you three or four good titles so there's a great propensity for doing that kind of stuff exactly but even if you don't, some ways that you can come up with your own titles is you can literally write what is the book about. I always tell people to keep the title to seven to ten words at the most. The shorter, the better – the zone diet you know what I'm saying? The Intentional Millionaire which is one of my books so you know what the book is about and you've got a trigger word in there that's really going to entice people to read it. So, you want to think of a trigger word, if you use numbers try to use popular numbers like 7, 21, 5, 1, 101 they are some good numbers.

Raven Blair Davis: Okay.

Fran Harris: So you play with the tricks and tools that are out there and then you'll come up with something great.

Raven Blair Davis: Well I just made it with I think nine numbers and how to turn your telephone to a cash cow – just made it, I should call Fran. Absolutely and boy it was hard coming up with a title so you have to have a special knack on that, that's for sure.

Fran Harris: They should check out www.5dayebooksolution.com and also check out www.franharris.com.

Raven Blair Davis: Check out Fran Harris because you will see her shoot the basket. You can play I don't play basketball. I am a volleyball person I can't help it. You're listening to Careers from the Kitchen Table. This is Raven Blair Davis I'm the host of this show I'm here visiting with Dr. Fran Harris and we are hearing something good in this talk today. We are cooking up in here, be back after this.

Raven Blair Davis: Alright. Welcome back, I'm here in Houston and Fran you're in Dallas?

Fran Harris: I'm in Dallas.

Raven Blair Davis: What a wonderful world we live in. You're listening to Careers from the Kitchen Table, we appreciate you coming and listening in and we invite you to next time bring a friend with you and check us out. I'm at the end of this show – boy time flies when you're having fun but I want to squeeze in a couple more questions real quick Fran. Once we've completed writing our book, how do we get the word out to start making some cash?

Fran Harris: Yeah, the first thing you need to do is to tell everybody you know, sounds simple but you'd be surprised how many people will just tell everybody in their address book that they've written a book.

Raven Blair Davis: Okay.

Fran Harris: They're too afraid to tell people that they've written a book and trust me, if you're too afraid to market your products, you'll never make a lot of money. The first thing you can do is to literally send out an email blast to everybody in your database.

Raven Blair Davis: Friends, family, subscribers...

Fran Harris: And ask them to forward it to everybody they know. There's no guarantee they're going to do it out of the goodness of their heart so ask them.

Raven Blair Davis: Yeah Jerry Clark says if you don't ask, you won't get. What about endorsements? Is there something you can suggest we do or is there something we should do on our first eBook and if so, how the heck do we get experts and gurus like you to agree to look at our book and give us an endorsement?

Fran Harris: A couple things you can do, first of all, once you write your book and you feel it's good enough to show the world, make a list of 10 people – your wish list people that you want to take a look at your book. Understand that I don't necessarily have time to read a 50, 60, 100 page book but you want to make sure that in your note to people that you just say 'can I send you a chapter, can I send you three to five pages' so the person receiving it knows this is gonna take a few minutes, goes to saying 'will you read my book' because the answer's gonna be no to that. I'm not gonna have time to read your book but if you say 'hey Fran do you have a second to read a couple of pages I'd love to get your endorsement – testimonial' sure, I mean there's a possibility I'll do that so that's the thing you want to do and also you don't want to discount the regular customer. If you've got a list of 10 people, make another list of 10 people who are just regular people who just love the information who're gonna evangelize for your book because a testimonial is great especially when it comes from regular people if you ask me.

Raven Blair Davis: Okay. Well thank you for sharing – you hear the music in the background and you've been through this so you know. I feel like I'm in Sao Paolo and they got the brooms. It has been a pleasure, thank you so much for coming and by the way do you have a few seconds to maybe just glance through my book, I'd like to send it to you. How to turn telephones to a cash cow...

Fran Harris: You can send me a couple of pages.

Raven Blair Davis: Mine is audio eBook so I'll give you a couple minutes of audio.

Fran Harris: Exactly, alright cool, thanks Raven.

Raven Blair Davis: Alright. Thank you everyone, you have been listening to Careers from the Kitchen Table and Dr. Fran Harris has been our guest and she is awesome. Go check her out at the www.5dayebooksolutions.com and until next week this is Raven Blair Davis and we'll see you next week. Until then, god bless and much prosperity to you.

To listen to the full audio of this interview visit:
http://www.careersfromthekitchentable.com/2ndEditionaudios

Plus be sure to visit http://amazingwomenofpower.com/radio and grab your free copy of *"Talk Your Way to Success – Unleash Your Dynamic Voice"* by Raven!

Khaliq Glover

Grammy Award Winning Recording Engineer, Producer, Songwriter

aka Khaliq-O-Vision, is a Grammy Award Winning Mixing Engineer/Producer whose clients include Prince, Michael Jackson, Justin Timberlake, Angie Stone, Herbie Hancock, Christina Aguilera, Marcus Miller, Jeffrey Osborne, Jamie Fox, Patti LaBelle, and many more.

He just completed work on the new upcoming Michael Jackson album since his passing. Khaliq also trains thousands of students online about all things related to recording, producing, and mixing music at a professional level by revealing many of the closely guarded secrets of the world's top recording artists, engineers, and producers.

Khaliq was one of the original musicians who worked on the "We Are the World" project with Michael Jackson and other noted celebrities. As a result he received a Grammy as one of the participating music engineers. Just recently, he was also one of the musicians who was asked to worked on the "This Is It" movie after the passing of Michael Jackson

Raven Blair Davis: I'm Raven Blair Davis your host and I'm just delighted because I'm about to bring on a Grammy award music engineer right to you. Sit back, relax – well don't get too relaxed, grab something lightly because you definitely are gonna want to take some copious notes on this one. Now, who am I speaking with? Well none other than Khaliq Glover also known as Khaliq O'Vision he's a Grammy winning recording engineer, 2001 Marcus Miller M2 producer and song writer based in Los Angeles California.   Khaliq worked for Kenny Rogers at Lionshare studios from 1982 to 1986 as an apprentice to learn engineering from the top engineers in the music industry such as Humberto Gatica, Tommy Vicari and John Guess. He soon became a first engineer on records by Jermaine Jackson, Donna Summers, Kenny Rogers, Jeffrey Osborne and many, many others. He also is one of many engineers to participate on "We Are The World" – remember that? Yeah, he participated on the "We Are The World" project produced by none other than Quincy Jones with an all-star cast including Michael Jackson, Lionel Richie, Stevie Wonder, Ray Charles, Bruce Springsteen, Bob Dylan, Diana Ross and many, many more. This man has so many dynamic accolades I could go on and on. The best thing for you to do is pay attention to what he's gonna be telling you. He's gonna give you all his information but you know what, you have to stay to the end because we're not gonna have him give you anything right now. We just want you to sit back, relax, enjoy and take some copious notes so without further ado I am delighted and excited to bring on my friend and my mentor Khaliq Glover. Hey Khaliq how are you?

Khaliq Glover: Hey Raven, how you doing?

Raven Blair Davis: I am dynamic. Are you kidding? I'm sitting here with you; we're getting ready to get some of your secrets. I am right on the edge of my seat my friend.

Khaliq Glover: So am I, I always love talking to you.

Raven Blair Davis: Wonderful. Well let's start out by catching the audience up a little bit about you. Just briefly, how did you get started in the music business Khaliq?

Khaliq Glover: Well it's truly one of those things where kind of by accident in a way – it only came I guess at age 13, 14, 15 - finding yourself. My father used to be a drummer but he never really encouraged me to get into music because it's a rough business you know? But of course I had to toy around with some of his stuff every now and then and hoped that I wouldn't get caught but eventually he ended up getting me a guitar and I just toyed with that and started playing it, teaching myself to play. And to make a long story short, after dealing with many vocal bands back east in Pittsburg where I'm from, I ended up migrating out here to Los Angeles and to record the songs that I was writing, I had to figure out some equipment that a publisher saw my talent and he gave me some free time to come in and just record whatever I wanted at night but I had to mind the equipment on my own. I just dug in and pulled out manuals and experimented and tried to figure it out on my own. Over the course of maybe a couple of years, a guy that was a friend of theirs was watching me do that and saw that I was serious and one day he offered me a job. He said 'how would you like to have a job working for Kenny Rogers and maybe learn about engineering?'

Raven Blair Davis: Now, how cool is that?

Khaliq Glover: I stumbled into it because like I said I was a guitar player. I'm not a technical engineer. I didn't go to school for it and that wasn't my first focus. I haven't even considered it at all but after I got into it, I liked the nuances of being around all these different stars I was working – at that time Kenny Rogers had a studio called Lionshare that had nothing but the greatest people at that particular time. The top artists, they were all migrating there. This is one of the premier studios in the world actually so I was very lucky.

Raven Blair Davis: Wow. My goodness, so this is a childhood passion and to listening to that, I said I have got to make sure that my grandson Christian hears the replay of this because he just informed me as of last week that he wants to play the guitar. So, he's gonna be truly inspired by your story. I have to get him all your teleseminars for sure.

Khaliq Glover: Absolutely.

Raven Blair Davis: We've got a lot of things we want to cram in so that those at home listening to this that aspire to be a musician or a song writer or a singer, they'll know how they can begin their home business. We're gonna go ahead and jump in to the questions. First of all, let me ask you this, how did you feel – coz I've got to ask you this before I go any further, how did you feel when you found out that you were getting that Grammy Khaliq?

Khaliq Glover: Are you kidding? I was just – the funny thing about the Grammy, there's two dramatic sides very diametrically opposed. One side of it I was just totally floured and ecstatic because when you're a young person, there are no limits to your dreams and possibilities so I always knew and told myself one day I'll get a Grammy but as you go through life and life just beats you down and beats you back into the reality, you have to pay bills and everything, I come to find out over years that while I was a good guitar player there were billions of great guitar players out here so what made me alter my reality is the engineering. That's a smaller pond and so there's thousands and thousands of guitar players and not a whole heck a lot of engineers and really good engineers shrinks down even smaller so I did what I could to try to learn how to be able to stay in the room with the greats and learn from them and then in the course of doing that, picking up some of their secrets, I won't call myself one of the greats but at least I figured – I was pretty open, I was a sponge to learn some good stuff that makes me able to still work now after all these years. The way I felt after I got that Grammy or when I first found out I was gonna get the Grammy was 'wow this is a dream come true' but also at the same time I had a reality check that I keep it very real in my mind because I know a lot of people that have gotten Grammys as well, artists, engineers and things like that and the bottom line it's a wonderful accolade to have but it's still just a trophy so you still really have to keep your career on forward momentum. I'm constantly trying to learn new things and constantly trying to stay in business because the industry is always changing so the reality of it is it's a great thing to have and it's great to be able to say about it but at the same time my reality is I want to do what I need to do to get the next Grammy, the past Grammy is done and gone. It's a trophy on the shelf, the next is what's important and I don't have that yet so that's my goal.

Raven Blair Davis: Yeah that's common. We speak in that in existence for sure. Let me ask you this Khaliq, do you work your music business from home?

Khaliq Glover: Partially. The nature of my business being in the music industry and being an engineer, I work with some good high level clients luckily so they usually have their own home studios and facilities and everything so many times I get called to work at their place. I was – when Jeffrey Osborne built his studio at his house, you know that I was the guy then that – that was the job that I left Lionshare for because Jeffrey hired me to be his personal engineer and then I worked with him for many, many years over a decade and then Herbie Hancock has a great studio. He has a massive facility and purple rate and all that stuff, he has a massive facility in Minneapolis so I go there but when I'm working with people that don't have those kind of massive budgets, I have a home studio setup at home that I put together – I used to have a pretty elaborate setup but I've scaled it down over the years because with digital technology and changing things, you don't really need as much equipment today as you used to need back even five years ago.

Raven Blair Davis: I'm glad to hear you say that because my next question Khaliq is how difficult is it to create a studio for those listening that want to get going and in their home and can you throw out a low and a high price range?

Khaliq Glover: Yeah and it really is across the board but it's a great time right now because technology is amazing especially with computers. If you've got enough money to buy any type of computer today, you basically have a studio that comes with it for free because most computers whether they're window or mac, mac's really great because they're meant for creativity, for music and creation so mac's come with a thing called garage band that you can start recording immediately as soon as you open it up you can start making songs and record and some people use it for podcasting and things like that and that comes with the computer so all you have to do is go out and buy mac and you get all that stuff. PC's are little more restricted but they have some things as well too and there are some free things that you can find on the internet just by searching. One of them being audacity which is a free program – I think you get it at sourceforge.net.

Raven Blair Davis: Oh yeah.

Khaliq Glover: Just do a search for audacity on Google and it has free software that comes up and that works for PC or mac for recording into your computer. Basically if you've got a computer, you can have a recording studio right then and there and we know you can get computers right now. You can get a laptop or used computer for under $500 even right now.

Raven Blair Davis: I know, so exciting for technology. Well that's good to know so they can probably even go out there and find something for between $500 to $1000 maybe?

Khaliq Glover: Absolutely.

Raven Blair Davis: Fantastic.

Khaliq Glover: You could get your computer but then I recommend auxiliary equipment – if you're trying to do a recording studio – whether you're trying to be a musician or a podcaster or radio show host or whatever, you need to have a good microphone or a decent microphone so that's probably – but a lot of great microphone now are being made, being manufactured in China and they come over here and you can get several things from companies without having to break the bank that'll get you started and get you a good decent quality sound until you can upgrade to better equipment and there's really a ton of resources right not to be able to have good quality.

Raven Blair Davis: That's fabulous to know that. There was a time where working in and building your music studio from home was either a real challenge or almost unheard of so it is just fantastic to be able to share with everyone today Khaliq.

Khaliq Glover: Yeah.

Raven Blair Davis: And they're hearing it from you that they can go out there and make this dream happen and they can get the equipment, it's not gonna break the bank, they're not gonna have to put up their homes or anything like that. Let me ask you this, if someone's listening out there and they say 'wow I'm inspired. I'm ready to do this thing' where should they start as far as building their music business, in other words, what are some of the key steps that you can recommend they take to get this in action?

Khaliq Glover: Well basically I use myself as what I've been finding and the stumbling along, there's a lot of ways to do things and you have to find what works for yourself so the first thing that I could think because I had to figure it out. I started out with the broad thing of saying 'I want to learn how to do my business on internet' but that's too broad so the first thing I started finding out is I did homework and research and finding out what other people did to lead me somewhere – you basically have to narrow it down, if you're gonna be in the music business and you want to make a music studio or become a recording artist or something, we have to focus what is it that you want to do. You have to focus it down into a smaller part of the business and once you do that, for example are you gonna be a recording artist or are you going to be an engineer or are you going to be a producer or a song writer, don't try to be them all. Too many people try to be them all.

Raven Blair Davis: Right. So you're basically saying niche it?

Khaliq Glover: Yeah.

Raven Blair Davis: Later focus on what you exactly want to do, pinpoint it down to the minute.

Khaliq Glover: And it doesn't mean you can't learn the other side but to get your business going, if it's too scattered in too many directions then you probably won't get anything down because there's too many things to learn in all the different directions so to get you at least started, if you're gonna be a song writer or if you're an engineer, then focus on what equipment you need or what skills you need to build and base your business from there. The second thing I would say is you need to figure out – if you get out of business, is it really business because you have to know who's the market, who are you trying to market to and if you don't know who actually might want to buy your stuff before you start trying to put together, you may spend a whole bunch of time making something that nobody wants and I had to find out by stumbling out and trying to figure out because music is so broad I actually tried a lot of different things and now I'm starting to zero in more and more on what people really, really want as opposed to just what I like and what…

Raven Blair Davis: Yeah, wow that's a good point and I'm glad you brought that up so let's go ahead and talk about that a little bit. What is the market looking for?

Khaliq Glover: Well as far as music and the focus of our call is trying to build a music business from home, the music industry is in tire streaks right now and the reason record companies are sledding and CD sales are at all-time lows and things like that is because the business is completely changed. People can find pretty much anything they want online for free so people don't want to pay for music anymore. Now, it's interesting because those that keep resisting and keep trying to follow the old business model, the old record company record label sign the deal keep the artist in this little box, that doesn't work anymore and there's a handful of artists – there's a group called Nine Inch Nails and there's a couple of other ones that have been actually marketing their stuff online directly to the consumer. They've been giving away a lot of stuff. They'll put their whole album up and you can download a lot of it for free and then decide to pay them if you like it and they take a chance on their popularity that they've build over the years that people will still – are willing to pay for them because they know they're getting quality for them without them having to brow beat them.

Raven Blair Davis: Right.

Khaliq Glover: Or without them having to go out and buy a CD and find out that there's only one song on the CD that you like after paying about $20. So the business has changed dramatically and what the industry I think is looking for now is – the music industry itself is trying to find a solution but the people are looking for what they always look for. They just want quality and a fair exchange for their dollar. People will give you their money if you don't try to rip them off and that's what the music industry quite frankly has been doing for say the last couple of decades or at least the last decade they've just been taking people's money and you get something and have one good song on an album. I know I get mad when I get that.

Raven Blair Davis: I used to get pretty mad at that too. So that's interesting that you brought this up. I want to ask you because we're getting down to our last few minutes here so there's a couple really, really important questions I feel I need to ask you on this and one of them is as a new person getting started, can you share with them maybe how they would go about marketing their first song and perhaps even touch real lightly on branding their self?

Khaliq Glover: Yes definitely I mean I've been watching it happen and I've been adjusting even what I do because it's a new day now so the first thing that I would suggest anybody do – it's funny because I do coaching classes for people to teach them how to get better things out of their songs so I sent out an offer to my list where I would give them a personal coaching telephone call where I get on the phone with them and they could play their song for me over the phone and I tell them what I hear until they found out what their concerns and tell them how to make it better or whatever and people were just floored by that and the thing is that I ran into one guy that I said 'would you mind if I – we need some real help with things so would you mind if I did that and post it in the internet or post it to anybody' and he was 'I don't want my songs heard by anybody else because they are not copyrighted yet and the funny thing is and I understand his concern but after all of these years that I've been in the business and that's been over 25 years now, I have not run into one single person and I don't even know one single person that ever had his song stolen from somebody else hearing it somewhere out there like – the old myth was you can't play your songs for anybody because somebody might steal your song and put it out and you hear all these myths – but I have not run into one single person out of everybody that I've met over the years that has happened to. The most that's likely to happen if it's somebody that you knew, one of your boys or if you write a song with somebody and then the co-writer runs off with it but the general population won't do that so my biggest tip I would say right now is get feedback from the public. Put your stuff up for free. Put it out on MySpace for free and get some feedback from people and see if they actually like what you do. See if they'll start building up and support what you do because that's how you're eventually gonna make some money. That's how the changing market place has started – as you know the people that are smarter started figuring that out and they're not worried about giving stuff away for free because they know if they build the following then the people will pay for the stuff later on because they know they're gonna get quality.

Raven Blair Davis: Right. Absolutely.

Khaliq Glover: With MySpace and YouTube you can put your CD for sale on cdbaby and a couple other places that you can get it out there but put a lot of free stuff out to get feedback from people and let them tell you what they think.

Raven Blair Davis: Absolutely. Well you know we've got about 3 minutes so I want you to share real quickly how the listeners can get in contact with you because you have some dynamic teleseminars and you just told us about something that is almost unheard of what you did so that's super – coaching individual over the phone like that and they're getting this information from a Grammy award winner, how fantastic is that? S o, share with us your website real quickly and then after that we'll have about a minute if you can touch on how they can begin to monetize right away like creating their own CD's or anything like that.

Khaliq Glover: Okay. Well first of all anybody that wants to learn how to make their music better or even just their vocal because I'm creating a product actually so I want you to get in my list which is at www.hypnotic-audio-secrets.com and there's a little sign up box that you'll see on it. Just give your name and email, you don't have to give a lot of information, just your name and email so I can contact you and I will have specials like the coaching where I will give it at an extremely discounted price but I'm also coming up with a product that may be of interest to your listeners, I'm coming up with a product that's specifically for how to record vocals.

Raven Blair Davis: Oh, wow, awesome.

Khaliq Glover: This will work whether you're a singer or podcast or radio announcer whatever, if you do anything with your voice, this will give you techniques that can transfer to anybody so sign up at www.hypnotic-audio-secrets.com.

Raven Blair Davis: Thank you and you have your teleseminars once a week right?
Khaliq Glover: Yeah it's depending on my work schedule because sometimes I'm in the studio for 14 to 16 hour days and you know how that goes.
Raven Blair Davis: Okay, close this out because I know we're gonna go in a commercial in about one minute, real quickly, what's the fastest way for them to start monetizing from their home music business.

Khaliq Glover: The fastest way to start monetizing is to make some samples of what you do and put up a web page or a blog or something like that and I would suggest try some of the single here and there for download for cheap price, do it cheaper than I-tunes. I -tunes is 99 cents, so audios for maybe 79 cents, most people will take a risk on that and see if they're interested, put a little free thing where they can hear it or even ask for donations, have a PayPal donation that you can put on a blog and things like that if they like it they can just give you a donation.

Raven Blair Davis: Alright. Well this has been absolutely wonderful. Thank you again my friend for coming and sharing. You've always been there for me.

Raven Blair Davis: Absolutely. I appreciate you so much for coming and sharing with us here at Careers from the Kitchen Table. We look forward to your product and one more time the website is...

Khaliq Glover: www.hypnotic-audio-secrets.com, www.mixingandrecording.com, www.eqsecrets.com and www.vocalrecordingsecrets.com

Raven Blair Davis: Alright. You have been listening to an interview with the Grammy winning engineer Khaliq Glover. I recommend if you're thinking about getting in the home business industry of music, make sure you check him out and be sure to check out his teleseminars.

To listen to the full audio of this interview visit:

http://www.careersfromthekitchentable.com/2ndEditionaudios

Plus be sure to visit http://amazingwomenofpower.com/radio and grab your free copy of *"Talk Your Way to Success – Unleash Your Dynamic Voice"* by Raven!

Kim Kiyosaki

Speaker, Author, TV Host and Investor

With a passion for educating women about money and investing, Kim Kiyosaki draws on a lifetime of experience—in business, education, real estate and investing in her mission to empower women to take control of their financial lives.

Her belief: The world would be a better place if there were more Rich Women. At first blush this statement may seem to be an obvious assumption, but Kim digs deeper into wealth as it relates to happiness, relationships, self-esteem/self-worth and celebrations of success.

A self-made Rich Woman, Kim hosts a national television show for PBS, is a sought-after speaker and a columnist for WomenEntrepreneur.com.

She's married to Robert Kiyosaki, entrepreneur, investor, teacher and author of the international mega-bestseller Rich Dad Poor Dad, but remains a fiercely independent woman.

Raven Blair Davis: I'm about to bring this lady on, her name is Kim Kiyosaki. Let me tell you a little bit about Kim. With a passion for educating women about money and investing, Kim draws on a lifetime of experiences in business, education, real estate and investing in her mission to empower women to take control of their financial lives. Kim's belief is the world would be a much better place if there were more rich women – I like that Kim. At first this statement may seem to be an obvious assumption but Kim digs deeper into a well as it relates to happiness, relationships, self-esteem, self-worth and celebration of success. A self-made rich women, Kim hosts a national television show for PBS, is a sought after speaker and a columnist for women entrepreneurs and she's married to the man, yes I'm talking about Robert Kiyosaki, entrepreneur, investor, teacher and author of an international mega bestseller – I got a chance to see both at Ellie Drake's big event in October and they are amazing couple in business. You know what; Kim knows her stuff so without further ado, our feature guest, none other than Kim Kiyosaki. Hey Kim.

Kim Kiyosaki: Hey Raven how are you? You're fantastic.

Raven Blair Davis: Thank you, how are you?

Kim Kiyosaki: I'm terrific.

Raven Blair Davis: Well you know what, I'm excited. You are just a delight to meet at the event and what I like about you is you are just you. You're just so authentic, I love that.

Kim Kiyosaki: Thanks, well people look at me and they see now where I am today and they see the fancy stuff but it wasn't that long ago that Robert and I were flat broke, we were homeless for a period of time, and we really struggled financially so I understand especially today with the economy and what's happening. I understand if people have some concerns and some fear about their financial lives because I've been there and it wasn't that long ago.

Raven Blair Davis: And that's what we're gonna be talking about today as a matter of fact getting pass that fear and taking charge of your money, taking charge of your life. A little bit from your rich woman book by the way nice cover. If you haven't got this book, you have to go get it its rich woman by Kim Kiyosaki, take charge of your money, take charge of your life, beautiful, purple which makes you think of money and I like that Kim and the picture is just awesome, kudos to you girl on the book.

Kim Kiyosaki: Thank you, thank you.

Raven Blair Davis: Listen, I want to jump right into our subject because you're right, people are scared to death right now and I'm a firm believer of what you speak about, you bring about and we have to get away from the fear, we have to get away from TV and the negativity. Before we get into our questions and a little bit of your story, can you just share your thoughts on that?

Kim Kiyosaki: Well when you look at the economy right now, there's an awful lot of opportunity, there's an awful lot of fear and which way is the economy gonna go – who knows and this is not just the US economy, this is the global economy. I look at down the road and one of the things I do Raven is I prepare for the worst and I look at what if the jobs don't come back? What if the markets don't come back and what if all this happens because I don't want to depend upon the government, if the government's going to continue printing money which I think they will – probably what that means is there's going to be inflation which means your money is going to buy you less and less and it also means that a lot of government services, they're taking about Medicare, social security, that may disappear if not diminish greatly. I'm looking at – okay I can't depend on the government.

Raven Blair Davis: Right.

Kim Kiyosaki: I'm not planning on depending on the government. I have to depend on me so what can I do today? I think that's the most important thing. What do I need to do to be in control of my financial life? What do I need to do to get my family financially secure? It's not even a matter necessarily of financially free right now for a lot of people it's just how do I get that financial security?

Raven Blair Davis: It's about being secure first and then the financial freedom. I like what you said when you said you prepare yourself for the worst.

Kim Kiyosaki: Absolutely. Its understanding the key for the rich woman philosophy and the key to whole rich dad philosophy is financial education. In this economy, part of what that is paying attention to what's happening, listening to some of the TV shows and radio shows like yours Raven, that's number one...

Raven Blair Davis: Thank you.

Kim Kiyosaki: Listening and then discerning what it really means to you. Go online, actually I really recommend going online and finding those newsletters, finding the sources that are not linked to advertising dollars which are not linked to an agenda that are not there to sell you something. Look for the specific plates that are really there to educate you.

Raven Blair Davis: Inform you, and give you insight.

Kim Kiyosaki: Inform you, right. There's one investor who I really enjoy listening to, his name is Jim Rogers.

Raven Blair Davis: Okay.

Kim Kiyosaki: He's with the Soros. He started one of the major hedge funds years ago and he travels the world and he just tells it like it is. You don't have to agree with any of these people but just start paying attention to what's happening so that then you can start to make better financial decisions for yourself. You have to be aware and a lot of women say 'I'm not good with money or my eyes blaze over when it comes to money' well you know what, that's BS. You have to start taking care of you and your money.

Raven Blair Davis: Yeah we have to step away from the fear.

Kim Kiyosaki: You know what I think the fear really is because I hear it all the time, I'm afraid of making mistakes, I'm afraid of losing money. I think most women – I think we know what we need to do whether it's our financial life or job, our career, a relationship – maybe a bad relationship. I think we know what to do, the question is do we have the courage to accept the consequences. If you're in a bad marriage and you need to walk away, do you have the courage to struggle a little bit in the short term. Do you have the courage to go through the tough times but to be a happier individual?

Raven Blair Davis: That takes a lot of courage.

Kim Kiyosaki: Yeah and the opposite of fear is courage and do you have the courage to accept the consequences of the actions you know you need to take. I know there are things I know I need to do. Am I willing to do it is the question?

Raven Blair Davis: Yeah and then just like you said earlier, just facing what could be the worst scenario.

Kim Kiyosaki: Right. What's the worst case scenario, look at it, how do you deal with it? I look at the worst case scenarios in my business. I look at the worst case scenarios in every investment I go into and I always have a plan to deal with if that happens. Now, 99.9% of the time that never happens. It's usually somewhere in between of what the reality is of here's the best case and here's the worst case. But because I prepared for the worst, if that doesn't happen, I'm stepping that much ahead of the game.

Raven Blair Davis: Yeah, you can handle it.

Kim Kiyosaki: Yeah.

Raven Blair Davis: You can handle it for sure. Tell us worth is deep and I can reason up on you girl. You've got a real deep passion for empowering women to financial independence. Tell us about that.

Kim Kiyosaki: Yeah I'm surprised because growing up; I really hung out with the men. I hung out with the boys, the men, I like sports, I like business and most of my mentors, teachers were men so that now I'm working with women is an idea that I didn't think would happen for me. And what happened is when Robert and I founded the rich dad company that was back in '96. We were traveling the world and we were talking about the rich dad principles and philosophy and I would get up and I would speak briefly to the women about women and money, women and investing and it didn't matter if I was in Los Angeles, Singapore, South Africa. After every talk, I would be surrounded by women and no matter what city I was in, same as you, same questions. Here's what I found is that most women do not make their financial lives the priority until they have a wakeup call.

Raven Blair Davis: Yeah that would be true.

Kim Kiyosaki: So it could be a divorce. Today, one out of two marriages end in divorce and typically if there are kids involved, the women gets the kids and the first year after divorce, a women's standard living drops an average of 45%. A wakeup call could be an illness where you can no longer work or could be a job layoff which is happening for a lot of people today men and women and for women, 58% of female baby boomers have less than 10,000 set aside for retirement. That's not gonna last very long. Another wakeup call could be the death of a spouse and this statistic has risen but of the elderly living in poverty, 75% are women yet 80% of those women were not poor when their husbands were alive. The wakeup call – all the sudden the woman goes 'oh my god I have to take care of the money' she doesn't know what do with it, Mr. & Ms. Financial helper comes along and the next thing you know she's broke and poor. I think so many of us have not had the financial education. One of the things I see happening in this economy which I see is a real plus is people are realizing more and more that financial education is priceless that they need to get themselves financially educated and not depend upon a spouse, the government, family but they have to depend upon themselves.

Raven Blair Davis: Yeah and I think it goes back to what you were saying. We're more back in the corner now and it's like you come out and fight, teach me all the information I need and you want to indulge in everything, get it all, consume everything.

Kim Kiyosaki: Absolutely and for women I think this really is – I'm working on a new book called "It's Your Time" because I think today when the economy is bad, there's more and more cases that show that it's when women do step up. It's when women take the lead. If there's a financial crisis in a family or a crisis of any kind in a family, it's typically the woman that stands up and says okay 'I'll handle this' but until she has to, until it's in her face, typically women – this is a very generalize statement, typically women may sit back and not take the necessary action until they're forced to.

Raven Blair Davis: Because they're forced to and I believe that and then we become unstoppable in our pursuit.

Kim Kiyosaki: Yes. I just came across a – there was a speech given by the CEO of Coca-Cola a gentleman by the name of Muhtar Kent and he said that the real drivers of the world won't be any nation but will be women.

Raven Blair Davis: I like him, what's his name again?

Kim Kiyosaki: Muhtar Kent

Raven Blair Davis: Alright.

Kim Kiyosaki: CEO of Coca-Cola. He says its women entrepreneurs and women in business, political leaders, he said that 21st century is going to be the women's century and I completely agree with that. I think we need more and more women leaders in all facets of life.

Raven Blair Davis: I know. I have to tell you I was really ruthless with Hillary. I wanted to see what a woman would do.

Kim Kiyosaki: I'm impressed with what she's been doing.

Raven Blair Davis: Yeah.

Kim Kiyosaki: I've been watching her and I'm really impressed with what she's been doing so good for her.

Raven Blair Davis: You talked earlier about it's important for us to get financially secure before financially free so I'd like for you to talk a little bit and explain to listeners what you mean about financially secure and the difference of being financially free and what exactly that means.

Kim Kiyosaki: That's a really good question. There's a famous investor Warren Buffet. I just heard this and I like what he said. He said there are many ways to get to financial heaven and I like that term financial heaven because financial heaven is different for everybody. Your financial heaven may be different than my financial heaven.

Raven Blair Davis: Right because everybody lives on several different levels or statuses.

Kim Kiyosaki: Yes, exactly so financial security for me is what do you need to survive, where do you need to feel secure and to be able to sleep at night not being worried about having enough to pay the bills, having enough to take care of the family, that would be financial security. Financial freedom for me – it's our philosophy; simply we have our money working for us so that every month, our investments and it's very simple. People think to be financially free; you need millions and millions of dollars, that's not my philosophy. The philosophy is we have money coming in every month from our investments primarily real estate that is greater than our expenses. For example, when Robert and I 'retired' which was back in 1994, we didn't have millions of dollars. We simply had $10,000 a month coming in cash flow from our investments but our living expenses were only $3,000. So at that moment we were financially free. We did not have to work for money anymore because our money was working for us. That's the formula of financial freedom and everybody knows what their living expenses are if they tell themselves the honest truth and the brutal truth about really how much is going out every month then figure out how much in cash flow you need to cover that. Here's the beauty of it Raven. This is what I like the best. When that happened for me in '94 and I could sleep well at night and I had peace of mind and I was in financial heaven, I pictured for the first time – asked myself what is it that I really want to do with my life and up until that point it was just about how to have enough money to pay the bills.

Raven Blair Davis: How to survive.

Kim Kiyosaki: How to survive. So that was when I started looking at the whole – this is when the rich dad philosophy – Robert and I created the board game cash flow, that was the first thing we did so that people could teach each other about money and investing. We didn't have to go around teaching ever body. The game taught people and people could teach one another so that's how we started the rich dad company and then from there, the rich woman emerged because I just saw this tremendous need for women to be empowered and educated and to take care of themselves financially.

Raven Blair Davis: Boy, are we glad you did. You showed a big time for it. We definitely appreciate that. So now that you've explained the difference of being financially secure and financially free, my question to you is it really possible for us to become financially free even during this recession and if so, how do we begin?

Kim Kiyosaki: Yes, in terms for finding opportunities, this recession is the best for that if you know what to look for.

Raven Blair Davis: Okay.

Kim Kiyosaki: I got two answers to that Raven. Number one is you have to get financially educated and there's so many ways to do that. My head is spinning because there's so much I want to say. Just every day, learn something new about money. Learn a new world, a new vocabulary word or read a book or an article or go online or watch a news program, listen to a radio program about money. Everyday learn something new about money because the key is in order to become financially secure and ideally financially free its' what you do in your spare time that will determine your success.   You're not gonna get rich at work. You're not gonna get rich at a job. It's what you do at your spare time and I know women especially are like 'oh god I have no spare time' everybody has spare time. You always have – it's your choice to do what you do with your time so if one of your priorities is to put aside even half an hour a day to learn about money, learn about investing because this is your life, your financial future, that's your life so I would say learn something new about money every day and then one other thing that you could specifically today is – one of the rules Robert and I follow is with every single dollar bill that comes into our household, it doesn't matter where it comes from but every single dollar, we take 30% off the top. That's how we started. We take more off now but it was at the time 30% off the top.

Raven Blair Davis: To save or invest.

Kim Kiyosaki: Yes we put 10% to a savings account, exactly 10% into an investment account and 10% into a charity and the key is it didn't matter what the percentage was as long as you did it with every single dollar and it became a habit. That was the key.

Raven Blair Davis: And what they say in 21 days...

Kim Kiyosaki: Yeah in 21 days it becomes a habit correct.

Raven Blair Davis: So it's just a matter of keep doing it.

Kim Kiyosaki: Right and you start learning – we're forming this rich women group throughout the world where women are coming together on a regular basis and meeting and learning and studying together because that's what it takes. The game of money, investing, of becoming financially independent is a process. It's not gonna happen overnight. It's not get rich quick. It's a process. And going back to your question of in this economy, in this economy right now, if you know what you're looking for, there are deals right and left because when the prices are down, and we women know how to find a bargain. We're great shoppers. If we can do it with shoes and handbags, we could do it with stocks and real estates. We know how to find that bargain and it's not rocket science but right now when the prices are low, I'm buying more today than I did several years ago because there are so many opportunities out there where the prices have come down dramatically which of course means the cash flow is better or the return on your money is better than it was several years ago when the markets were so high.

Raven Blair Davis: This is time to let go the person so to speak and it's so funny because when this life – people hold on to their money when it comes to things like that, investing – I've talked to many people about advertising 'oh no I don't want to do anything' then I'm saying well if you don't want to do anything your business is gonna go away but they don't get it. That's the same thing with investing. However they'll go out and buy these big expensive games for the kids to sit on TV or they'll go buy the dress and the shoes and you're saying just take a little.

Kim Kiyosaki: Yeah. Just start small. Get the financial education and then start small. Don't bet the ranch, your house mortgage, just start small. Take baby steps. We bring out two really good points in the world of business, when people cut back first is their advertising and the advertising and their PR is what they need to expand upon in tough times and to grow your business. So, you have to start small. Put a little money down and if people are saving money, I think saving money right now is probably one of the worst things you can do because as the money prints more and more money your money becomes worth less and less. It's gonna cost you more dollars to put food on your table and put dinner on your table in six months than it did six months earlier than it did today. One thing that Robert and I do and I'm not saying to do this but you might want to start researching it is instead of holding cash, we're holding silver and gold because as more and more dollars get put into the economy and the value of your dollar goes down, the price of silver and gold typically will go up. We've been seeing it go up a lot lately, we're hoping it's gonna come back down but right now I think it's a good place to hold my cash.

Raven Blair Davis: Like you said, we just have to go out and educate ourselves, read these things and instead of watching the housewives Raven just start watching some good stuff.

Kim Kiyosaki: You know what's fun too? You put a little money down, let's say you go out today and you buy a one ounce silver coin. It's gonna cost you about $30 today but what it does is you've now bought this commodity and I like silver because it is a consumable. It's used in computers, light bulbs and cell phones, it's used up and so there's gonna be more and more demand especially with the new countries coming online, new infrastructure being built, but you put a little money down and all the sudden your interest is gonna go through the roof. I don't care if it's $30 or $3,000 it could be $10 whatever it is so you put a little money down and you're gonna start watching the price of silver every day and you're gonna go online and you're gonna go see TV shows on it and you're gonna start looking at articles and newspapers and magazines and just because you put $30 down you're gonna start to become more and more educated and smarter and more sophisticated in the world of silver investing. It's that simple.

Raven Blair Davis: That's good. I'm glad you shared that with us and so many times I'm sure you would agree Kim, at the end of the week; we waste that $30 or $50 and cannot even account for where it went.

Kim Kiyosaki: Yeah, easily and that's a great piece because from the beginning you really have to know where you are. One of the first steps really is – your financial education is to know where you are today financially and this again goes back to you have to tell the honest truth. You have to be brutal. You have to admit to how much you spend on restaurants and how much you spend on clothes and shopping and who you owe money to and where is your money. I mean if you're married, do you know where the money is, do you know what investment you have and do you know where all the accounts are? That's step number one – to understand where you are today financially because when I talk about financial independence and about financial heaven, financial heaven to me is not cutting up your credit card, it's not living below your means, pinching pennies, clipping coupons, it's not about that because that does not inspire a person. That actually – to live below your means really to me means be less of who you are. I want to instead expand who I am. I want to grow who I am and I want to expand my means. So in your plan, you may in the beginning need to really pay attention to your money and you may need to do some things differently and not spend as much as you were spending on things that make you no money. So people spend money on things, you might need to cut back on those and start putting your money into accounts where you – put in investment accounts and tied in accounts and things like that but the overall plan in my opinion as the rich woman philosophy is to be more of who you are and to create your financial life to have what it is you want. Not to drive the old beat up clunker car and downsize to a smaller house but to really create your plan so it gives you what it is you want and inspires you to be more of who you are.

Raven Blair Davis: Inspire you to be more of who you are. I like that because a lot of times we're not quite sure who we are and then when we do something that's so positive it's like – unleash the greatness within us.

Kim Kiyosaki: Yes and discovering who you are and being true to you, that's 99.9% of the game to me, to business success, to investing, you have to be true to who you are.

Raven Blair Davis: Absolutely. Thank you so much Kim Kiyosaki for this amazing interview and thank you all for listening in as I interviewed on this portion of this show none other than Kim Kiyosaki, author, speaker, financial adviser, investor and her book "Rich Woman Take Charge of Your Money, Take Charge of Your Life," Kim Kiyosaki, give them that website one more time Kim.

Kim Kiyosaki: Its richwoman.com.

Raven Blair Davis: This is Raven a.k.a the talk show maven. I certainly hoped you enjoyed that interview I did with Kim Kiyosaki but you know what, that's only half of what Kim and I talked about. I'm gonna give you a website where you can go hear the entire interview which was over an hour long because I tell you it just gets better and better.

Go to www.careersfromthekitchentable.com and you will be able to hear the entire interview that I did with Kim and it is incredible. Lots of good information that I plan on putting into action and I hope you do too.

To listen to the full audio of this interview visit
http://www.careersfromthekitchentable.com/2ndEditionaudios

Plus be sure to visit http://amazingwomenofpower.com/radio and grab your free copy of *"Talk Your Way to Success – Unleash Your Dynamic Voice"* by Raven!

Michael Senoff
"The King of Interviews"

Michael is an experienced internet marketer and talk show host and a popular professional interviewer. Michael has taught 100% online around the country & around the world to more than 50,000 students.

His web site Hardtofindseminars.com started in 1992 buying and selling pre-owned Jay Abraham seminars, Gary Halbert seminars and Dan Kennedy seminars, books and tapes for pennies on the dollar. Now his over-the-top online audio interview web site is listed in the top 1% of most visited web sites in the world. Michael has also worked as a coach and advisor to other famous marketing consultants.

He is the author of the book: "Talk Yourself Rich": (86 of the most revealing, proprietary secrets on the subject of how to make more money with audio interviews and the soon to be released sequel: Audio Marketing Secrets; How To Make Your Own Information Product Using Audio Interviews. With "Over 117 Hours of FREE Downloadable Audio Interviews With Sales, Marketing and Business Success Experts."

Michael Senoff's hardtofindseminars.com is the world's leading FREE digital audio business library that uses the power of personal interviews and storytelling to capture and relay the advice of world-class business experts.

Get free audio interviews of the experience and guidance of business leaders on the subjects of business growth, direct marketing, business buying, writing, effective advertising, referral marketing, negotiating, product development, marketing consulting, and the art of buying advertising.

Using Little More Than A Telephone And Your Voice

The beauty of audio is that it costs very little to produce, can be used in many different ways to make money, and is convenient for users who want to fill up their iPods and listen while they multitask.

In this interview Michael shares the cheapest ways he knows how to put together quality audios, along with some real-life examples of how to land interviews and make money right away.

Raven Blair Davis: Welcome to Careers from the Kitchen Table, the show that teaches how to cook without the cooking. As you know, each and every week, we bring you straight talk from the experts giving you some good old home recipes of success so that you my friend can begin to build a business from your home or maybe you just want to do your career from the home. The choice is yours. We always tell you we like to show you how to get from that hectic highway to the smooth sailing hallway and you are at the right place at the right time especially today because I'm so excite to have the guest that I'm gonna be bringing you today. I want you to think of something as you listen to our full hour today and I want you to think that there is power in your voice. Yeah, there's power in your voice and our guest today is gonna show you how much power there actually is and how you can make money from your voice. How cool is that? My guest today – wow, this is definitely a dream come true interview. You know I always tell you when it's one of my dreams and he is a dream come true interview. I met Michael a few months ago through my sister Tracy. She said 'you have to check out this site' and when I did, it was just phenomenal. His name is Michael Senoff and he's the founder and executive editor of www.hardtofindseminars.com.

Michael is an experienced internet marketer and talk show host and a popular professional interviewer. He has taught 100% online – doesn't do a whole lot of travel at all and he's taught people around the country and around the world to more than 50,000 students. His websites www.hardtofindseminars.com started in 1992 buying and selling pre-owned Jay Abraham seminars, Gary Halbert seminars and Dan Kennedy seminars, books and tapes for pennies on a dollar. Now he's the top online and interview website and is listed in the top 1% of most visited websites in the world. Michael has also worked as a coach, an adviser to the famous marketing consultants; you name 'em, he worked with them for sure. He's the author of the book "Talk Yourself Rich" revealing proprietary secrets on the subject of how to make more money with audio interviews and the soon to be released sequel audio marketing secrets, how to make your own information products used in audio interviews. Michael, welcome to Careers from the Kitchen Table. I'm so excited.

Michael Senoff: Wow Raven, I really appreciate that. I am flattered and what a great, great introduction. I really appreciate that. Thank you.

Raven Blair Davis: Well you're very welcome, you deserve another and I know we have lots to cover; I want to give you the full hour because you are just the man when it comes to interviewing that's for sure. Definitely have mastered the art and there is an art to that isn't it?

Michael Senoff: Is there an art? I don't know if you've ever met or your listeners have ever met good listeners or maybe net people who just talk damn too much. If someone just talked too much, they can't be a good listener so I think the art is shutting your mouth and being a good listener and I don't know where I heard this quote 'god gave you two ears and one mouth so you'd listen twice as much as you talk' I wouldn't say it's an art. I think it's just common sense and there isn't a listener right now listening to your show who cannot do this and cannot do what I have done.

Raven Blair Davis: Well before we zap into our questions, I know you're a man of stories and our listeners here at Careers from the Kitchen Table; they love a good story so let's start with yours. What got you into doing this?

Michael Senoff: Okay. What got me into all this blabbing and talking and interviewing and asking questions? I think first of all I'm just naturally a curious person and all these interviews I've been doing over the year's really they're all from a selfish point of view. It's all because I wanted to learn stuff but I had a magic little tool and that is a little recorder where I could get on the phone with someone just like you're talking to me and we are recording and we're capturing that magic. We're capturing the words that I'm saying and the questions that you're asking and we're able to harness that and hold that and we don't ever have to remember because we got it "canned and cloned" and that's a quote from a great mentor if mine, a guy named Gary Halbert. But how this all started was years ago when eBay was just getting going and I was living in San Diego California down at the beach. I came out here to follow that California dream and I'm from Atlanta, Georgia originally and I came out here involved in a multilevel marketing industry. I graduated college from the University of Alabama so I'm a southern boy and grew up in Atlanta and then came out here for that California dream, wanted to check out the sunshine. I lived right on the ocean for the first nine months in a little two bedroom place and drove out here with a buddy of mine from college and I didn't know what I was going to do. I just knew I wanted to come out here and just – like the early settlers, come stake my claim. I didn't know what I was gonna do and I floundered from multilevel marketing to marketing jobs and multilevel marketing was a good experience. I learned a lot from that. There was good training but I can never make any money from it and I needed to do something where I could support myself and I got involved with eBay and as I had a quest for learning marketing, there was this marketing dude named Jay Abraham and I didn't know anything about him but someone said 'go check him out' just like your sister told you to check me out. So I checked this guy out and I had studied a lot of the Zig Ziglar and Brian Tracy – some of the real commercial names in selling. I've always had a quest for learning. So I checked this dude named Jay Abraham out and I found that this guy was putting on these seminars $20,000 to go to one of his seminars and I said 'what? $20,000 to go to a seminar?' What is this guy doing at these seminars you know? So $20,000 and I'm like 'man this has have to be good' I mean c'mon when you hear someone doing a seminar for $20,000 that gets your attention. You want to know what in the heck is this guy teaching for $20,000.

Raven Blair Davis: I know.

Michael Senoff: I called his office and there was a guy who answered the phone and I said I heard about these seminars and what other kind of products do you have and I was broke. I had no money and he pitched me on a set of these two videos, a set called optimization. It was Jay Abraham's main philosophy at that time on marketing and the three ways to grow a business and it was recorded at a Tony Robbins seminar. Everyone's seen Tony Robbins, the guy with the big teeth on TV. So I knew who Tony Robbins was since I'd seen him on TV and I think I even ordered his personal power trying to get some more power for myself at the time and I watched it and this thing, it just blew me away because I've been studying sales and stuff but this was the marketing part. If you know how to sell, that's great. Let's say you're knocking on doors and you can only knock on so many doors in a day but when you understand marketing, marketing is like the salesmanship. If you're a good salesman, multiply it. And then I really got into this stuff and I found the guy who had gone to the seminar and I asked him if he would sell me his used seminar because when you pay $20,000 to go to his seminar, you get to come home with all the recordings of the seminar on cassettes. At that time CD wasn't going but he'll give you the transcripts, written word per word transcripts, and he just threw in a huge pile of all his material like his life's work up until that point and that was in the early 90's. So, you know how people are, most people will get a book and never even finish the first chapter would you agree?

Raven Blair Davis: I totally agree.

Michael Senoff: Well you have people who went to this $20,000 and you have to keep in mind a lot of businesses likely paid for their employees to go or they used it as a write off and they just didn't value the $20,000 seminar and they came home with all this stuff and they would be looking at it and they never did anything with it. So I got a list from this guy and I found someone in San Diego where I was living who had gone to the $20,000 seminar. I called him up on the phone. I said 'hey this is kind of a weird call but I got your number as someone who went to that Jay Abraham seminar seven years ago and by any chance would you still have those tapes and stuff sitting around' and they said 'we sure do' and so I negotiated and was able to buy a set of those tapes for $50. He had everything. He paid $20K, I got them for $50 and I went over there with my wife and we picked them up. I went inside, there they were all in a box, the books, the tapes, everything. And I came home and I just started devouring it and this seminar was a seminar on how to make money as a marketing consultant. Jay Abraham was a real good marketing consultant where he would approach businesses and show them how to grow the business and he'd say 'if I can make you a dollar would you pay me 25 cents?' and he was real good at that and made millions and millions of dollars and I thought wow that would be great thing and I wanted to get into that. I started all that stuff and just honing my knowledge and learning more and more but then eBay was coming around and I had studied that and I wanted to learn how to sell something on eBay. I had this digital camera and I was engaged at that time and I think I moved in at that time with my fiancé and I wanted to buy this big blue barbecue grill. Now, this isn't any ordinary grill. This is called Kamado. Kamado is an ancient cooking method I think all the way back from Japan thousands of years ago but this thing looks like a big genie bottle and it's a smoker. You know when you smoke ribs or you smoke something at low temperature. I love cooking and I love barbecue so you could barbecue with it or you could smoke meats with it but there was a problem Raven. It was $1,700 and I was getting ready to get married and my wife did not want me to spend that money.

Raven Blair Davis: Oh no.

Michael Senoff: And I said 'fine, then I'm selling my Jay Abraham tapes' and I put them on eBay and I said pre-owned Jay Abraham tapes and sure enough I sold them. Don't quote me I think it was about the same price as the grill.

Raven Blair Davis: Oh really?

Michael Senoff: Yeah so I sold the set of tapes on eBay and I couldn't believe it. I paid for $50 and I made myself a nice profit and I bought my grill and I thought this may be a good business because the guy who sent me the list of the people in California who went to the seminar, I started calling all those people and seeing how many of those Jay Abraham seminars I could collect from people.

Raven Blair Davis: And I see you're like me. You're a telephone person.

Michael Senoff: Yeah I just hit the phones. I found probably five or six more in California and then I had people ship them to me and I had people sometimes give them to me for free. Sometimes I pay $200, sometimes $500 for the set because I break it all down and resell it and then in one of the boxes was a master list of 900 people who went to that seminar.

Raven Blair Davis: Oh, what a list.

Michael Senoff: And it had the name, phone number, address and so I was selling these things, it was a very hot market on eBay for pre-owned Jay Abraham stuff because eBay was new. There was no one else doing what I was doing. No competition and for a single guy selling Jay Abraham stuff on eBay, I was doing pretty well because I wouldn't pay much for it. So, fundamental concept in business, buy low, sell high. Find a market demand and eBay is a great for that. For your listeners, eBay is just such a little laboratory where you can determine markets and what sells and what doesn't sell and so I worked eBay in buying and selling hard to find seminar material for years and years. That's why I call it www.hardtofindseminars.com.

Raven Blair Davis: Wow. So that is really interesting and I was wondering how that name came about so thanks for sharing that story. There's a lot of meat in that story. I want to advise listeners to go back and listen to that again on the replay. Okay but I understand how you got going as far as getting your tape and audios of seminars and sell them on embay but how did it transition that into saying 'hey I want to interview people.'

Michael Senoff: Okay, great question. Well I knew with marketing, with what I had, it wasn't gonna last forever. Remember I told you there were only 900 names on that list? Well first of all this list was about seven years old so I couldn't get in touch with all of these people and I knew that my stores for pre-owned Jay Abraham seminar material was gonna dry up. I couldn't go print these. I wasn't counterfeiting stuff. I wasn't going to Kinko's making copies. I was only selling original material that people paid for and went to the seminar. So everything I sold was original stuff that people paid money for. The writing was on the wall. I needed to get something else going besides this pre-owned marketing seminars. I needed to develop my own products and so it just happened by accident.

There was some marketing buddies that I had made during those years who were into this Jay Abraham stuff and I started learning about marketing and I had some software on my computer that could record a conversation and there was a guy who called me and we said 'let's do a recording' I asked him questions about marketing and I asked him how he was making money. Really, I didn't have any plans of doing an interview site but it went so well that I just started doing recordings as a way to make it easier for people to absorb the information on my website because I figured you got these websites and these real long sales letters and some people don't want to read. They maybe don't have time or they're too lazy and I learned to do a recording and to turn that recording into what's called an mp3 file. When I first started my website www.hardtofindseminars.com it was only a one page website and it was a story of the blue barbecue grill and how I found all these Jay Abraham tapes and how I buy and sell them and it was just one page but at the top of that page, I put this mp3 recording that said 'hey if you're too busy to read the sales letter, you can download this mp3 so it was just a way to help the visitors who came to my site to give me an extra edge for the visitor who came to my site to get the information about what www.hardtofindseminars.com was about so they could download it and listen to it. They could click on it and the little player on their computer would play it for them almost like spoon feed them the information because when you have a website, you're trying to get your information to somebody's brain, you have to make it easy for people and that's all I was trying to do. And then I just started doing these interviews. I told you at the beginning it was all from a selfish motive. I just wanted to learn everything I could form business experts and marketing people and I said 'hey could I interview you?' and I like to ask questions. I think I'm pretty good at it and I think I'm a good listener and I was just interviewing these business experts really just for myself so I could learn. But I was also doing it as a way to keep people coming back to my website. I was also enacting at natural law. Give and you shall receive. I wanted to give some real good value and I wanted people to remember the name of the site, they say 'man there's this site out there and he's got these great interviews and they're not bad interviews. They're pretty good. I can't believe he's giving all this stuff away for free' and that's how it all started and just kept doing it and doing and building it and making it bigger and better and longer interviews and more topics and four or five years later, all that stuff adds up.

Raven Blair Davis: Yeah and for those listening, you have to go check him out. We'll be taking a break pretty soon. Again its www.hardtofindseminars.com and when you get there you'll see that Michael has over 117 hours of free downloadable audio interviews and they pertain to sales, marketing and business success, experts. Remember, this man is the world's leading free digital audio business library. You've got to check him out. You know what Michael, before we go to commercial break, we have listeners here that – most of them have just lost their job and they're here to listen to Careers from the Kitchen Table to think of different creative ways that they can get going in a business. Then we have other people that listen to our show that already have a business and they're looking for ways to advance in that business. Things that they can do that they haven't done, step out of the box and get more creative. That's why I wanted to have you on the show and me being a talk show host, I understand that there is power in the voice and what all you can do with this. I like to jump in with a series of questions and we're gonna start up with a person that is not in business, thinking about it ,doesn't have a lot of money, is it gonna take a lot of money for them to get going and becoming interviewing experts in their particular industry?

Michael Senoff: No, it does not take a lot of money at all. Hopefully you have a telephone. You can download a free trial of products that allow you to record a digital audio recording. There are websites that offer this service; they'll give you a 30 day free trial.

Raven Blair Davis: I know www.freeconferencecall.com is one.

Michael Senoff: Excellent. Freeconferencecall.com is a resource that allows you to record a telephone conversation. There's a device when I first started that I used from RadioShack which you don't even need today. If you have internet service and a quiet place to talk on the phone, you can create a digital audio recording. Now there are some tricky things like editing the recording and you may be confused about what an mp3 file is but don't worry about that. Don't let that stop you. You can go on to www.craigslist.com or you can go on to a website where there are freelancers, people who know all the technical stuff who know about how to edit recordings, who know what an mp3 file is. All you have to be willing to do is sit on your bum, invite someone to be interviewed. You can do it by phone or you can send an email that says 'hey would you like to be interviewed, can I interview you, can you do me a favor can you help me out, I'm putting this website together – I'd love to interview you, I'd love to talk about how you got to where you are, you're so great and you are such an expert at this or that can I ask you a few questions about how you got there' and you know what, most experts at something love to talk about themselves and their wife or their husband or friend probably never asked them about what they do. Experts are passionate about whatever their expertise is and in many cases there are probably a lot of people who never shared that passion so when you approach them to say 'tell me about your passion, about your expertise, will you share this with me?' they are flattered because no one in their life has ever asked them that before because no one really cares enough to know about it, sometimes not even their spouse. So you're gonna be real surprised at if you ask how you shall receive – someone would say sure I'd love to help you out. And experts generally got to the top of where they are because they're probably pretty good people, nice people too. And nice people like to help other people out so it's not gonna be hard to invite someone to be interviewed and it's not gonna cost you a lot of money whatsoever. You just have to have the courage and the confidence to just do that first one, like diving off a diving board. It's always gonna be scary at the first one and people are going to think their voice sounds stupid because we all sound different when we listen to ourselves.

Raven Blair Davis: Yeah.

Michael Senoff: Or they think that they don't know how to ask a question or all these little voices in your head are going to keep you from doing it, they're all nonsense. Plus, no one cares how you sound. People aren't listening to my interviews to hear how I sound. Maybe your listeners are but when you go to my site, I'm always the guy doing the interview.

Raven Blair Davis: Right.

Michael Senoff: Raven, when people listen to your show, I'm sure you're a nice person but let's get real here. They don't care about you.

Raven Blair Davis: Yeah they want the content that the experts bring in.

Michael Senoff: They want to hear your experts. You're just a conduit just like Oprah Winfrey. Oprah's great but they want to see her guest Dr. Oz and all the great guests she has on the show. That's what they're interested in so you have to get out of your own way. You have to get your ego in check because if you're all concerned with how you sound and what people are gonna think about me, get over it, no one cares. They want to hear your guests.

Raven Blair Davis: I 100% agree and that's one thing I had to tell myself at the beginning because when I first started interviewing, because I was one of those people who are – my voice is deep for a woman and all that stuff. I really was not in love with my voice but I've been doing telemarketing for over 25 years so I was very comfortable with being on the phone. I'm like forget it. My thing is I'm gonna bring the best of the best on and people will listen because they will give great, great information and that's what you do Michael. You're giving people an opportunity to hear from people they normally would not hear from about all kinds of topics and you're giving it free. That's amazing because you have tons and tons of audio in every subject and I just find your site fascinating. I could talk to you about that all day but we're gonna go ahead and move on.

Michael Senoff: Okay.

Raven Blair Davis: Let me ask you this. We know that it doesn't take a lot of money for them to get started and you said that they don't really have to be someone famous to get a high profile person on their show but doing their interview for their book or audio, that's where most people have a problem because they're looking at where they are now and saying how in the world am I going to get Michael Senoff or how am I gonna call Jay Abraham or someone at that level and I don't have a book. I barely got my business up. What would you say to them?

Michael Senoff: Well you do have to have a plan. Sometimes people will do it for nothing but if you want to increase your chances of getting the interview, you could have what we call intention. I don't want you to lie or anything but let's say that you're planning on doing a collection of interviews with the world's greatest smartest women business owners and let's say that's something you're really interested in learning about and you have this list of all these great women business owners, then when you call their secretary or you email them directly, you give them a reason why they may want to be interviewed. Think about Oprah Winfrey, think about Larry King, think about all the famous people who go on this shows that you watch on your TV set being interviewed. Why are they doing those interviews? Are they doing it for their help? They're doing it for exposure. What are they doing? They're promoting their latest movie, a book, promoting a cause, charity, they're on there for some reason so they get to plug whatever they're promoting at the end of the interview or during the interview or maybe several places during the interview but at the same time they have to be willing to be interviewed. That's the tradeoff. Tom Cruise goes on Oprah. Oprah says 'c'mon Tom I'll put you in front of millions of millions of people' and Tom says 'that's fine' but it's understood that Tom gets to talk about his new movie. That's the deal, that's the negotiation so when you're approaching a woman business owner and you contacted her, what is your reason why she wants to do an interview with you? When you contact her you can say 'hey I'm Michael Senoff. I am putting together the world's leading website of interviews with women business owners and I'd like to invite you to be one of our guests on our show. And a website could be a show and your website may not even be done yet because you are putting it together. Now, why would that woman business owner say yes? She's gonna say yes for potential exposure because she's gonna come on the show, she's gonna get potential exposure – you know when people are interviewed on radio stations, there's no guarantee that they're gonna get tons and tons of business. People do interviews hoping that they're gonna get more business. Hoping that they're gonna get more notoriety, hoping that it's going to comeback to them in some positive way but Raven when you approached me, I know there's no guarantee other than me giving good value to your listeners that I'm gonna get anything back for that. I'm doing it because I know something good will come out of it and even if it's not monetarily, at least I'll be able to expose your listeners to my site www.hardtofindseminars.com and you'll just never know down the road but I think that's how most people view it doing an interview. So there is an understanding between an interviewer and the interviewee so I would tell your listeners when you approach – come up with some reasons why they want to do the interview with you.

Raven Blair Davis: Right. Well that's good that you brought that up because you're right. I think a lot of times we don't get going in different types of business because we're setting ourselves with all these fears and what ifs but if they get the ego out of the way, forget all that, just move forward and what you really are passionate about and what you believe and the doors will open. I always say it's not what you say; it's how you say it. If you speak with confidence and assuredly, most likely you're gonna get what you want. But if you speak like Willy Timid and not quite sure going and making the call like this person's probably gonna say no then you've already set yourself up for failure that's for sure. We're gonna come back. We are speaking with Michael Senoff and this man as you can see is just absolutely incredible. He's the founder and executive editor of the famous www.hardtofindseminars.com if you have not checked this man out, I recommend you go right now to www.hardtofindseminars.com and take the tour. It's unbelievable. Over 117 hours of free downloadable audio interviews on sales, marketing and business experts, Michael Senoff, he's the man. Check him out.

Raven Blair Davis: Alright everyone, welcome back to the second part of our show. You're listening to Careers from the Kitchen Table. My name is Raven Blair Davis. I'm the host of this show. My guest today is Michael Senoff, founder and executive editor of www.hardtofindseminars.com and if you've been wondering how we've been cooking today, yes we have been cooking it up in here. As always we are giving you lots of good old home recipes for success so that you can begin to start the career from the home that you always wanted or the business from your home that you've always dreamed about so you can get off that highway and start going on that commute to that smooth sailing hallway because I can tell you how sweet it is right Mike?

Michael Senoff: That is right.

Raven Blair Davis: That's right. We're gonna jump back into our questions for the second part. Michael has shared his story on how he got going in being a true master of doing nothing but top interviews and hopefully if you haven't had the chance to check out his site, you definitely will by the time we finish this interview. Mike thank you for sharing all that you've shared with us so far. I want to jump into some questions now to get these listeners really going in there. You've given us a really good idea. In fact you've given us two or three short scripts on how to go about doing that. Let's talk about the different ways you can do the interview once you land it. Obviously on audio but you can repurpose in that many different ways. Can you share a little information on that for us?

Michael Senoff: Absolutely. Some of the interviews I have to tell you, when you come to my site, I am going to try and sell you something. Now, you come to my site, there's a lot of free stuff and it's just gonna be great content and it's gonna give tons and tons of value but sprinkle throughout these interviews, I have got a master plan that's really sneaky and you may come across one of my interviews say for an example, let's say you're in selling. Raven you said you did some telemarketing at one time?

Raven Blair Davis: Yes I did.

Michael Senoff: Well I've got a recording on my website called cold calling techniques. Let's say you're in sales and someone's out there hitting the phones and they see cold calling techniques, well that applies to them. I bet they're gonna go click on that link and they're gonna see my interview with this master expert cold calling trainer. I call him the cold calling king and they're gonna read the headline about what's it about and they're gonna read the description and they're gonna have the ability to play the recording on the internet from their computer. They can download the mp3 file which allows them to put it on their iPod or to burn it on to CD to be able to take that interview with them on the road. They are not stuck in front of my computer.

Listen to the audio for the rest of this great interview!

To listen to the full audio of this interview visit
http://www.careersfromthekitchentable.com/2ndEditionaudios

Plus be sure to visit http://amazingwomenofpower.com/radio **and grab your free copy of** *"Talk Your Way to Success – Unleash Your Dynamic Voice"* **by Raven!**

Careers from the Kitchen Table Home Business Directory Second Edition

Be sure to join award winning talk show host and celebrity interviewer Raven Blair Davis each week for insider secrets, tips, strategies and formulas for success to help you grow your business faster rather than slower!

"Careers from the Kitchen Table"

http://www.careersfromthekitchentable.com

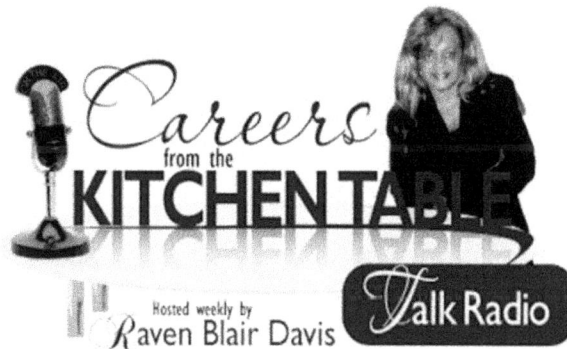

America's Hottest Home Business Radio Network

Hosted weekly by Celebrity Interviewer and Award Winning Talk Show Host Raven a.k.a. *The Talk Show Maven*

Broadcast every Thursday and Saturday at 11:00 AM Central on
www.awoptalk247.com

Raven International presents
World's Leading Positive Programming Network 24/7!

AWOP is under the umbrella of **"Raven International Media Productions"** as: *"Amazing Women of Power Talk 24.7 Network Radio."* The network consists of Raven's award winning talk shows: "Women Power Radio" and "Careers from the Kitchen Table," as well as her Celebrity Rave Reviews Talk show, plus over 20 other Amazing talk show host shows ranging from empowerment, round table discussions, health, law of attraction, business finance, spirituality, family programing, as well as an ALL Men line up of shows on Fridays.

Interested in hosting your show or being a guest on the network? Contact Raven toll-free at 800.431.0842 or email: radio@amazingwomenofpower.com

We love social media too! Connect with us on FACEBOOK by visiting https://www.facebook.com/groups/awopradionetwork/

To Listen to the network LIVE visit http://www.awoptalk247.com and click the flashing pink on air button!

We are extremely excited about the AWOP Network! Our hosts are DYNAMIC and the content of their shows are compelling! Be sure to check them out, tell your family and friends!

Not only do we have a worldwide platform to broadcast our shows but, one of the things that we are really thrilled about, is that with the **Amazing Women of Power Radio Network,** we are able to air the shows on one platform! -- reaching millions with our message!

Checkout Our Awesome Weekly Lineup

Monday: Empowerment, Inspiration and Motivation

Tuesday: Roundtable Discussions - Entertainment, Book Reviews, etc.

Wednesday: Health, Beauty, Metaphysical, Law of Attraction

Thursday: Finance, Business, Careers, Job

Friday: Amazing Men of Power & Music

Saturday: All flavors (Monday through Sunday mix)

Sunday: Spiritual, Family and Children

Each day between shows, enjoy smooth jazz to relax you – listen while you work!

Meet The Amazing Women of Power Hosts

Bonnie Terry – Learning Made Easy Talk Radio

Cathy Hansell – Safety Breakthrough Talk Radio

Christina Suter – Ask Christina First

Consuelo Meux – **Seasoned Women Health Radio**

Cynthia Lee – **Christian Leaders Talk Radio**

Ginny Vasquez – **The Holistic Way**

JJ Frederickson – **Stress Less Radio**

Keva Larthridge Mack – **Funky Mystic Radio**

Lorena Douglas – **Destiny Driven Radio**

Lynn Hidy – **Sales Coaching Over Coffee**

Sherry Prindle – **Make Money Making a Difference**; Social Media Marketing

Sonya Stockhaus – **Get Out of Your Head and Into Your Life!**

Meet The Amazing MEN of Power Hosts

Barclay Fisher - <u>Connecting To Your Greatness</u>

Blair Boone - <u>A Toast to Song</u>

Ced Reynolds – <u>The Entrepreneurial Pastor Speaks</u>

Fred Simkovsky – <u>Visions of Success Internet Radio Talk Show</u>

Tom Cunningham - <u>Amazing Life Stories</u>

If you are a business owner and would like to air a 30 to 60 second commercial during Raven's show, call Raven via800.431.0842. All commercials remain in each interview for a minimum of six months and for celebrity interviews a minimum of a year. You will also receive a MP3 recording.

Women Power Radio has been chosen one of the Top 100 Best Small Biz Podcast for THREE years in a row by Small Business Trends.com.

<u>Click here</u> to hear empowering and inspiring interviews of Unstoppable Women of Power

Visit **http://www.careersfromthekitchentable.com** *and listen to nearly five years of archived audios from these experts and more, sign up for the free newsletter!*

Want to have "your" own radio show and interview your favorite thought leader, author or celebrity?

Now you can get my easy to follow step-by-step formula for creating and launching your radio show and land that dream interview! You'll get exact steps to go from zero to launching your first show in less than six weeks!

Raven Blair Davis Presents Kitchen Table Radio

How to Produce, Post and Profit From "your" very own talk show

Discover the real secrets to:

- Just how easy it really is to create and launch your show without having to buy expensive equipment

- How being a talk show host can be a great platform for you and your business

- What type of format is best for you and how long your show really should be

- The easiest way to create content for your show that will keep your listeners coming back for more

- How to get the guest of your dreams without paying them anything

- The fastest, easiest and simplest way to attract and build a worldwide audience

- When you should do a free vs. paid internet radio show or podcast

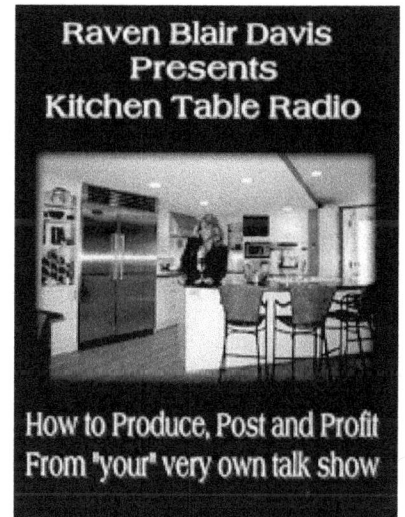

Why be mentored by Raven? See what others have to say...

BONUS AUDIO: Join Raven and many celebrities as they congratulate and celebrate *Graduation with the students!* http://www.audioacrobat.com/play/Wfrz1xSh

---

I have appeared on more than 800 radio interview shows in the past 20 years, and my time with Raven Blair Davis on her show "Careers from the Kitchen Table" was one of the most enjoyable ever.

She is a rare combination of dynamic, spontaneous and fun, as well as thoroughly prepared, deeply insightful and a great listener who responds with great follow-up questions as well as her own experiences in a way that moves the conversation forward without stealing the focus. I would highly recommend being on her show to anyone who is serious about getting your message out to more people–and enjoying the process at the same time.

Jack Canfield
America's #1 Success Coach
www.JackCanfield.com

The Kitchen Table Radio Personal Broadcasting Course, was a god-send for me. As the widow of, radio legend, Earl Nightingale, many of my customers today first heard of Earl over the airwaves of early radio. His, "Our Changing World", radio show was heard daily around the world, but it was always his desire for the two of us to have a radio show together one day. In the mid-eighties, we came close to seeing that dream come true when we were approached by a group of people who wanted to start a "success radio station" with Earl and me as their main commentators, however the incredible costs involved with starting a new radio station were prohibitive and we saw our dreams dashed.

Through the years, many station managers have confirmed the need for positive programming, and could see a program hosted by myself as filling a great yawning need in radio, but said that "sponsors won't pay for that kind of programming".

When I learned about, The Kitchen Table Radio Personal Broadcasting Course, I just about jumped for joy! The Course, is incredibly informative and provided me with every tool I needed to be on the air and sharing the Nightingale messages. The only thing Raven asked me to bring, "to the table" was, my own personal desire!

Raven, thank you from the bottom of my heart!
Diana Nightingale,
Speaker/author
Nighingale Radio, Host
http://earlnightingale.com

KITCHEN TABLE RADIO
INSIDER SECRETS TO PRODUCING, POSTING AND PROFITING
FROM YOUR OWN TALK SHOW

Unleash the power of your voice! **Order your copy today!**

http://www.kitchentableradio.com

FREE CONSULTATION

Call or email Raven today to schedule your no cost, no obligation 15 minute consultation!

Email: Raven@Womenpower-Radio.com
Call 800-431-0842

OR Visit http://www.kitchentableradio.com now!

Careers from the Kitchen Table Home Business Directory Second Edition

Stories from the Kitchen Table

Enjoy these engaging stories from Entrepreneurs, Solopreneurs, and Founders of Non-Profit organizations as they share their challenges and how they've come to where they are today!

Say Yes to Success

Are you ready to say yes to success?   As you read through the stories from our featured guests, do you see a pattern? We all know starting your own business, whether brick and mortar or run out of the comfort of your home, can be a real challenge.

What's the pattern? All of our contributors have made the commitment to **SAY YES TO SUCCESS!**

That is our driving force in providing to you the **"Careers From the Kitchen Table Home Business Directory"** each year. We hope you find the inspiration to go forward with your dreams and…

Here's a link (http://www.audioacrobat/play/wbct5kxk0) where you can hear Raven on the other side of the mic! Valorie Nelson Parker, speaker, author and Les Brown's booking agent recently interviewed Raven on the topic:

Say Yes to Success!

Alanna Levenson

"I am not what happened to me, I am what I choose to become."
Carl Jung

Turning Transitions into Transformations

In her previous 15-year career as a sales professional representing various technologies, Alanna became an expert at reinventing herself thanks to the volatility of the dotcom industry, after being laid off a total of six times and relying on her instincts to get through these difficult transition periods. But these seemingly negative transitions bred a new opportunity. Some friends pointed out to her that she might want to consider becoming a coach and expressed that she is someone who has the openness, faith and courage to keep transforming; finding new skills and experiences; someone who is a great listener, astute, passionate, trustworthy, and most importantly, true to herself.

Her inspiration for wanting to help others comes from her own life experiences where she uses her intuition and multifaceted breadth of experience to see the possibilities for others even when they can't. From acting, improvisational and stand-up comedy training, she learned about the power of our emotions and how we can use them to our advantage. She empowers her clients to use their own unique way of taking some of life's biggest challenges, creating new perspectives and turning them into opportunities.

Working with entrepreneurs and executives between the ages of 30 and 65, Alanna's techniques address many issues including: finding one's purpose; pursuing a career change; staying focused; obtaining financial stability and thinking abundantly; changing undesired behavioral patterns to healthier ones; enhancing relationships and identifying those that are congruent with who they are; and being able to love oneself and others again following a divorce or a break-up. Using her previous career experiences, she is also a great coach in teaching others to practice successful sales, networking, and marketing techniques. Clients are able to identify with Alanna because she's been through many of the same transitions that they're going through. One of her strongest qualities as a coach is her ability to listen to her clients without imposing her own agenda. Two powerful questions she feels everyone should ask themselves is, "Who am I now?" and "Who do I want to be?" The coaching process is a safe place to raise these questions and pursue the answers with joy and enthusiasm.

Alanna's ideal client is an entrepreneur, solo enterprises or executives who are looking to take themselves to the next level in his or her personal and professional transformation. She notes the following challenges in her business:

> Being confident and a really great listener. Alanna is now able to react to her clients' needs without an agenda. Her business prospered and so have my clients.

> Knowing what she's good at and when to ask for help in other areas of business, such as Marketing and Public Relations, being able to do what she does best.

Alanna Levenson

Recipe for SUCCESS!

1. Make a list of what your fears are and how they're getting in the way of the tools you need to succeed

2. Write down your values and make sure your business and personal values are in alignment

3. Understand the process of using SMART goals and apply that process to each and every accomplishment you want to achieve

4. Acknowledge your relationship to money and make sure it's a healthy one

5. Define success for yourself and make sure it aligns with your values and your healthy relationship to money

6. Know what you can control and what you can't — and then most importantly, let go of what you can't

7. Own up to your strengths and know when to ask for help in other areas

About Alanna Levenson

Using an organic transformational process, and the power of the unconscious mind, she coaches her clients one-on-one, by phone, Skype and in person. She also conducts ongoing workshops and is available to customize workshops for various groups. Depending on the needs or requests of her clients, her sessions encompass the use of powerful coaching principles and techniques, NLP tools for a particular issue. She strongly believes in creating awareness of how the unconscious mind works, so her clients can use to that their advantage. The kind of clients she mostly works with are entrepreneurs or executives between the ages of 30 and 65.

Alanna Levenson
I Love My Life! Coaching
13547 Ventura Blvd., #242,
Sherman Oaks, CA 91423

Email: Alanna@i-love-my-life.com
Phone: 213-400-7970
Website: http://i-love-my-life.com
Facebook: https://www.facebook.com/pages/I-Love-My-Life-Coaching/192310894122167
LinkedIn: http://www.linkedin.com/pub/alanna-levenson/0/3a0/7a0

Careers from the Kitchen Table Home Business Directory Second Edition

Angie Monko

"It is better to be hated for what you are than to be loved for what you are not"
Unknown

From CPA to Certified Hypnotist – What?

Angie has always had an entrepreneurial heart. She graduated from college in 1990 with a B.S. in accounting and was in the financial industry for 20 years, passing her CPA exam right out of college on the first try. During this 20 year period, she was a consultant with Pampered Chef for a couple of years and a financial planner with Primerica Financial Services for a couple of years after that. Angie found it difficult to get either business off the ground while working full-time in positions of responsibility, and so she quit.

Angie found it difficult to make good money with either endeavor because she was often tired from trying to balance her FT job, her business and her family life. She is married and has two teenage daughters.

In 2002 Angie joined a 12-step group for compulsive eating. This led her into pursing information about the life coaching profession. From her networking efforts, Angie learned about emotional freedom technique (EFT) and how this drastically helps people. She studied EFT, practiced it on her friends and family and herself and then launched her business, Harmony Harbor, in March of 2008.

All the while Angie was working fulltime at AT&T as a regional finance manager. Her heart ws tugging at her to leave and pursue her passion, but she was afraid to give up the benefits, the guaranteed nice paycheck, bonuses, etc. Angie used her EFT technique to overcome this fear, and an opportunity presented itself for her to leave AT&T with a severance package. Angie left AT&T in February 2011, and she also incorporated a perfect tool to partner with EFT (hypnosis) by becoming a certified hypnotist in 2010.

Angie loves helping people discover and live their most passionate life by helping them to change their mind. She now happily works from home, with clients all over the U.S. via telephone as well as in person. Angie overcame many fears to follow her dream life and it keeps getting better.

Angie says her challenges have been:

Feeling like there isn't enough time to get all of the responsibilities done and have time to relax. I surrender my daily schedule to my Higher Self and ask for guidance on what the next step is. She also says that sometimes she is not selective enough of her clients and work with them because they pay. She's now raising her standards and letting people know that she wants to work only with decisive and forward moving people.

Angie Monko

Recipe for SUCCESS!

1. Focus on what you want, relax and have fun

2. Truly care about how you feel and be willing to take great care of yourself

3. Have more of a need to be happy than to be right

4. Express your authentic self even if it doesn't please others

5. Know your values and align your business objectives with them

6. Master your mind and reclaim your power from others

7. Surrender your life, your business results and everything to your Higher Self, the Power Presence within you

About Angie Monko

Angie Monko launched Harmony Harbor Hypnosis, Inc., a safe haven to heal your habits, in March 2008. Angie has gone from Victim to Victor in several areas of her life, through a compulsive eating disorder, a challenging divorce, custody of her child, her relationship with her stepdaughter and in her career. Angie has nearly five years of meridian tapping (a/k/a emotional freedom technique) experience and has been coaching for nine years. She was certified as a hypnotist in 2010, as she found this a natural complement to tapping. On the business level, Angie uses a powerful combination of hypnosis, tapping and coaching to help successful entrepreneurs earn six figures, have plenty of quality time with family and friends, and live a life of passion & adventure! For personal services, Angie specializes in helping professional women in their 30's to 60's release weight permanently without diets and willpower and heal their habits surrounding food and body image and in the process achieve health, wealth and happiness.

Angie Monko
Harmony Harbor Hypnosis
2476 Pheasant Run Drive
Maryland Heights, MO 63043

Email: 4monko@att.net
Phone: 314-422-6520
Website: www.harmonyharbor.com
Facebook: www.facebook.com/HarmonyHarborHypnosis
LinkedIn: www.linkedin.com/in/harmonyharbor
Twitter: www.twitter.com/angiemonko4monko@att.net

Anita P. Kirkman

"Now to Him who is able to do exceedingly and abundantly above all that we ask or think according to the power that works in us"
Ephesians 3:20

Picture it...

...a young engineering major at the University of Alabama. She has dreams of becoming a CEO of a huge firm, she see herself in an expensive suit, high heeled pumps, a French roll hairstyle and big corner office with a gorgeous view of the Pacific Ocean.

That was Anita BEFORE she fell in love with and married her college sweetheart. This sweetheart would go on to become a commissioned officer in the US Army and suddenly there went Anita's hopes and dreams...or did it? Anita endured much over the years moving from place to place, giving up one career after another. On top of that, she had children and often found herself feeling like a single Mom as her husband was off serving the country.

With all of that going on, Anita, woke up one day looked in the mirror and did not recognize herself. What happened to that young woman that was supposed to be a CEO with the large corner office? At that point, she decided to work for herself starting in a cosmetics direct sales company. She moved up and earned her place in the top 3% of that company. She went on to do the same in a nutritional and financial services company.

That experience helped to start her own company, Vision in Purpose (VIP) Coaching and Training. Long story short, Anita, did not sacrifice her dream of being of CEO, though it did not materialize the way she thought it would. God has granted her something even more special and everything she went through made her the dynamic lady she is today.

Anita says the two biggest challenges in business she's faced are:

1. Moving around a lot to different areas, as a military spouse. She used this as a reason to get out and meet new people and establish new networks which allowed her to grow and make contacts all over the world.

2. Having to start over after each move and establish a new customer base. Though it was often difficult, she began to get the hang of starting over in a new area. It helped her to have a positive attitude and she was always sure to join a networking organization

immediately so that she could get exposure. One means of networking was and still is doing speaking engagements.

Anita P. Kirkman

Recipe for SUCCESS!

1. Stay connected to your inner power source daily

2. Create a written vision for your business and life using present tense words

3. Know and honor your values, without exception

4. Get a coach or mentor to help you right away

5. Believe in yourself and your capabilities, don't sell yourself short!

6. Find your uniqueness and use that to set yourself apart from competition

7. Learn to master your mindset and make your thought work for you, not against you.

About Anita P. Kirkman

Anita P. Kirkman, founder and CEO of Vision in Purpose (VIP) Coaching and Training, is an inspiring and dedicated certified life and business coach, trainer, and speaker. She has been featured on several internet and local talk radio and TV shows and is a proven leader with 20+ years' experience from an impressive array of business sectors including engineering, government, financial services and direct sales.

Anita is committed to empowering home office business women to prosper in their businesses by transforming their mindsets about time, money, self and leadership. She utilizes her invaluable, combined, and successful experience in these areas, along with her extensive training to help her clients achieve their goals. Through her passionate and energetic coaching combined with her unique ability to inspire and train, her clients have experienced better financial control, increased self-awareness, and have overcome known and hidden challenges in order to attain and sustain their desired goals.

Anita is the author of "Master Your Money Mindset: How to Transform Your Relationship with Cash" Program.

Anita Kirkman
Vision In Purpose Coaching and Training
254 Wedgewood Terrace Rd,
Madison, AL 35757

Email: anita@visioininpurpose.com
Phone: 256.721.4553
Website: www.visioninpurpose.com
Facebook: http://bit.ly/visioninpurposefb
LinkedIn: http://linkd.in/coachanitak

Careers from the Kitchen Table Home Business Directory Second Edition

Anne Duffy

**"We can all do small things, with great love, and together we
can do something wonderful"**
Mother Teresa

Change is a good thing!

Shortly after accepting a job transfer to Charlotte, NC, Anne's husband Tom quit his corporate job to begin a business venture of his own. As it is for most new business entrepreneurs, financial hardships were among the growing pains they encountered. "It wasn't long before our dreams of financial freedom fell apart," Anne recalls. She was suddenly forced to either find full-time hygiene work or another significant source of income. "If Tom's business had taken off from the very start, it is doubtful I would have pursued this dream but God knew better. He knew I needed this for myself. Oxyfresh gave me something to focus on and kept me sane when things looked pretty bleak."

Every day she focused on her vision of being financially free and treated her opportunity like a part-time business, not a "some-time" business. By developing her own leadership skills she was able to help others do the same.

Anne's unwavering pursuit of balance in all areas of life has paid big dividends for the Duffy family. Not only is Anne financially richer as the recipient of the Oxyfresh Super Star Cash Award, she now enjoys a level of personal freedom that most people only dream of. And she's done it without sacrificing the people or values that mean the most to her. "Oxfyresh was a choice I made because our family needed more income to stay in our home and keep our kids in private school. How great it is that I have been able to always be there for my children and husband because I wasn't working 40 plus hours a week in a small operatory for someone else's dream. I did it my way - slow, but certainly sure!" Anne's devotion to balancing home, work, friends and finances is reflected in the way she models leadership and integrity in the field. She encourages people to just be themselves, and in doing so empowers them to discover their true power. "Start and don't stop" is her mantra.

Anne's two biggest business challenges are:

1. Finding enough prospects to get the momentum going – Staying excited, listening to people's needs and realizing that everyone is a prospect is key.
2. Thinking she had to know everything – knowing where to find the information and teaching the others to do the same keeps her on track.

When asked who her ideal clients are, Ann says that the Oxyfresh flagship line offers the best products for healthy mouths and fresh breath. So she looks to anyone in the Dental or

Veterinary fields, authority figures with success habits and credibility along with anyone who has an external outlet for health and wellness products.

Anne M. Duffy

Recipe for SUCCESS!

1. Believe in yourself and your opportunity

2. Find a Buddy –Empower others

3. Always Follow up

4. Be Organized and prepared

5. Be Attractive

6. Develop a Marketing Plan

7. Just do it and keep doing it!

About Anne M. Duffy

Anne began her career in network marketing 16 years ago – a choice she made to help pay the family bills and put gas in her care. She quickly rose to the top of Oxyfresh Worldwide while practicing dental hygiene two days a week and publishing Dental Entrepreneur magazine. She has a strong commitment to health and wealth, environmental conscious, philanthropic focus, fun and personal development. She is married to her college sweetheart and has raised three adult children that are now pursuing their own successful careers.

Anne M. Duffy
Oxyfresh Worldwide, Inc.
12233 Pine Valley Club Dr.
Charlotte, NC 28277

Email: Aduff2@aol.com
Phone: 704-953-0261
Website: www.oxyfresh.com/anneduffy
Facebook: Anne Linesch Duffy
LinkedIn: http://linkdin/AnneDuffy

Anne Gordon

"One day you finally knew what you had to do"
Mary Oliver

Realize Your Purpose, Passion and Power!

Anne was just 7-years-old when she first recalls having a sense of purpose in life. This was followed by a period of depression, because she knew her formative ideas for what she would do with her life had nothing to do with her family's strict expectations of her. She was born the eighth child to a family of entrepreneurs. Her family operated a very successful business and felt they had an elite reputation to uphold. They made it clear what their expectations were — how Anne should conduct her life and who she should become. Most of her youth she felt stifled, unable to speak her desires. She turned to writing and time in nature for inspiration and peace.

In 1998, she began charting her own course, despite being confronted by stern disapproval from family. She stopped working for the family business, left home, met the love of her life and opened a healing arts center in Mt. Shasta, California.

Years later, Anne and her husband decided to move to Bend, Oregon to focus on raising their three children. Although Anne enjoyed the task of motherhood, she felt driven to do more, perhaps as a result of the obstacles she faced growing up. She began searching for her life's work and discovered life coaching. Immediately, she knew it was right for her because, without realizing it, she had been coaching friends and family for years. When she decided to go for it, magic began to happen and things fell into place easily, confirming that she was on track.

Anne now lives her passion operating Glow Life Coaching from home. She is dedicated to helping people realize their purpose, passion and power by connecting clients to the wisdom of their bodies, the teachings of native cultures, creative expression, joyful curiosity and inquiry. She coaches individuals, offers tele-classes and holds nature-based group retreats for women. She does inspirational speaking, weaving in her love for poetry. She coaches the next generations of family businesses and loves to help young adults explore their passions through creative writing.

Anne's greatest challenge was creating meaningful life work that reflected her gifts and talents. She took various personal assessments*, researched life coaching extensively and talking to many people in the industry. Ultimately she used her "inner compass" as her guide.
*Kolbe Index A and assessments offered at:
http://www.authentichappiness.sas.upenn.edu/Default.aspx

Anne Gordon

Recipe for SUCCESS!

1. Clarify your purpose and passion

2. Know your "mission." This is how you realize your purpose and passion in the world

3. Sit everyday with your soul. (i.e., meditate, pray, journal, dance, sit quietly in nature)

4. Find a mentor and coach and talk to them regularly

5. Develop your own personal support team and ask them for help! Emotional supporters, intellectual supporters, spiritual supporters, financial and "techie" supporters

6. Everyday take a turtle step forward in growing your business Think small and easy

7. Play and rest more, push less

About Anne Gordon

Anne Gordon is the founder and owner of Glow Life Coaching. She is a life coach and nature coach trained by bestselling author and columnist for O magazine Martha Beck and master life coach and founder of The SageFire Institute Michael Trotta. She is also a student of master meditation and Feldenkrais instructor Russell Delman. She was a manager of corporate communications for a successful family-owned California winery. She co-founded and operated a Healing Arts Center in northern California where she practiced massage therapy. She is a poet and holds a black belt in the martial art of Aikido. She lives with her husband and three children in beautiful Bend, OR.

Anne Gordon
Glow Life Coaching
2521 NW Coe Ct.
Bend, OR 97701

Email: anne@glowlifecoaching.com
Phone: 541-306-4445
Website: www.glowlifecoaching.com
Facebook: www.fcebook.com/annegordonor
LinkedIn: www.linkedin.com/pub/anne-gordon/23/848/7a5

Annie Kirschenmann

"We are what we do repeatedly. Excellence then is not an act. It's a habit".
Aristotle

"Right Brain" Meets "Left Brain" in Business

Annie's original passion was the dance. This quickly became a three-way love affair with theatre and engaging these creative activities dominated her childhood. Her experience as an actress cultivated a fascination with motivation and human behavior; she got her B.A. in Psychology. The dance, never far behind, she went on to earn her Master of Science degree in Dance/Movement Therapy. In the process, she won an award for her thesis on the Beneficial Aspects of Laughter, Smiling and Humor. She worked for years in hospitals, as well as with special children and in private practice.

Then, through a series of circumstances she used to call accidents, Annie suddenly found herself in the world of business, running a company as its President and CEO. With zero background and training in business, she learned what she needed, when she needed it and usually on the fly! More and more, she found herself drawing on her training and experience in the arts, thus deeply engaging her core Creative Energy, in order to absorb these new skills.

The allure of human behavior now captured her interest in the form of how people "are" in organizations and the workplace. This led her to corporate business coaching; she received her training and certification from Corporate Coach University.

In 2005, U.S. Senator Kent Conrad named Annie the very first Marketplace Entrepreneur of the Year. When presenting the award, he stated, "Annie is a true entrepreneur in every sense of the word. She is excited, driven and most importantly, has true entrepreneurial spirit that can turn a good idea into a reality."

After 16 years, she stepped down from her position as a CEO to focus entirely on her own business: A.K.A Coach and Company. She considers it to be one of the most exhilarating creative acts she has ever engaged, and it opened the space for the Creativity Matrix™ to come into being. Annie is delighted to be discovering that business is not all that different from life; and that when we are truly creative about our businesses and our lives – success is inevitable.

Careers from the Kitchen Table Home Business Directory Second Edition

Annie landed quite suddenly in the corporate world with zero training, so business itself was a challenge! A "right brainer" by nature, she also had some trouble structuring for success. The solution? The Creativity Matrix™; bridging the "right brain - left brain" gap in business and providing others the tools do that with ease instead of angst!

Annie Kirschenmann

Recipe for SUCCESS!

1. Create enough structure in your calendar or work plan to stay focused; balanced with enough space to stay flexible and able to respond to unexpected opportunities

2. Organize your most important or demanding tasks during your peak energy time of day

3. Make sure there is at least one item on your to-do list every day that absolutely delights you

4. Stare out the window. (This is Annie's A #1 tip to executives to help them access their creativity)

5. Write a list of what is unique about you. Review it every morning

6. Creativity and structure in business are both essential. Use yours in the right order and at the right time to create unstoppable success

7. Have fun! (If what you are doing is not fun, change something small about it – right now -- so there is more fun in your workday.)

About Annie Kirschenmann

Annie Kirschenmann was born in Bismarck, North Dakota; however has been very mobile ever since then! She has lived in the Dakotas, Connecticut, Germany, Ohio, New York City, Boston, Chicago, the Twin Cities and London.

She received her B.A. from Macalester College in St Paul, MN and earned her Master of Science at Hunter College in New York, where she won an award for her thesis. She is a Board Certified Coach, Certified Corporate Business Coach, a Board Certified Dance/Movement Therapist, a

Nationally Certified Counselor and a Certified NLP Practitioner. In 2005 she received the Marketplace Entrepreneur of the Year award.

After many years as the CEO of an international company, she stepped down to run her own coaching, strategy and training business – A.K. A Coach and Company and its divisions: The Creativity Matrix™ and Simple Stress Solutions™. Since then she has worked with amazing entrepreneurs, business owners, executives and companies, including Peak Potentials and Microsoft.

Annie Kirschenmann
A.K. A Coach and Company
6844 35th St. SE
Windsor, ND 58424

Email: annie@akacoachandcompany.com
Phone: 701-763-6406
Website: www.akacoachandcompany.com
Facebook: www.facebook.com/pages/AK-A-Coach-and-Company/26696788139?sk
LinkedIn: http://www.linkedin.com/in/anniekirschenmann
Twitter: www.twitter.com/#!/AnnieKCoach

Arris Charles

"Comfort makes cowards of all of us"
Michael Gerber, The E-Myth Revisited

From Corporate Cubicle to Christian Coaching

At the start of her career journey, Arris worked as a Network Engineer/Project Manager. After years of working, her desire to be true to her purpose and true self and to express her passions led her to transition to Leadership Training & Development. Her satisfaction increased, but with corporate pressures and repetitive motion injuries, she had to decide to either have multiple arm surgeries or quit. She prayed for the right answer, really not wanting to choose. Then an outsourcing of her position beat her to it—same fate, but with severance pay! God's timing was perfect!

She decided not to return to the corporate environment and stayed home to start a family and find a fulfilling career. While raising two young sons, she began to build a Life Coaching practice. But her progress was limited because her inner life was filled with self-defeating thoughts that kept her in her comfort zone, and her body was plagued with fatigue and chronic pain from lack of self-care. Her spiritual journey brought her to believe in her personal value and power to reach her goals through her faith. She took intentional steps to balance life to reach her full potential not only in her career, but in spirituality, thoughts, emotions, fitness, relationships, finances, homemaking and recreation.

Seeking God's will and strength, she has created a life with joy, peace and passion as the norm instead of the exception. Viewing the importance of our body as the vehicle for our journey, she also obtained her certification as a Personal Trainer to help clients shape their life from the inside out.

Arris serves clients through Christian Life Coaching and Personal Fitness Training to build up mind, body and spirit to step boldly into God's extraordinary calling for your life. She helps you weave together extraordinary personal vision, spiritual focus and tailored practical actions to develop custom life strategies for lasting results. She named her company Heir to Life^{SM} because she sees her clients and herself as heirs to an abundant, powerful and fulfilling life...right now!

Arris' biggest challenge as a wife and mother of two, was the tension to balance the multitude of business start-up tasks with home, family and self-care. Her desire to fulfill her calling was so strong that it was very easy for her to get caught up in striving to get the groundwork done, while other core areas of life were left competing to win her time and energy, but often not getting adequate attention. Though she was accomplishing much, this dilemma often left her with a feeling of discontent or guilt, stealing the fulfillment she was meant to experience.

Something had to change so that she would have no regrets in any area of life, not just career. Through prayerful contemplation, she understood that her calling was not only to build a ministry and business to serve others, but also and more importantly, she had a purpose to care for her needs as well as serve her home and family with the same passion. Making the choice to set her priorities in order and exercise the self-discipline to pull back the reigns when and where necessary to live a more balanced life, the rewards in both her personal and work life were all the more plentiful and fulfilling.

Arris Charles

Recipe for SUCCESS!

1. Never forsake your spiritual, physical or emotional well-being or relationships for the sake of career success

2. Take captive your self-defeating thoughts so you can step out beyond your comfort zone and fears

3. Understand how all areas of your life connect to your purpose in life to increase fulfillment

4. For more peace, effectiveness and productivity in running your business stay true to your unique personality, gifts, talents, needs and stage of life

5. Stay connected with supportive people, some that think differently than you do, to gain new perspectives, encouragement and accountability

6. Manage expectations of yourself and others to minimize unnecessary stress and disappointments

7. Strive for excellence, but know that it's okay not to be perfect in everything.

About Arris Charles

Arris Turner Charles is a Christian Life Coach and NASM Certified Personal Trainer. She empowers her clients in mind, body and spirit to step boldly into ALL that God intended for them to become and fulfill. As a writer with a passion to encourage and call to action, her blog equips her readers to live more effective and fulfilling lives. Arris also serves non-profit ministries through mentor coaching and workshops to help the clients they serve believe in themselves and become equipped with ways to transform their lives from the inside out.

Arris has also served as a ministry Discipleship Coaching Director, developing and managing a Discipleship Coach Training program to equip Life Coaches to help clients in their community and churches to discover and fulfill their unique calling. She is a graduate of Coach U and has been trained as a Biblical Counselor with a focus on women's ministry through the American Association of Christian Counselors. She holds a BS degree in Electrical Engineering with an emphasis in Telecommunications, with corporate background in Leadership Training and Development, Project Management and Network Engineering. She is a member of the Christian Coaches Network. Arris is married with two sons.

Arris Turner Charles
Heir to Life, LLC
11601 Shadow Creek Pkwy #317
Pearland, TX 77584

Email: Arris@HeirToLife.com
Phone: 832-729-6317
Website: www.HeirToLife.com
LinkedIn: http://www.linkedin.com/in/heirtolife
Twitter: CoachArris

Ashley Dais

"Everything you want is on the other side of what you refuse to do to get it."
Darnyelle A. Jervey

Do Better. Be Better

When Ashley decided to venture into the life coaching business, she had no idea how hard it would be to be a soloprenuer. Building relationships and strategies to help build the brand was a phenomenal task. She struggled with confidence, balance, and how to make it all come together. Once she made up in her mind to make that non-negotiable decision to do better and be better, then she was able to gain focus and continuity in her business structure and begin to gain paying clients.

Without making that step to dedicate herself to the growth of her business, lack of confidence and imbalance would have held her back and eventually defeated her and the business. So, moving forward and taking action regardless of her feelings and mistakes, she was able to profit and be successful!

Ashley says her biggest challenges in being a soloprenuer was doing all the necessary start up work, while still trying to work to bring in income for business growth and maintaining family.

She also learned about branding. If no one knows you...it is challenging getting the clientele you seek after.

Ashley Dias

Recipe for SUCCESS!

1. Make an informed decision to give your all

2. Stay focused, diligent, and determined

3. When it gets tougher, you get tougher

4. Don't quit, find a different way to move forward in your goal

5. Understand that mistakes are how businesses are developed

6. Be willing to learn and go out and seek answers

7. Get a mentor to help you along the way...don't

About Ashley Dias

Ashley is a mother, counselor, and life coach helping people become better than their circumstance. She graduated from a HBCU, Livingstone College, in Salisbury NC, with a Bachelor's Degree in Psychology. Ashley has always been in mind-frame of helping others. She joined a national sisterhood dedicated to the community service of others, Delta Sigma Theta Sorority, Inc because she is committed to the betterment of helping others, which ultimately helps the community. Ashley has worked with children and youth in the capacity of a residential counselor, helped people with debt as a credit counselor, performed duties as a social worker in the department of social services, and currently helps individuals with substance abuse issues as a substance abuse counselor and as a life coach. Ashley helps people who have displaced emotions which affect them mentally and socially. She is passionate about seeing and helping people live better lives!

Ashley Dais
Couch Talk Life Coaching
326 Kingsport Drive, NE
Concord, NC 28025

Email: couchtalklifecoaching@gmail.com
Phone: 704-619-7028
Website: www.ashleydais.com
Facebook: http://www.facebook.com/#!/CouchTalkLifeCoaching
Twitter: http://twitter.com/#!/AshleyDias

Bonnie Terry

"Successful learning requires action, without action you are just gathering information"
Bonnie Terry

Follow Your Dream!

As a 3rd grader, Bonnie struggled with learning to read. Being in the lowest reading group was life changing. Bonnie decided to teach to make learning easy for those that struggled.

So, Bonnie became a teacher, even taught reading methods classes at the university. But, once she had her three children, she stayed home to take care of them.

Eventually, it was time to get back to teaching.

Re-entering the workforce was difficult! School districts preferred to hire new teachers rather than experienced ones so they could pay lower salaries.

Bonnie's dream to teach was not to be stymied. With no business experience but years of teaching experience, space in her home, and the courage to fulfill her dream of helping children learn with ease she opened her learning center.

Within days she had her first student and within a week she had three. Her business grew by word of mouth and before she knew it she was hiring teaching assistants.

Bonnie started creating her own teaching materials from methods she had honed over her years of teaching.

The books, games, and guides she created were popular with both students and parents. Parents started asking if they could purchase them. Bonnie decided that she could do it – she could publish her books and games and provide them to others.

Then life happened...her husband of 27 years had a freak accident and died. As far as she was concerned her life was over. She was left a widow with 3 children to support.

The "extra family income" now was her only income. Bonnie knew she needed to do more to support her children and herself. She created a website and started selling her learning books, games and guides online.

Parents using the products got the same great results as she did. Phone calls started coming from parents asking for more than just her products; they wanted her! So, Bonnie learned how to do webinars.

Now Bonnie's company, *Bonnie Terry Learning* also teaches parents how to improve their children's learning skills in just minutes a day with her online *Awaken the Scholar Within* program.

One of Bonnie's biggest challenges was learning how to move forward when her husband of 27 years died. Every day was difficult, not having her husband, her support, her sweetheart there any longer. Out of the depts. Of despair and grief, Bonnie had to learn how to go on and support her family. Thankfully, with much counseling and family support, she started living again and realized she was a survivor.

Bonnie's second biggest challenge was to believe and trust herself enough that she could succeed and could do whatever it would take to support her family. Bonnie knew that in order to really make a living she had to do things differently, she had to close down her learning center and focus on marketing her books, games and guides online.

Taking that leap of faith, closing down the center, was one of the hardest things she had to do, but she knew that not taking it would not change her future. With prayer, coaching, and listening to her inner wisdom, Bonnie changed the way she did business, and ultimately broadened the impact she has on families worldwide through her learning products and Awaken the Scholar Within coaching program.

Bonnie Terry

Recipe for SUCCESS!

1. Believe in yourself; trust yourself and your inner wisdom, you have the natural abilities, recognize and use them

2. Be passionate about your business, otherwise it's not worth doing. Enjoy your business and your customers

3. Be the expert in your field by keeping up with the latest practices, research and trends

4. Listen to others whether it is family, friends, clients or prospective clients. Listen with emotion, filter out what doesn't apply. Learn from what you've heard and then Do-act on what you learned

5. You don't have to be the expert in everything. Build a support system that you can reach out to. You don't have to know or do it all

6. Surround yourself with advisors and coaches that pull you up and push you forward

7. Don't re-invent the wheel, instead model after other successful businesses

About Bonnie Terry

Bonnie Terry was born and raised in Chicago, Illinois. Bonnie graduated from Illinois State University with a B.S. in Special Education Learning Disabilities, Physically Handicapped and Elementary Education. Bonnie also earned her M.Ed. in Special Education: Learning Disabilities. She is a Board Certified Educational Therapist and Learning Disabilities Specialist with a home based business. Bonnie has been a California resident for the last 33 years.

Bonnie is known as America's leading learning expert and has lectured both nationally and internationally. She appears frequently on education on FOX Morning News. A highpoint of Bonnie's career was to be one of only four speakers in a Reading Education Delegation sent to China.

She is the founder of *Bonnie Terry Learning* and the *Awaken the Scholar Within* program. Bonnie's company has earned such noted accolades as: Top 101 education blogs to follow http://bonnieterry.com/blog; Top 50 special educators to follow on twitter http://twitter.com/#!/bonnieterry_btl; and Top 101 education websites and #1 in reading category http://bonnieterrylearning.com

Bonnie and her company have been awarded *Special Needs Company of the Year*, *Who's Who of Professional Educators* and have been recognized for her *Contribution to the Field of Educational Therapy*.

Bonnie books and games have received *Teacher's Favorite* and *Teacher's Choice* awards.

Bonnie Terry, M. Ed., BCET
Bonnie Terry Learning

Email: info@bonnieterrylearning.com
Phone: 530-888-7160
Website: http://twitter.com/#!/bonnieterry_btl
Blog: http://bonnieterry.com/blog

Carmen Chandler

"To think you can, creates the force that can."
Orison Swett Marden

Who am I? What am I?

Carmen worked for many years in Corporate America, loving the challenges of her job for various companies. She was a mother of two and always knew her most important job in Life was to take care of her family and to raise her beautiful son and daughter. It was a good life, but in her forties she decided to leave her employment to take care of her father –in –law who was diagnosed with Alzheimer's. After he passed away, her husband said, "This is your time! Do something for you!" She was in her fifties, and thought was it too late to venture out? Start a new business? She started questioning herself. Who am I? What am I? She seemed to have "all" the answers for other's but, none for herself! Then one day she read the story of "Grandma Moses" who started painting at the age of 76. Grandma Moses was discovered by the art world 2 years later. Known for happy scenes of rural life, her work was widely sought after in America, Europe and Japan at the age of 80! Carmen thought, if Grandma Moses could do it, so could she! After all, age was just a number!

Carmen loved fashion and found her passion in the design and making of jewelry. She loved the shapes and colors of stones and crystals and so began her journey. So far, after creating so many designs, she has not duplicated a piece! Her clients know that when they are wearing a "Chandler Creation" it is indeed a very special piece. Some has asked her to duplicate a design. She will instead create something "similar" but, never exactly as the original piece. To view her designs visit her online shop at www.etsy.com/shop/chandlercreations.

Finally, Carmen has said, "I am a person who loves making jewelry!" What am I? "A creator of original, unique jewelry designs."   She believes that one is truly happy in business, when they are doing something they are truly passionate about!

Carmen shares her business challenges:

Finding **TIME** is a huge challenge! Learn to set up your "ME TIME", so that your family can share your success during "WE TIME"!

Find ways to **PROMOTE** your business can be a challenge. Know your target market. Be inventive! Use all sources available to you! I advertised, did private showing parties, trade shows and developed an online store.

Carmen Chandler

Recipe for SUCCESS!

1. Remember it's never too late to make your dreams come true!

2. Value yourself! Believe in you!

3. Find your passion!

4. Do not procrastinate! Our time on earth is so sweet and so short!

5. Turn negatives into positives (There is always a way to overcome)

6. Trust your instincts!

7. Envision it! Create It! Live It! (Whatever it may be)

About Carmen Chandler

Carmen was born and raised in Honolulu, Hawaii and moved to Houston, Texas when she married.

At a young age, she started designing and sewing clothes. While living in Athens, Greece she found a way to earn money by drawing horses on shirts for the jockey's at the race track. She knew that she loved fashion, drawing and designing! Carmen finally found her passion in the design and making of jewelry. Her unique designs can be viewed at www.etsy.com/shop/chandlercreations or, if you reside in the Houston area, contact her to book special events or a fun "Bling Party" at chandler.creations@ymail.com.

Carmen Chandler
Jewelry Designer
Email: chandler.creations@ymail.com
Phone: 281-380-2022

Carol Mazur

"Don't be afraid to give up the good for the great."
John D Rockefeller

A Promise Kept

Carol's journey into real estate coaching was driven by years of mixed messages in the real estate training industry and a desire to help agents succeed faster.

Carol began her real estate career at the age of twenty-two. She spent thousands of dollars on training and struggled for years. She'd build a thriving business only to have the real estate market collapse. She blamed the market, but looking back it was not entirely the market.

Everyone had different advice about how to be successful. It was confusing. She jumped from one training program to the next. Each time she threw out the old system and began a new one.

While searching for ways to end her continual up and down sales cycle, she found some old audios that changed her mind set and her life. Carol opened her mind, stopped limiting her beliefs and blocked out negativity. She set goals, achieved them and set bigger goals. Success followed.

Determined to cut through all of the confusion in real estate training; Carol went back to college at the age of fifty and earned her AS in Education. On a mission, she moved from Point Pleasant, NJ to Wilmington, NC. She accepted a sales director position to create a cutting edge real estate sales training "Success Center."

Carol taught advanced real estate training and business building techniques. Agent results skyrocketed. Carol was doing what she loved every day. Real estate companies down the block and across the nation were folding as their company was quickly growing to one of the top ranked affiliates in the nation. Surprisingly, that's when it happened. Carol was instructed to bring in outdated training she did not believe in and to charge the agents a hefty fee. She'd have to break her promise to only introduce proven training that works. She found she could not break that promise and left with her 95% approval rating in hand. It was one of the darkest days of Carol's life.

Out of darkness came light and the Top Producer Group, LLC was born. Today Carol runs her business by the Integrity Rule: Everything they use is tested and proven by current top producers.

To increase her productivity Carol uses an excel sheet to list her everyday activities. She then assigns tasks from the list to virtual assistants and experts in those areas. This frees her time up so that she can focus on what she does best: creating content for the agent.

Carol Mazur

Recipe for SUCCESS!

1. Stay true and be good to yourself

2. Find a way to give back and monetize it

3. If you make a promise keep it

4. Never let anyone get in the way of doing what is right or best

5. Remove all negativity from your life or as much as possible

6. Outsource all of your everyday unproductive tasks

7. Keep learning and sharing

About Carol Mazur

REAL ESTATE COACH CAROL MAZUR is well-known for running an innovative "Success Center" for a 300 agent Coldwell Banker affiliate where she developed the "Advanced Certificate of Education" sales training program.

Today Carol is owner/founder of TopProTraining.com – an online success center for real estate agents to be top producers. Her innovative ACTIONAR® training coaches agents to top results with easy step by step top pro systems.

Carol holds an active Broker ‑ in ‑ Charge license. She is a Certified e ‑ Marketing Specialist, Summa Cum Laude – Ocean County College, a Certified Negotiation Specialist and holds a Graduate Realtor Institute designation. She is a Member of the International Association of Coaching, the National Association of Professional Women and UN Women.

Carol has coached hundreds of agents to be the best of the best. An innate love of learning contributes to her ability to implement new and improved ideas and to create top results. She works with new agents, top producers and company trainers. Together they continuously discover and share new ideas, the latest technology and proven wealth creating marketing systems that lead to success in real estate.

Carol Mazur
The Top Producer Group, LLC
8722 New Forest Drive
Wilmington, NC 28411

Email: coachcarolmazur@gmail.com
Phone: 910-681-1110
Website: www.topprotraining.com
Facebook: http://www.facebook.com/RECoaching
LinkedIn: http://www.linkedin.com/in/carolmazur

Careers from the Kitchen Table Home Business Directory Second Edition

Chris Barnett

"Enjoy the Little Things"
Chris's Grandmother

Cookie-Cutter Medicine?!? Not from Christina!

Chris decided while in sixth grade that pharmacy would be her profession, but it wasn't until she was halfway through her doctorate degree at the University of Kansas that her specific career path became clear.

While working as a pharmacy technician at a busy chain-retail pharmacy throughout middle and high school and her undergraduate and professional degree programs, Chris most enjoyed the aspects of pharmacy that had her speaking with patients. As her training became more advanced, though, she realized that traditional retail pharmacists are rarely allowed the luxury of spending time with their patients. That wasn't the kind of pharmacist Chris wanted to be.

Compounding pharmacy, though, enables – indeed, requires – the pharmacist to speak personally with each patient, discuss treatment options with his or her physician, then make the medication "from scratch" to meet that individual patient's needs. This personal level of care appealed to Chris and catered to her interpersonal communication skills and creativity.

After working with the Professional Compounding Centers of America (PCCA, the industry leader in compounding pharmacy) for 3 years, traveling across the continent to teach pharmacy students at virtually every pharmacy school in the U.S. and Canada about modern-day compounding pharmacy, Chris began her entrepreneurial path. She opened her own compounding pharmacy on the west side of Houston in 2008.

Since then, the pharmacy has become an established component of the West Houston and Westchase District communities and complements the growing medical community on the expanding west side of town. Chris enjoys working with her patients and their diverse needs. Whether they need customized hormones or thyroid medicine, personalized pain management, simplified medication regimens (liquids and lozenges instead of pills), or hand-crafted nutritional supplements, Chris and her team recognize that people aren't made from cookie cutters; their medicine shouldn't be, either.

Chris explains her challenges since opening her own pharmacy in 2008 have been to be patient and to find balance. In every aspect of her life, Chris was accustomed to setting a goal with a timeline and promptly achieving it, but building a business from scratch doesn't follow such an easy pattern. Creating a successful and productive business entails forging relationships and trust, which takes time. Chris also struggled with how to reserve some of her time, her energy, her*self* for priorities other than the pharmacy: family has always been her first priority, and it was hard for Chris to reconcile the essential nature of the business as a priority versus her personal belief that family is paramount. Fortunately – and maddeningly – "patience" and "balance" tend to be elusive but also one other's solution: Chris has found she has to be patient for the business to grow to the point that her attentions can be shared, and in finding balance in small ways, it is easier to be patient with the pharmacy's growth.

Chris Barnett

Recipe for SUCCESS!

1. Patience

2. Supportive family

3. Perseverance

4. Determination

5. The ability to truly listen to others and identify their needs

6. Steadfast loyalty to your standards in the face of competition, especially that of lower quality

7. Flexibility

About Chris Barnett

Chris was born in raised in Kansas and graduated from the University Of Kansas School Of Pharmacy with her Doctorate of Pharmacy in 2003. She married her pharmacy-school sweetheart, Chad, right after graduation. Luckily, both Chris and Chad applied for and were accepted into amazing job opportunities in Houston, Texas, so after being out of school and married for only 4 weeks, the Barnett's moved to Houston. Chris's passion is ballroom dancing, especially East-coast wing, in which she used to compete and perform. Also, she and Chad renovated their kitchen soon after purchasing their first home and now enjoy their time together cooking, learning new recipes, cooking techniques, and enjoying the fruits of their labor.

Christina Barnett, Pharm.D.
Westchase Specialty Pharmacy
11301 Richmond Ave, St K-101
Houston, TX 77082

Email: CBarnett@WestchaseRx.com
Phone: 281-497-5214
Fax: 281-497-5215
Website: www.WestchaseRx.com
Facebook: www.Facebook.com/WestchaseRx

Christal Mercier

"For I know the plans I have for you, declares the Lord. Plans to prosper you and not harm you. Plans to give you a hope and a future"
Jeremiah 29:11

Follow Your Dreams

Christal Mercier is a business women specializing in damaged for over 30 years. She was different than most children, starting to comb her own hair at the tender age of 6. Christal would comb her baby sister's hair and fix her classmates hair.

After trying many unsuccessful professions, Christal decided to apply to beauty school, since styling hair was always a passion for her. She loved trying to make people's hair compliment them instead of taking away. Since then, Christal has been applying hair weaves for over 25 years. She knew she had a gift from "GOD." About ten years ago, a lady came in, who was badly burned at the age of two, and asked for a weave, Christal thought, "Lord, what am I going to do?" But right in the midst of the application process, God showed Christal a vision of how the base and application was to be placed.

Christal's sister, Timothy, also inspired her to get into the hair augmentation industry. Timothy suffered from hair loss. Christal remembers back in the day, when a stylist would say, "The perm needs to stay on a little while longer so your hair can get straight," instead of just rinsing the relaxer off. Due to this misconception, Christal's sister, Timothy, was severely chemically burned. She watched her sister go from being an Ebony Fashion Fair model, the first black to model Jordache' jeans, to an inward, depressed and very self-conscious person.

Knowing how depressed Timothy was about her hair loss, her sister Cathy, paid for a hair replacement system from a very reputable company (which I choose not to name). Unfortunately, it looked very unnatural, and she was still depressed. Christal prayed, "Lord" you've got to let me learn how to do hair replacement systems, and make it look more natural."

Six months later, Christal got the opportunity. She perfected her craft and she made her sister a promise that she would make to others like her, to have a more natural appearance. After Christal applied her sister's hair replacement system, it was like letting the cat out of the bag.

Later, Christal discovered that her sister, Timothy, had another battle to overcome--cancer. This devastating situation made Christal even more determined to give her sister, and others like her, the opportunity to feel good about themselves. By enhancing their outward appearance with a non-surgical hair replacement system, Christal was able to rebuild their self-confidence and restore their self-esteem.   Her motto is: "You can be sick, but you don't have to look sick."

Since then, Christal began to give free consultations to both women and children. But during these meetings she noticed that her clients, with hair loss, had self-esteem that was so low that they couldn't even look her in the eyes; they were broken and they didn't feel whole. They didn't feel good about themselves. For that very reason, Christal made sure that all consultations and services are performed in a private setting.

A year before Christal's sister passed in 2009, due to breast cancer, she started a non-profit organization called "Hair Dreams by Christal, Inc."   Recognizing the importance of self-esteem in a person's everyday life, her non-profit organization provides non-surgical hair replacement systems to underprivileged women and children who suffer from extreme hair loss, long or short-term, beyond their control.

One of Christal's biggest challenges was to figure out how to form a non-profit organization, when she had a profitable salon providing the same services. She began researching unnatural hair loss in women and children, and found that it is more prevalent than we think. She talked to other non-profit organizations for one year, prior to coming up with an amendment, and she was granted the 501(c)(3) non-profit organization, Hair Dreams By Christal, Inc.

Christal's challenge now, is locating funding for her non-profit in order to provide non-surgical hair replacement systems to under privileged women and children. What she provides is not considered as main stream; but it is needed. Hair loss reaches across all social, racial and economic boundaries; therefore, it doesn't pick and choose who it will affect.

If you would like to make a tax-deductible donation to Hair Dreams please visit www.hairdreamsbychristal.org and make someone's hair dream come true.

Christal Mercier

Recipe for SUCCESS!

1. Put God first and pay your tithes

2. Treat others the way you want to be treated; do a quality job and you will get quality results

3. Don't take peoples "disadvantage" to your "advantage"; you can't do wrong and get by

4. Keep your business and personal life separate

5. Have integrity and character in your business as well as your personal life

6. Be willing to learn; you're never too old

7. Love what you do and you will never have to work a day in your life!!!

About Christal Mercier

Christal, the owner and founder of Hair Dreams by Christal, Inc. has been fulfilling hair dreams for more than 30 years. She has been blessed with a talent to assist people of all ethnic backgrounds with hair restoration. Her client base spans across several states and various nationalities. Christal specializes in non-surgical hair replacement systems that give the illusion of restoration which help to rebuild confidence and self-esteem while providing a solution for what they thought could not be resolved.

Christal Mercier
Hair Dreams By Christal, Inc.
514 Texas Parkway, Suite A
Missouri City, Texas 77489

Email: HairDreamsByChristalInc@yahoo.com
Phone: 877-499-9433
Website: www.HairDreamsbyChristal.org
LinkedIn: http://www.linkedin.com/pub/christal-mercier/20/238/8a5
Twitter: HairDreamsInc

Christina Suter

"To tell the truth is an act of mercy for myself"
Byron Katie

From Ideals to Leadership

Christina started her first venture with a passionate dream to change the way a business was run. The Ground Level Center was a small meeting space in Venice, CA, rented out to conscious-minded teachers who shared a spiritual message. Based on an innovative win-win philosophy, she let each teacher pay according to what value they received from using the space. For two years, the minimal overhead was not even covered and the group expressed resistance to contributing more. Christina's disappointment led to an honest, deeply introspective evaluation of her business that was a major turning point for her as an entrepreneur.

Examining her underlying purpose for the business, Christina acknowledged that she found the experience of running Ground Level Center deeply fulfilling and loved being a leader. She realized that, as a business owner, it was her job alone to know what the business needs financially and make it work. She also learned that people's relationship with money is not always clear-cut. The teachers relied on her leadership to make sure the meeting space was supported; they were understandably focused on their own businesses, not hers. Once she set a standard room rental price, every teacher was supported, not just that one who used the space that day.

Those hard-learned lessons augmented Christina's existing entrepreneurial ideals, while instilling a deeper sense of confidence and clarity about her contribution to the world through her business. As a result, she began consulting with other entrepreneurs, drawing on the wisdom she had gained firsthand. In fact, that experience has been consistently instrumental in giving Christina the understanding to support her clients to embrace their passion, make it real and access the internal strength required to step into being a leader in such an environment.

Over the last decade, she has fine-tuned the process of streamlining a company so it not only performs successfully, but brings the owner a sense of peace and fulfillment that can often be lost in the daily pressures of operating a business, making a profit and solving problems.

Christina had accumulated several boxes of uncompleted paperwork. Intending to "get around to it" a friend trained her on how to file items, when to throw them away, how to create a To Do list and the difference between a task and a project. In the first month, Christina greatly improved her capacity to respond to her clients.

Christina Suter

Recipe for SUCCESS!

1. Follow your vision and dreams

2. Know and honor your ideals

3. Take and implement a good time management course

4. Learn how to read the numbers for your business and do so every month

5. Schedule in time for yourself and your family every week – in PEN!

6. Know how much you are able to get done; do that and no more

7. Get enough sleep every night

About Christina Suter

As the founder and lead consultant of Ground Level Consulting, Christina L. Suter brings two decades of real-world experience as a small business owner and real estate investor. She developed her extensive financial and operational skills firsthand as she faced and overcame each difficulty that appeared along the way. She started up, managed and sold one business, while establishing herself as a successful consultant and simultaneously developing an extensive real estate portfolio. In 2002, Christina made the decision to leverage her experience into helping other small business owners and property owners through a consulting practice that works the way an entrepreneur works, dealing with the pressing problems of a business on the ground level and in real time. Since then, she has supported numerous companies throughout southern California and the western United States move beyond surviving to thriving. Christina's solid background and education—including a Bachelors in Business, an Associates in Teaching and a Masters in Psychology—strongly influence her work with Ground Level clients. Not only does she offer keen insights into what will make or break the success of any given business, but she teaches the skills every entrepreneur needs to move forward. And she does this in a warm, supportive, non-judgmental way that is always highly respectful of her clients' personal values.

Christina Suter
Ground Level Consulting
3579 E Foothill Blvd #320
Pasadena, CA 91107

Email: Christina@groundlevel-consulting.com
Phone: 310-463-5942
Website: www.grourndlevel-consulting.com
LinkedIn: http://www.linkedin.com/in/christinalsmith

Deb Scott

"Be yourself - everyone else is already taken"
Oscar Wilde

Against All Odds

You would never think growing up in a dysfunctional family where depression and alcoholism lived routinely, being sexually abused by a teacher at a young age, or fighting daily demons of doubt and despair - anyone could come through with a happy ending - but it's true.. And YOU can too.

Easy - No. Possible - Yes.

What did Deb need to transform the tragedy into a triumph? Good mentors, loving kindness, faith in God. Awareness was the first step towards acceptance, and ultimately a translation into better everyday action.

It's not about perfection - it's about progress.

Deb would tell you to never quit, never give up hope, never stop believing in the best possibilities. The very thing you don't want may be exactly what will give you everything you need, and more.

The Sky is Green & The Grass is Blue - turning your upside down world right side up, is the book and advise she wished someone had given her.

You're not finished yet - the best is yet to come

Face it - everyone who has been extremely successful has probably also experienced great failure and a whole bunch of nay sayers. If you have either of these - good news - you're in great company with the winners in life!

Deb found that what you resist will persist, so don't make the goal eliminating moments of discouragement or negative people from your existence - accept they are prowling around to destroy everyone's dream - be strong, practice your defense, take control of the inevitable in advance.

When the time to prepare has arrived - the time to prepare has past. Use the 7 ingredients listed in the recipe for success below as a constant daily habit, and you will automatically be immune to the disease of those who only destroy and displease.

If it doesn't kill you - it will only make you stronger!

Deb Scott

Recipe for SUCCESS!

1. Vision - If you don't know where you are going - you will never get there

2. Outcome - Always begin with the end in mind. What is your best case scenario when your business is at its best?

3. How do you feel when? People don't change because they see the light - they change because they feel the heat. You will only be motivated in the long run by a feeling - not a word or even money. It is the feeling you want which having the money gives you. Go down your list of goals and create a feeling you desire for each one

4. Mentors - Eleanor Roosevelt said it best when she commented "you can't live long enough to make all the mistakes yourself in this world - learn from others." You must have good mentors - coaches - advocates - who already have what you want. Follow the steps of those already walking in their greatness - and you will arrive at yours must sooner having a lot more fun

5. Successful Sabotage - Don't set yourself up for failure - set yourself up for success!

6. Mind Vitamins - Feed your whole soul with people, places, and things which move you towards creation your vision. You don't take a vitamin a month and expect it to have any significant effect on your health - and your business success is no different. People who win have good daily habits. If you don't think small things matter - you never spent the night alone with a mosquito

7. Celebration - Be sure to always celebrate your success. Have fun, keep a good sense of humor, and emphasize the positive. Take what you like and leave the rest - but remember - you need to begin in order to win

About Deb Scott

Deb Scott, BA, CPC, Certified Professional Coach, specializes in working with individuals, businesses, and corporate environments, transforming ineffective group and personal dynamics into high-powered, successful, dynamic individuals and teams. As a Biology major in college, Deb became an award-winning sales and leadership specialist. With 20 years of background in cardiac surgery sales, she now applies her sales and business background to motivational speaking and consulting. She speaks and writes about how you can turn things around whether you're in sales, marketing, advertising, hiring, or teambuilding. – "The Sky is Green and The Grass is Blue." Turning Your Upside-Down World Right-Side-Up!" is her debut book, and has won THREE National Book Awards for excellence.

Deb Scott
Discover the Amazing YOU! Coaching
PO Box 551
Newburyport, MA 01950

Email: deb@greenskyandbluegrass.com
Phone: 978-462-2215
Website: http://www.greenskyandbluegrass.com
Facebook: http://www.facebook.com/authorandmotivationalspeaker
LinkedIn: http://www.linkedin.com/in/debscottauthorspeaker
Twitter: @greenskydeb

Deborah Bishop

"May you always know the truth and see the lights surrounding you."
Bob Dylan

A Little Bit About Deborah

Deborah's personal success story has had so many ups and downs, challenges and victories that she has often joked that if she ever published her life's story, she would title it a work of fiction! Born in Vancouver Canada, she debuted onstage at the age of four. Deb has performed internationally and been so close to massive success that to say she tasted it wouldn't do it justice.

 Growing up in the arts, with a bent for all things spiritual, Deborah has heard her fill of what's not possible and that it's all about struggle, sacrifice and having to be discovered. It was almost seen as noble to be a "starving artist" or within the healing arts, to give her "gifts" away.

It was in her teens that Deborah took on her first business; "Performing Arts Magazine." A visionary beyond her years, the magazine she created was backed by two prominent business men who ultimately wanted a tax write-off and thus the first issue never saw the light of day. It was as tough lesson, but one that placed Deborah firmly on the road of independence and self -reliance.

Dabbling in the occasional JOB, Deborah had to admit she was not happy working for someone else and took on the role of freelancer and full on entrepreneur.   It was in Los Angeles where she established herself as a force to be reckoned with, within the Entertainment and Personal Development Industries. Struggle however, was never far behind as her past demons and beliefs followed her and continued to deny her entry to the life she truly longed for.

A survivor of family traumas, serious health issues and a brutal attack, Deborah's past stood firmly in the way. Developing her own methodology, Deborah uncovered the lies that trapped her and learned how to rewrite her story and claim her success which included taking herself from earning less than twelve thousand dollars a year, to over three hundred thousand within fourteen months. Deborah has literally helped hundreds of others to do the same.

Deborah Bishop

Recipe for SUCCESS!

1. Dream big and dream often, build your vision

2. Tell only those who will support your vision

3. Do something every day that moves your vision forward

4. Act as if you are already successful

5. Make decisions quickly and keep focused

6. Take actions that generate income versus just keeping busy

7. Learn from your mistakes, love yourself anyway and keep going

About Deborah Bishop

Deborah Bishop currently resides in Nashville TN. She was raised in Vancouver, BC and spent several years in Los Angeles, CA. A Personal Development Performance Artist, Speaker, Author, Conceptual Consultant and Strategic Life Coach; Deborah's education was both diverse and non-traditional, from private schooling and studying with the Royal Conservatory of Canada, to a performing arts program and one on one mentoring and apprenticing. Throw in a large dose from the school known as life and the knowledge acquired from being involved in founding and running three Theater Companies, a Production Company, a Personal Development Business, an Interactive Entertainment company, a Direct Market Company and her current business which is her own Personal Development / Positive Entertainment company featuring; The "U"Factor, and you have a potent blend of wisdom and real life experience. Deborah is a published author and a loved Talk Radio and TV Talk show personality. She excels at helping others to attain a life filled with wealth on every level and showing them how to monetize their ideas, talents and passions. Deborah currently balances her work with her philanthropic endeavors and believes that giving back is the only way to truly achieve life success.

Deborah Bishop
JSYI a Division of Right On Enterprises
414 Munn Rd.
Nashville, TN 37214

Email: livealimitlesslife@gmail.com
Phone: 615-376-9905 / 800-582-8772
Website: http://www.deborahbishop.com
Facebook: http://www.facebook.com/deborahbishop

Fred (Coach Doc Fred) Simkovsky

"Simple Solutions for Complex Challenges"
Dr. Fred Simkovsky, CMCP

Does the Eternal Optimist Still Exist?

 Coach "Doc Fred" got his education at night over 23 years while holding down a full time job and raising four children with his wonderful wife of 43 years. He is now the proud grandfather of 15 grandchildren who he loves all dearly. He has been successful because he would not accept defeat, learning from his mistakes and having a lot of great people who coached and mentored him along the way. He still has 2 mentor/coaches who he gets help from monthly.

He is the eternal optimist and believes he can make a difference in peoples' lives.

It's been a challenge growing my coaching, organizational development, training business through networking and soon to be Visions of Success Internet Radio Show. It's important to keep current and relevant in this ambiguous world by doing a lot of research and networking.

Dr. Fred Simkovsky

Recipe for SUCCESS!

1. Listen before you speak. Listen to what is said and not said

2. Ask for help

3. Collaborate when possible

4. Learn something new daily

5. Start with a prioritized "To-Do" list daily

6. Don't procrastinate EVER

7. Be positive ALWAYS

About Dr. Fred (Coach Doc Fred) Simkovsky

Dr. Fred (Coach Doc Fred) Simkovsky is a certified master coach, organizational development/learning consultant, and speech mastery trainer with over 25 years of experience in multi-disciplinary environments both nationally and internationally in the USA, Canada, Germany, Japan, India, and China. Doc Fred has successfully guided over 750 individuals, at all levels, to their Visions of Success in the last 10 years alone

Dr. Fred (Coach Doc Fred) Simkovsky
Life Career Business Coach
3076 Paige Ave.
Simi Valley, CA 93063

Email: fredsimkovsky@yahoo.com
Phone: 510-506-8281
Website: http://www.lifecareerbusinesscoach.com
Facebook: http://www.facebook.com/fsimkovsky
LinkedIn: http://www.linkedin.com/in/fredsimkovsky

JJ Frederickson

"And men are, that they might have joy."
Nephi 2:25

From Dance Coach to Life Coach

Before becoming a Life Coach, JJ owned a dance studio for almost 9 years. She was also a perfectionist, and this combination worked fine until JJ gave birth to her daughter. Once a baby was in the mix, it was impossible to be a perfect in every role.

All of a sudden, nothing seemed to work. Her daughter was clingy; her students were unruly; the parents were dissatisfied; and her husband was neglected. Walking into the studio felt like walking into a war zone and at home she felt like Cinderella ... never getting a break.

The stress came to a head when her infant daughter was fussing while JJ was prepping for the annual dance recital. She looked at her daughter and said, "I just wish you'd go to sleep!"

Now that's a reaction most parents have on occasion. But on this day, JJ noticed that she wanted her daughter to sleep all the time so that she could get her "important" work done. She realized that her priorities were screwed up, and she didn't want to model this for her daughter.

JJ needed help getting things back into perspective, so she hired a Fearless Living life coach and laid down her perfectionism. She learned that her mental patterns and habits had run amok, and now it was time to shift her brain and claim the joy she always wanted.

JJ's life changed dramatically in just three months of coaching. She decided she wanted to become a Life Coach and started training with the Fearless Living Institute. Eventually she retired from the dance studio, so that she could work from her home as a Life Coach and fully enjoy her family. Now instead of helping people express themselves on stage, she helps people express themselves in their life.

Challenges that JJ has met and conquered include time constraints of having children and a home business: I made a schedule of my available time. Even with just a few hours/week for clients, it was better focusing on hours available than on the time I didn't have.

Fear of sales calling: I review positive feedback from those I've already helped, reminding me that I make a difference.

JJ Frederickson

Recipe for SUCCESS!

1. Be yourself; don't set out to impress

2. Remember that you make your own rules

3. Set business hours and family hours

4. Savor the experience you're having right now

5. Do things that feed your soul

6. Stop stressing; find joy in everything you do

7. Stay open to inspiration; it can come from anywhere

About JJ Frederickson

JJ Frederickson CFLC is the creator of The Live Life Easy Stress Solution, taking people from midlife stress to their midlife best by introducing them to their caveman (or cavewoman) brain. Once the connection between stress and the caveman brain is made — that's when magic happens!

She's the original Expert Life Coach for Milwaukee's WTMJ4 and a certified Coach and Trainer with The Fearless Living Institute. Through her broadcasts, seminars, blogs and articles, people learn how to get rid of stress and have more fun! In her private practice she's helped mid-lifers around the globe tackle issues with their jobs, relationships, blended families, finances, and retirement.

JJ earned a BA in Broadcast and Electronic Communication from Marquette University, with a Journalism emphasis. She was a writer and editor for Southern Lakes Media and a news reporter for WIN-TV and WMIR. She was also a founder of Sage Street Dance Company in Burlington.

Now, JJ the Life Coach feels like she's found her calling. She says, "Life Coaching brings everything in my life together. I can pull together all my skills and experiences to help people reduce stress and fall in love with their lives. How amazing is that?"

JJ Frederickson
JJ the Life Coach
PO Box 113
Honey Creek, WI 53138

Email: JJ@JJthelifecoach.com
Phone: 414-732-3320
Website: http://www.jjthelifecoach.com
Facebook: http://www.facebook.com/jjthelifecoach
LinkedIn: http://www.linkedin.com/in/jjthelifecoach
Twitter: http://twitter.com/jjthelifecoach

Jean Jones

"The biggest adventure you can ever take is to live the life of your dreams"
Oprah Winfrey

Unique and Passionate My Arbonne Story

Jean Jones teaches one to dream big and encourages our children to do the same, achieve to become successful. Work hard with commitment, perseverance, guidance of a supportive family and incredible mentors, as lifelong learners as she has. Arbonne International may be a company that can help one nurture their passions and dreams.

With Arbonne, she is able to share her passions and expertise to help others strive and acquire their dreams. It has certainly brought hope and newfound optimism and success to many others. She believes as women today, we feel that we can do it all, as super women – balance our lives well. One to be constantly present for our children, maintain a successful home and career and also be a great-loving wife, a good friend , give back to society and adequately take care of ourselves last. Tough balance!

Jones earned a BS degree in Health and Physical education and a MLA masters in history, literature and art history. She worked in her profession for over 30 years. She was feeling partially unfulfilled. Constant self-evaluation led her to and on Arbonne International as an independent fitness and wellness consultant. She needed a beautiful new lease on life.

During her 36 year marriage she was dealing with a severe physical and mentally abusive relationship while protecting her 3 children and grandson. God brought her through as the biblical character Job. Jean was feeling inadequate with a severe broken heart and very used, lingering effects are still visible today. Still she continues to bring out the best in others, Arbonne gave her the incentive: she had been looking for a legit home based business, to help her son finish his university degree. To help pay off extensive private debt, left by the vindictive divorce and to extend her professional career and passions. This new challenge set her on a new course to succeed and help others to do the same. It set a new style where dreams are real and achievable. One can build on Airbonne as a new business in network marketing and obtain success.

Jean Jones

Recipe for SUCCESS!

1. Schedule and introduce Arbonne and its benefits and opportunities

2. Keep it simple, teach and educate others about the great product and business

3. Never pre-judge people as new business builders, because of their circumstances, God calls all the shots. The best cream rises to the top

4. Share all the options, create interest with a prospect. They will decide if it's best for them

5. Arbonne sponsor people and educate them, who are willing to do the course work

6. Train people who want success as badly as you do

7. The Arbonne success plan is worth looking at

About Jean Jones

Jean Polk Jones is a dedicated woman who has worked at her career as a fitness health educator, teacher and English professor. She continues to work and search for her ultimate, ongoing purpose in God's vision for her life. Born in Erie, PA and raised in Flint, MI, Jean currently resides in Missouri City, Sugarland Texas Area.

Jean earned a BS degree in health and physical education, life time certificate from Texas Southern University in Houston and a master's degree, MLA in History, Literature and Art History from Houston Baptist University. She has studied in Madrid, Lisbon, London and Mexico in addition to many locations in the US. Jean is the proud mother of Kila Jai, Khara Brittany, Delorean Jones, and a 13 year old grandson, Cam'ron.

Jean Jones
2601 Cartwright Rd Suite D259
Missouri City, TX 77459
Email: jaepolk4@aol.com
Phone: 281-969-8492
Cell: 281-702-2207
Facebook: #18706595

Jeff Tollefson

"Your imagination is your preview of life's coming attraction"
Albert Einstein

Living Naturally

Jeff's original occupation required a great amount of manual and physical labor which was the initial driving force in his desire to get away from the mental and physical deterioration caused by this work and the freedom he longed for as a human being to create his own source of income and excel at and in it.

Originally, his company TheraPure was born out of many, varied injuries having taken their toll on him, as well as a need to supplement his family's income. What started as a loving hobby in 1994 on a DOS-based computer given to him by his sister would prove to be a precursor to just the experience he would need to endure a life-altering episode.

In 2005 his youngest son was diagnosed with leukemia. After the struggle through traditional therapies, he was in a search of finding the most pure and non-harmful life-style for his family. TheraPure was no longer a side business but more of a mission. His passion for this business was exponentially increased with the diagnosis of his son. It was apparent to him that there was a natural approach to living a healthy, simple existence. It would enable his family to strive for a more peaceful life in this sometimes overwhelming world.

With his computer, his desire to "change the world" and a lot of hard work, he has built his company from its humble beginnings in his home office to an Internet-based, nationally-distributed line of holistic and life improving products, as well as manufacturing his own aromatherapy accessories and products.

Research has shown that a positive outlook strengthens body, mind and spirit - all the while increasing your happiness. TheraPure strives to find the best life-enhancing products that may assist us on our journey by reaching higher levels of awareness through optimum wellness. His mission is to educate and emulate what nature has proven since its inception. Living naturally is truly living.

Jeff's biggest challenge was to walk away from a very well-paying job and into the unknown abyss of success or failure on his own as a self-employed business man. He jumped in with both feet and everything else he had while continuing his regular job.

Success did not come overnight, but has definitely come and now he's his own boss duplicating his previous income while celebrating the freedoms he now has with his own business.

He's also noted that finding the right resources to work with to help your business succeed is super important. He has found Amazon, Google and Facebook are paramount in catapulting your business out the front door and into every home in America and beyond.

Jeff Tollefson

Recipe for SUCCESS!

1. Have a streamlined website

2. Fast delivery of goods and services

3. Stay organized

4. Block your time to insure you get what's needed done

5. Don't be afraid to make big changes

6. Always call customers and follow-up

7. Finding the right resources is super important

About Jeff Tollefson

Jeffrey Tollefson was born in New Rockford, ND and grew up on a farm near a town of less than 1800 people, with his parents and siblings. His beginnings were simple and basic.

Jeff later attended college, then began his travels to Washington State, Florida, Utah, and Texas and then finally settled in California. He bought a home and started a family.

He took some college business classes, just enough to stoke the fire that drives him to be his own boss. He continued working to meet his obligations although spent all his free time at night and on long weekends developing, reading, and building his now flourishing business.

He is now working from home, focused on his successful business and has refined that old saying 'burning the midnight oil' into producing and distributing high grade, certified organic Essential Oils!

Jeff Tollefson
TheraPure.com Health Essentials
30776 Mirage Circle
Menifee, CA 92584

Email: jeff@therapure.com
Phone: 877-846-8669   951-679-3519
Website: http://www.therapure.com
Facebook: www.facebook.com/therapure
YouTube: www.youtube.com/therapure

Joan Day-Gilbert

"Life does not consist of thinking it consists in acting"
Woodrow Wilson -1912

The Empowerment of Being Empowered

Committed to her job, family, and marriage, at age 50 Joan found her life spiraling with unimagined events. The major loss of a brother, mother and workmate all within a six month period was taking its toll.

Fighting depression and a failing marriage, Joan was sure she was about to lose her job too. She knew she could not handle everything alone, and turned to much needed support from family, friends, church and prayer.

Joan noticed a new found strength. An inner strength that she knew would take her through whatever life brought to her. She also recognized that that new inner strength was a direct result of the support she had received. Joan then had a realization.

Knowing firsthand the despair that comes with loss and the lack of hope for the future that can creep up on one, hardly without notice, Joan realized that through her journey, she had learned how to overcome the despair and depression. She had become strong, viable and able to move to the next stage.

With this new found strength, Joan realized that her new found passion was to help others. She knew she could empower others to visualize themselves as more than they could ever imagine.

Out of her experience, Joan launched her very own radio show called "The Sweetness of Living Radio." She now can help numerous people to find themselves once again, and live the life they've always dreamed of.

Joan also did something she had always dreamed of. She started her very own business selling a line of Christian jewelry, apparel and gifts. She calls her new business "Bless-D."

While not without hurdles along the way, Joan says her two biggest business challenges were really personal challenges as well. Learning how to market herself was something new and unknown. She also learned the importance of balance and prioritizing the many things she had on her to-do list. Joan says working with her coach was the best way to get a handle on these challenges. Joan learned one of the toughest rules of being in business, and that's taking care of herself.

Joan Day-Gilbert   *Recipe for* SUCCESS!

1. Try, try, try, try, try, try, then try again!
2. Build trust in your clients
3. It's ok to fail – just learn
4. Keep Trying
5. If you don't know, don't be afraid to ask someone
6. Stay motivated and keep positive
7. Keep in mind it does not happen overnight

Joan Day-Gilbert
Bless-d
6454 Park Central Way #D
Indianapolis, IN 46260

Email: sweetnessoflivingradio@juno.com
Phone: 317-989-8601
Website: http://www.bless-d.com
Website: http://www.sweetnessoflivingradio.com

Judy Winslow

"I'm not a genius. I'm just a tremendous bundle of experience."
Richard Buckminster Fuller

"Your Journey Holds the Clues..."

The journey into business began early, though she didn't realize it. For years she was a misfit, an outsider on the sidelines, shy, observing others. It wasn't until college that she began to feel proud to be different, noticing that those who were truly memorable dared to be themselves. After moving to New York City, she found herself sitting around a table one evening with about a dozen women, all chattering happily. She realized that each had a very distinct personality yet they shared the willingness to be authentic, exactly 'as is', even at the risk of not being liked or accepted by all.

During these years Judy noticed this quality was exactly what allowed businesses to extremely successful. From participating in a redesign/rebranding of Woman's Day Magazine, to assisting Elizabeth Taylor's first perfume launch, each related their business model and offerings to this endeavor. Later she would call this 'Being Unforgettable', though during this period she was simply following her intuition.

Her first business began after approaching her boss at Woman's Day to open shop. It was SO exciting to work with Fortune 100 companies and make an impact. If only they had applied some of their wisdom to their own company, things may have turned out differently. The first big lesson came early. After billing a surprising solid six figures the first year, the accountant made a major mistake that almost ruined the business! As business owners we need to stay on top of everything. Four years and multiple awards later, it was time to resign and move on, although that business thrives today.

Now, over 20 years later, life and work are still enjoyable. From being a graphic designer, to planning marketing strategies, then adding coaching and consulting to the mix, her journey has been filled with new challenges, joyful unfolding's and wonderful clients. That shy girl now happily speaks to groups, conducts workshops and trainings and tells anyone who will listen that the road to success is paved with brave souls willing to be Unforgettable, to forge their own way, bringing their gifts to the world.

When you're on the 'grow' there's a point when you can't get it all done alone. Sleep time dreams are filled with a particular task, days spent frustrated with a challenge, or when someone else would do the job better with absolutely no stress, why struggle? Hire it out or lose your mind. Getting help will change your life.

Judy Winslow

Recipe for SUCCESS!

1. Believe you CAN!

2. Identify & appreciate your own skills and talents – read your testimonials daily if need be

3. Be willing to be different and stand out

4. Keep learning

5. Understand the difference between busy vs. productive

6. Create a sustainable business model

7. Make time to re-charge, play and laugh!

About Judy Winslow

J. Winslow, (the 'Brandologist') has the unique ability to help business owners, entrepreneurs and careerists find the core of who they are. Mixing existing elements, their passion plus innovation builds a presence with clarity and intention rather than by accident. Branding, NOT just for cattle, is key to business success. Winslow has assisted in creating Unforgettable Brands throughout her career for clients ranging from Fortune 100's to start-ups seeking creative business building strategies including Madison Avenue biggies Elizabeth Taylor, Clairol, Noxell, Woman's Day Magazine plus others you may not read about, but whose lives and businesses have been changed forever.

Judy Winslow
Unforgettable Brands
5592 Eastwind Dr
Sarasota, FL 34233

Email: jw@unforgettablebrands.com
Phone: 941-921-7440
Website: http://www.unforgettablebrands.com
Facebook: https://www.facebook.com/judywins
LinkedIn: http://www.linkedin.com/in/judywins
Twitter: http://twitter.com/#!/judywins

Kathryn Reeves

"The Universe doesn't call the qualified - it qualifies the called"
Michael Beckwith

Kathryn's Journey

Kathryn has been in and out of the spiritual path all of her life. She's studied various branches of Christianity, Judaism, Islam, and Hinduism. S he's been a student of meditation.

When not on her journey, she felt unfulfilled, and knew there was something missing in her life. When the Universe sent her the message that she was to speak of her journey openly and honestly to help others along the way, she jumped in with both feet!

It's been difficult to figure out how to make a living with this work, but it finally came to me to simply do the work and the money will take care of itself.

Upon reflection of my past I realized how many times the Universe had tapped me on the shoulder ~ from standing on a stool to practice sermons in the bathroom mirror, to converting to Catholicism then applying to become a num. I've been to Hajj, the Islamic journey to Mecca and studied Judaism for 4 years. Finally, I realized the answers were within rather than without.

I'm sharing my journey and whatever wisdom the Universe chooses to share through me in satsang. I have given satsang at Many Rivers Books & Tea in Sepastopol, CA and in Auburn Alchemy in Auburn, CA. You can also find me on YouTube by searching my name.

Kathryn Reeves

Recipe for SUCCESS!

1. Rid yourself of negative self-talk

2. Always work with integrity

3. Never promise what you can't deliver

4. Be consistent

5. Keep service uppermost in mind

6. Be transparent about your own goals

7. ALWAYS be authentic

About Kathryn Reeves

Dr. Kathryn earned her Psy.D. from California Coast University at age 52. She started a private practice in the Sacramento area, which resulted in her book, "Take Charge! A Pocket Guide for Coping with Life." However, that was not her true path and she came back to her journey in spirituality.

Kathryn Reeves
Take Charge! With Dr. Kathryn
102 Lifton Ct.
Roseville CSA 95747

Email: drkathryn@drkathrynonline.com
Phone: 916-663-8266
Website: http://www.drkathrynonline.com
Facebook: http://www.facebook.com/TakeChargeCoach
Twitter: drkathryn1

Keiko Hsu

"Be the change you want to see in the world"
M. Gandhi

What Do YOU Want to Do for the Next 50 Years?

A crisis can be a huge catalyst to reinvent your life. Keiko had a successful 28-year career at General Electric Company. But her world came crashing down when her 26-year marriage unexpectedly crumbled during the same year her job was eliminated due to layoffs. Truly a double-whammy crisis.

Keiko soon realized there was no point in being miserable. At age 52, she predicted she had 50 more years to live, so she asked "What do I want to do for the NEXT 50 years?" She decided to reinvent herself and follow her passions, triggering her journey to find her purpose, passions, and start the next chapter of her life.

She realized she no longer needed to work for a large organization to have credibility. She could fly solo, start her own business, enjoy the rewards of working for herself. She had plenty of management experience, so it should be easy, right? Here are some lessons she learned the hard way:

Follow your heart. After deciding to become a Life Coach, Keiko went through training, certification, and started her business Wings for Women, coaching women through life transitions, especially divorce. Although life coaching was very gratifying work, she also wanted to leverage her business expertise by becoming a management consultant. Starting up this second business turned out to be a costly endeavor that distracted Keiko for several months until she finally decided her heart wasn't in it. Her life coaching was truly her passion.

Get help from other professionals. Keiko discovered the value of investing in mentor coaches to push her and teach her effective techniques for business success. She also recognized the importance of hiring specialists for certain tasks - a housekeeper, accountant, business attorney, web developer, writer, newsletter producer. She learned that paying others for the value they provide to you also helps you develop confidence to charge what YOU'RE worth! Keiko's personal metamorphosis and entrepreneurial journey has clarified her mission for Wings for Women, to enable women to live a joyful life after divorce and attain new heights in their career, life, and relationships.

After working in large corporations, Keiko initially found it lonely and distracting to work in a home office as a soloprenuer, even though she was serving clients by phone as a Life Coach. To address this challenge, she:

- Established a weekly routine including scheduled exercise, networking, and social activities

- Had weekly calls with an "accountability partner"

Keiko Hsu

Recipe for SUCCESS!

1. Be crystal clear on your target market and why they would buy your product or service

2. Develop relationships with your team members, clients, prospects, and potential collaboration partners

3. Listen to your internal procrastinator. There's usually an important message from your subconscious mind

4. Allow other people to help you with tasks that aren't in your sweet spot

5. Invest in continuous learning for your personal and business growth

6. Pay other people for the value they provide to you. It will give you the confidence to charge what YOU'RE worth!

7. Always be positive, even when things don't go as expected

About Keiko Hsu

Keiko Hsu, CPC, ACC is a Life-After-Divorce Mentor, certified Life Coach/Business Coach/ Dream Coach®, and CEO-Founder of Wings for Women®. Her mission is to inspire and enable women to live a joyful life after divorce ... and attain new heights in their life, career and relationships.

Her personal experiences in transforming her own life after divorce, plus her expert coaching skills and corporate leadership experience uniquely enabled Keiko to help recently divorced executive and professional women by providing them with clarity, courage, mentoring, and a step-by-step process to transform their lives.

Keiko is well known for being positive and resilient during challenging situations, seeing the silver lining in the clouds, living life full out, and manifesting her dreams and deepest desires. Her clients say she is courageous, inspiring, focused, accomplished, honest, and very professional.

Keiko is a certified professional coach, Vice President of the San Francisco chapter of the International Coach Federation (ICF), and a graduate of the Institute for Professional Excellence in Coaching (iPEC). During her 28 year career at General Electric Company, Keiko held many leadership and executive positions and led numerous strategic corporate initiatives.

Keiko Hsu
Wings for Women
152 Lombard St #704
San Francisco, CA 94111

Email: keiko@wingsforwomen.net
Phone: 415-738-2313
Website: http://www.wingsforwomen.net
Facebook: http://www.facebook.com/pages/Wings-for-women/197249213658076
LinkedIn: http://www.linkedin.com/in/keikohsu
Twitter: wingsforwomen

Careers from the Kitchen Table Home Business Directory Second Edition

Kelly Poelker

"If you can dream it - You can do it"
Walt Disney

Once an Entrepreneur, Always an Entrepreneur

Kelly gained early exposure to sales and being her own boss, following her Mom about as she sold Avon door-to-door.

When it was time to make money, Kelly became a budding entrepreneur. From her early teens, she cashed in green stamps, sold social security nameplates door-to-door, and walked dogs. Later, she sold Tupperware and Avon. She often did those jobs alongside her straight gigs in retail — if that's what you call being the Easter Bunny and Santa's elf at the mall!

True to her quest for complete independence, Kelly graduated early from high school, started college, and moved into her first apartment. Bam! Reality hit when rent came due, with no parties on the books and no hours scheduled. She opened the yellow pages, turned to "Banks" and didn't go farther than the letter G to get a job — but it took 18 years and three more employers to get back on her own.

Kelly re-entered the entrepreneur pool in 2000, opening her virtual assistant company, Another 8 Hours. Once again, she worked her business part-time in tandem with her full time job of 10 years (ah… benefits!).

After carefully stockpiling the coins in her car for years, Kelly took $140 in unwrapped quarters and opened her business checking account. Nine months later the corporate job was impeding her business growth. When her employer frowned upon her working from home as an independent contractor Kelly gave notice. On January 1, 2001 she was a full-time business owner — and, she signed her employer as her newest client!

After a few years, carving time and space from her home, she took the next leap of faith and moved the business to an outside office. Scarily, she lost her entire client base. Kelly-like, she re-focused, developed six-figure revenues, and became a bestselling author. Kelly loves going to the office every day. Her clients love her warmth, persistence, process and results. To this day she's never looked back — unless you count her pride and satisfaction in a job well done.

The biggest challenge Virtual Assistants face is misinformation: We partner long-term with clients, providing remote administrative support for business or busy personal lives. Owning a computer, an internet connection and wanting to work from home doesn't make you a VA. Outsourcing to under-paid overseas labor doesn't get people the consistent professional support they deserve and their business needs met.

Kelly Poelker

Recipe for SUCCESS!

1. Find your passion in life

2. Research, research, research

3. Develop a solid plan

4. Develop a solid marketing plan

5. Create your USP (Unique Selling Proposition)

6. Establish an external support system

7. Communicate with your internal support system

After 18 years in the corporate arena, Kelly left her cubicle behind to start her own empire as a virtual assistant. A career that is now noted as one of the Entrepreneur Magazine's top four in-demand businesses for 2011.

Kelly was in the forefront of the VA industry when she started her company, Another 8 Hours, in 2000 and began partnering with clients to help them manage and grow their businesses. Her client list includes Fortune 100 and 500 companies; TV and radio show hosts, small business owners, internationally recognized speakers and coaches as well as award-winning authors.

Kelly is co-author of Amazon bestseller and VA industry bible, Virtual Assistant - The Series: Become a Highly Successful, Sought After VA--the longest standing book in the industry that has helped thousands of virtual assistants get started in business. Her books are the most widely used training material in college VA programs across the country.

Kelly is the president of Another 8 Hours and Director/Founder of Academy of Virtual Professionals.

Kelly Poelker

Another 8 Hours, Inc.
106A East Fourth St.
O'Fallon, IL 62269

Email: kp@another8hours.com
Phone: 618-624-3080
Website: http://www.another8hours.com
Facebook: http://www.facebook.com/kellypoelker
LinkedIn: http://www.linkedin/in/kellypoelker
Twitter: http://www.twitter.com/kellypoelker

Careers from the Kitchen Table Home Business Directory Second Edition

Khatira Aboulfatova

"Service to many leads to Greatness"
Jim Rohn

Lifestyle by Design

Since her young age Khatira knew she was thinking differently than her peers and cultural upbringings. She had a strong belief in treating people better than she would treat herself. After graduating from Medical School, she became a successful expert in the area of preventive health and treating her patients with compassion and care. With all her heart she knew that she needed the freedom of choosing what is best. After her life transitioning and moving to the United States, her very first job made it clear for Khatira – working for someone and working 9-5 job wasn't an option. She wanted her life and a career working for her and her client's advantage, so it was up to her to design the lifestyle she would love.

After many interviews with Medical schools and professors she realized going back to traditional medicine wasn't for her, and she chose to become a holistic healer and jump start a part time business as she was working full time as a research associate at BCM (Baylor College of Medicine). There are many personal challenges, and obstacles she's gone through as a single mother, as a professional and a business woman - building her business. As she grew her business, she grew as a person. Khatira dedicated herself to self-growth and development and believes in healing one's self before healing anyone else. In her own words: "You can't teach what you don't have it."

Khatira says being her own Boss and the flexibility to work on her own schedule is great but leads to a big challenge - if she doesn't work – she doesn't get paid.

Khatira says she loves marketing and enjoys networking, meeting new friends and potential clients, where she learned her second challenge in business – following up! to follow up.

Khatira Aboulefatova

Recipe for SUCCESS!

1. Make a commitment

2. Have an integrity in your word and your work

3. Keep a positive attitude

4. Give more than you receive

5. Clear communications with clients and business partners

6. Listen more, talk less

7. Professionalism

About Khatira Aboulefatova

Born and raised in Azerbaijan, formerly known Soviet Union Republic. Khatira graduated from Medical University with Medical Doctor Degree in Pediatrics, and specialized in Tuberculosis and Pulmonology. She completed her Internship in Azerbaijan National research Institute for Tuberculosis and Pulmonology. She then transferred to the second biggest Region in Azerbaijan, as Pediatric Tuberculosis Specialist.

Khatira has lived in Houston for past 16 years and as she recalls it – Loves it!

After transition of her life Khatira got employed as a Research Coordinator here in Houston. Then as a Research Associate at the Baylor College of Medicine. Knowing there is no job security, and having an entrepreneurship goal she chose to continue her education and become a professional massage therapist. Along with her full time job at Baylor College of Medicine - Khatira started her mobile Massage Therapy business part time and in no time she became full time doing what she loves; helping people to achieve healthy body, mind and spirit. Khatira educates her clients on importance of balanced nutrition, exercise, healthy weight, anti-aging technologies for skin and body.

Khatira Aboulfatova
Wellness Beyond Belief
230 Westcott St. Suite 215
Houston, TX 77007

Email: Khatira_a@wellnessbeyondbelief.com
Phone: 832-876-9147
Website: http://www.wellnessbeyondbelief.com
Facebook: http://www.facebook.com/khatira.aboulfatova
LinkedIn: http://www.linkedin.com/pub/khatira-aboulfatova-m-d/1/255/921

Careers from the Kitchen Table Home Business Directory Second Edition

Kim L. Miles

"If you want to make good use of your time, you've got to know what's most important and then give it all you've got"
Lee Iacocca

Find your calling and enjoy your life!

Throughout her life Kim was good at math and science so when it came time to select a college, she was encouraged to go to an engineering college. Kim graduated from Colorado School of Mines in 1993 with a BS in Electrical Engineering and knew that it wasn't the field for her. Kim's commitment to "get her money's worth of my degree" and not disappoint anyone, motivated her to stay in engineering for many years. Finally after years of experience in various roles and searching for the right fit, Kim found her true calling – Coaching.

In 2007 Kim hired a coach, attended the top coaching school, CoachU, and completed the Core Essentials program. She opened her practice and maintained a corporate job while building her practice. While the practice slowly grew, Kim's focus with her business was less than desirable and the results reflected it. Once Kim became fully dedicated to her coaching practice, she became more skilled as a coach, attracted more clients and her practice grew faster than I ever imagined.

Through her experience, Kim as learned it is never enough to just be good at something; you must find joy and meaning in ALL you do to really add value to your own and others' lives. Every experience I had added value to who I am today and my clients ultimately benefit from. Plus - It's ok to try different things (careers, extracurricular activities etc.) but when you realize it's NOT a good fit, help everyone out and just move on

Kim has learned that not aligning her business actions with her personal values resulted in useless expended energy, in authenticity and lack of business building. Once she started living her values in EVERY business action, she found sales and marketing much easier and attracted more clients.

Feeling alone as an entrepreneur is one of the most common experiences when starting out in business - even for folks in networking marketing. Surrounding yourself with other entrepreneurs, friends and family helps fill the gap. Hiring a coach provides the outside perspective and support needed to help you accelerate the good times and move through the challenges with much more easy, joy and peace.

Kim L. Miles

Recipe for SUCCESS!

1. Align your personal values with that of your company/business

2. Live every action in your business in alignment with your values

3. Focus your development in better serving your clients NOT better serving your business

4. Hire a coach

5. Know your ideal client - "anyone" or "everyone" is NOT an ideal client

6. When you increase your price, increase the value added two fold

7. Focus on your calling not the outcome

About Kim L. Miles

Kim L. Miles loves coaching clients who are highly motivated and willing to utilize internal and external resources to achieve maximum success and fulfillment. She connects with people on all levels and utilizes her coach training, God given talents, and professional and personal experience to enhance her work with clients.

Kim's life purpose is to connect with people and establish meaningful relationships that support, encourage and allow for personal development and growth.

Kim is a professional with over 15 years of experience in various industries including engineering, telecommunications, aerospace and direct sales. She has experience in Project Development, Integration of Strategic Plans, Business Development, Sales, Training and Personnel Development in roles such as Project Manager, Corporate Account Manager, Technical Recruiter, Project Engineer, and Program Controls Analyst.

Note from Kim: Throughout my life I was good at math and science. When it came time to select a college, I was encouraged to go to an engineering college. I graduated from Colorado School of Mines in 1993 with a BS in Electrical Engineering and knew that it wasn't the field for me. After years of searching for the right fit in various technical and business roles, I found my true calling – Coaching.

Kim L. Miles
Kim L. Miles, LLC
3931 S Jebel Way
Aurora, CO 80013

Email: kim@kimlmiles.com
Phone: 303-690-7661
Website: http://www.kimlmiles.com
Facebook:http://www.facebook.com/media/set/?set=a.2256864113100.118499.1593278215& saved#!/CoachKimMiles
LinkedIn: Kim Miles (ACC)
Twitter: Kim_Miles

Kimberley Borgens

"The problem is never how to get new thoughts into your mind, but
how to get old ones out."
Dee Hock

Commitment & Accountability Creates Your Success

Kimberley got married right out of high school and had a son right away and within two years was a single mom on welfare. What changed? Kimberley said she had to take a hard look at what she had created in her life and where she was going. She asked herself, "Who am I holding responsible for my life?" Kimberley decided to go to community college and progressed on a double major in Administration of Justice and Business Management. She surrounded herself with people she wanted to be like.

Kimberley remarried and she and her husband became entrepreneurs. They started a private security business. They had both came from similar back grounds of training and decided to take what they knew and put it to action. With two kids and working from home they found it was not an easy to do. They organized their calendars to make sure they did not forget anything important.

Kimberley shared about those first years in business. "He would work a grave yard shift, come home and work for a few hours trying to get more clients while I was taking care of the kids, doing the business books and working a part time job in retail." "These first few years were a rollercoaster for relationship!"

Kimberley already knew what it was like to be a single mom on welfare and knew she had to stay focused and keep herself dedicated to her business. "We could never think that the business would not be successful because there was no other option in our minds!" Kimberley shared how one of their sons came down with a rare disease and had to have in home care. She worked her business schedule around his health needs. Kimberley says "Keeping my priorities straight and my values in alignment was important for our personal wellbeing and our business success!" Recipient of several awards she has shown that values and reputation matter in business.

Over the years Kimberley has found herself sharing information and helping women create businesses as a way to support their families, build confidence and self-esteem and not be a victim to the circumstances and situation

There are "how to's" everywhere in business. The biggest challenge is taking action on what you know is right for business. Business is a choice. You can decide at any time to quit, to improve, or be indecisive and let your business fade away. If you blame others for your success, you aren't taking responsibility for your choices.

Kimberley Borgens

Recipe for SUCCESS!

1. Care about your reputation – Do what you say you will do!

2. Know your personal capacity – delegate what you don't do best!

3. Keep a notebook of ideas – When ideas come to you write them down in a special notebook

4. Create a team – Even if you are a one woman operation working in your own business create a team of advisors, mastermind or fellow business people to brain storm and be a mentor with

5. Make the hard decisions – it is more important to be respected than liked! Remember this is business and take your emotions out of the decision

6. Get yourself out there – Whether you are networking in person, on social media or the internet get out there and be noticed. Know what is unique about your business and communicate exactly how your products and services will benefit those who work with you

7. Be willing to change your recipe. You may need to add a little more marketing, customer care and community effort to your recipe based on what is happening in the world around you. Business is ever changing and if you are not willing to adjust the recipe a bit your batter won't work!

About Kimberley Borgens

Kimberley Borgens is an award-winning entrepreneur, WABC - Certified Business Coach, Coach Trainer, Speaker and Author. She is known as the "Queen of Accountability." She works with business owners to challenge them to excellence. Focusing on working with leaders to reach their goals and build on their personal and professional development.

With 20 years, experience as an entrepreneur and ownership in five companies she has the skill from trial and error for you to be successful quicker. Kimberley has the ability to coach, consult and train in a wide entrepreneurial arena. Yet her favorite is in accountability. Her consulting helps to set small businesses up with compliance and vision systems to sustain long term business. Her coaching creates tangible results through accountability and compassion. Her training helps people to gain skill, improve communication and save money.

She has earned business awards from the Chamber of Commerce – Small Business of the Year and the Small Business Administration (SBA) Small Business of the Year Northern California Region.

Kimberley and her husband live in California with their four children and enjoy helping others begin business and be successful too. For more information visit www.bealegacy.com and learn more about the "Queen of Accountability" on Facebook.

Kimberley Borgens, CBC
Be A Legacy – Queen of Accountability
PO Box 8633
Stockton, CA 95208

Email: dreamteam@bealegacy.com
Phone: 209-993-7632
Website: http://www.bealegacy.com
Facebook: http://www.facebook.com/QueenofAccountability
LinkedIn: http://linkedin.com/in/kimberleyborgens
Twitter: http://twitter.com/BeALegacy

Careers from the Kitchen Table Home Business Directory Second Edition

Kristen L. Baker

"A person is what he or she thinks about all day long"
Ralph Waldo Emerson

The Fight to Her Dream

Kristen is a multifaceted person, she owns a catering business, and she is a Life Coach and an author. She started her journey as a Pre-Law major, with a dream of wanting to be a lawyer to help children. Her self-esteem was low due to people telling her she could never make it as a lawyer.

She went to help her mom out in the family catering business and made many changes to improve business and that was 22 years ago. She saw that not only was she able to make successful changes to the business, she was able to help others in the process. She became the owner of the business in 1998 and is still going strong. What makes her so successful is her easy going personality and her true willingness to make every event the best. Customers come back over and over and she never has to advertise, she has a reputation of top quality foods, service and she gets to know her customers.

Kristen became a Life Coach as well in 2005 after finding her purpose and passion to help others and change lives, one at a time. It was a struggle for some time, not knowing how to market her coaching, not trusting in her abilities at first. That all changed once she realized the gift she had and donated her time for one year to coach people and saw the amazing results. She gave to grow and now is a successful coach and loving it.

Kristen is a successful entrepreneur because she has passion, desire and focus on the end results.

Her challenges in business have been getting clients and marketing herself. She's joined many groups and wrote for sites to become visible and credible, and found this was the solution!

Kristen's ideal client is someone who truly wants to improve their life, is not afraid to think outside of the box and is prepared to commit to themselves the process in which to get to where they want to be.

Kristen L. Baker

Recipe for SUCCESS!

1. Define your goals, goals in which are attainable and realistic

2. Visualize your success

3. Take action

4. Listen to your gut

5. Be excited and positive

6. Proper Planning

7. Keep your eye on the ball

About Kristen L. Baker

In 2002, Kristen was going through a very stressful time in selling her home and moving into her dream home that she had set as her goal. Things did not go well and she began to have panic attacks and to fear just about everything - much to her surprise, because she was always so confident and successful. She was anxious all the time, avoided nearly everything that she loved out of fear. Nearing a year of laying in the fetal position and begging for signs to help her, she took matters in her own hands. She began creating tools to help herself and she decided to write her first book, "It's Okay To Have Anxiety..Really!" to share her story. During this very down time for her, she found her true person and is now living her dream changing other's lives through coaching. She is grateful for the bad as it brought her to the dream.

Kristen L. Baker
Life Coaching World Wide
2 Waterview Circle
Litchfield, NH 03052

Email: lifecoachbaker@aol.com
Phone: 603-204-9728
Website: http://www.lifecoachingworldwide.com
Facebook: http://www.facebook.com/pages/Life-Coaching-World-Wide-Where-Your-Dreams-Become-A-Reality/169934022691

Kristi Pavlik

"Do or do not, there is no try"
Yoda from Star Wars

The Best of Both Worlds

With the birth of our second child, I became a stay-at-home mom. I wanted something that would keep my mind busy, as well as add to the family finances. I dabbled in medical transcription - hated it! About the same time, the company I left asked if I would work as a consultant, from home, to help them through a major project. They paid me more per hour, and I was able to do this all from home.

Shortly after that, I was researching stay-at-home jobs and came across the term Virtual Assistant. I was doing everything these people were doing and a huge light bulb went off. I had found something I could sink my teeth into, and boy did I. In fact, my first client was the contractor who built my office and the kids play room.

This July we celebrated our 10-year anniversary. Adonai has changed drastically over those years. From working exclusively in the Real Estate industry to having no real estate clients and focusing on entrepreneurs and those in the coaching industry "I" has changed into a "we" as I have a group of specialist that are part of Team Adonai. And from being a "jack of all trades" to being known as "The Systems Chick", where we now offer our clients the best of both worlds - system design, business management, and ongoing virtual support.

It wasn't easy getting to this point though. I have gone through the "this is awesome," to "do I really want to do this," to "this should not be this hard," to "I cannot imagine my life getting any better."

Looking back, I would not have changed a thing. All that I, as well as Adonai, have gone through has brought us to the point we are at today - I am able to be the mom my kids need, and run a successful business - and that is a great thing.

Kristi says finding great team members is a challenge that was fixed by getting clear as to who our ideal team members are and what the position descriptions are.

Too many balls in the air: we set up systems & processes for how the routine things were to be handled. We now delegate, and focus on growing the business.

Kristi Pavlik

Recipe for SUCCESS!

1. Have a vision

2. Be determined to see it through

3. Do what you love, love what you do

4. Have a plan

5. Set up systems & processes

6. Delegate

7. Have fun

About Kristi Pavlik

From chaos to clarity, from task "overwhelm" to task mastery—this is what happens when Kristi Pavlik takes business professionals under her wing. For more than a decade, Kristi has been helping entrepreneurs and small business owners transform big ideas into effective systems that support profit and growth.

Active in the administrative management field for over 18 years, Kristi is a skilled professional who helps business leaders "get out of their own way". She helps them learn how to apply "systems thinking" and practical processes to their daily routines, resulting in improved efficiency, increased productivity and more time for what's really important. Clients who work with Kristi are amazed at how she uses simplified processes in order to calm chaos. They are thrilled at the reduced stress and increased time available for growing their businesses. When Kristi isn't working directly with clients, she's teaching virtual assistants and online business managers how to apply the art of systemization to their own practices.

In addition to a bachelor's degree in Business Management and Organizational Development,

Kristi is a certified Product Launch Specialist, proud graduate of AssistU and founding member of the Michigan Virtual Assistants association.

Kristi Pavlik
Adonai Business Solutions, LLC
332 Stoll
Lansing, MI 48917

Email: kristi@adonai-llc.com
Phone: 517-507-5939
Website: http://www.adonai-llc.com
Facebook: https://www.facebook.com/#!/TeamAdonai
LinkedIn: http://www.linkedin.com/in/kristipavlik
Twitter: http://twitter.com/KristiPavlik

LaTricia Smith

"You have brains in your head. You have feet in your shoes. You can steer yourself in any direction you choose."
Dr. Seuss

Follow Your Heart

LaTricia knew early in life that she was born to help people. Helping others has always been her passion. Because she is non-judgmental, people find it easy to talk to her and tell her things they may be afraid or ashamed to tell others. In 2007, LaTricia stumbled upon coaching and instantly knew that this was her calling. Because she had such a great passion for love and marriage, she decided to specialize in love and relationships. LaTricia began her coaching practice in 2007 part-time. It just seemed like a natural fit for her.

In July 2009, she decided to follow her heart. LaTricia resigned from her job to pursue a full-time coaching career. That was one of the best decisions she ever made. It was not an easy decision and it definitely came with a price. Although LaTricia had been coaching on a part-time basis for two years, the income was nowhere near what she was making at her job and the clients were not pouring in. She knew that she had not made a mistake because her heart doesn't lie. The truth truly dwells in the heart and she had followed her heart. LaTricia spent countless hours reading books, attending webinars, teleseminars and going to classes learning whatever she could about getting clients and having a full practice. Not only did she spent countless hours, she also spent a ton of money on business coaching, marketing coaching and programs to teach her how to keep her business from sinking.

Over the last four years, LaTricia has been no stranger to challenges, but none of the challenges, or rewards for that matter, would have come had she not followed her heart. Her heart told her that she could help people through their relationship challenges. No one said it would be easy, but the rewards totally outweigh the challenges. The look in the eyes of a couple who went from hopeless to happy or a single woman who finally found the man of her dream makes it all worth it.

The biggest challenge LaTricia had was learning to market her business effectively. Like many people she thought that opening the doors would equate to people running through them. When that didn't happen, LaTricia began to learn all she could about marketing. She took classes, hired a marketing coach and a marketing consultant to help with marketing efforts. As a result, her perspective on marketing changed and so did her business.

The other big challenge LaTricia had was staying focused and free from distractions. It is very easy to get distracted when you are working from home. There is housework to do, children to tend to and calls to answer. To keep from being distracted, LaTricia established office hours, a "to do" list and a schedule.

LaTricia says her ideal client is the nearly-wed couple who wants to have a truly healthy, happy, lifelong marriage.

La Tricia Smith

Recipe for SUCCESS!

1. Start each day with a positive attitude

2. Have a daily plan

3. Get a mentor, an accountability partner and a strong support group

4. Run from Perfectionism

5. Build a team

6. Give it your all

7. Constantly seek improvement

LaTricia Smith is a Relationship Coach, Ordained Minister and Certified Wedding Officiant. She has been married for 22 years and knows firsthand what it takes to create a successful relationship, having experienced the peaks and valleys of married life while still maintaining a loving relationship.

As a Relationship Coach, LaTricia helps singles develop the skills required to find a compatible mate, and helps couples resolve relationship issues and conflicts so they can remain together, create a stronger bond and live happily ever after.

As an Ordained Minister and Certified Wedding Officiant, LaTricia supports couples through one of the most memorable and meaningful experiences of their lives. She has a real affinity towards love and marriage and wants to help couples create ceremonies that espouse their love for each other and their feelings, beliefs, and ideas about marriage.

In her free time, LaTricia enjoys hanging out with her family, reading, writing and learning how to keep her plants alive.

LaTricia Smith
A Stronger Bond
PO Box 48522
Cumberland, NC 28331

910-816-9270
toll free: 888-568-9619

www.astrongerbond.com
info@astrongerbond.com
www.facebook.com/astrongerbond
www.linkedin.com/in/latriciasmith
www.twitter.com/LaTriciaSmith

Careers from the Kitchen Table Home Business Directory Second Edition

Leslie Cunningham

"Whatever you can do or dream you can... Boldness has genius, power and magic in it. Begin now"
Goethe

From Pinching Pennies to Six-Figure Success

At first Leslie didn't realize that the journey to create a successful business would involve time, commitment and dedication (in spite of her dreams of becoming an overnight success). Many times during the first couple of years she found herself doubting whether she could succeed. But she knew in her heart of hearts that she wanted to create a successful thriving business and personal financial life and that she had a burning desire and passion to teach other women entrepreneurs how to do the same.

This occurred in two areas of her business. One area was an inner shift from being a money manager to being a money creator.

The other area was getting on the same financial page with her husband. They had contrasting approaches to how they handled money in their marriage and to top it off they had acquired over $43,300 in credit card debt over a three year period.

She asked her husband if he would be willing to set up a time each week to talk about finances and develop a plan for getting rid of the credit card debt. They came to refer to their weekly meetings as their Financial Dates®. Surprisingly, instead of finances being a source of divisive tension that pulled them apart, it became the glue that held them together as they became a unified team.

With their debt gone Leslie is now on track to achieve 6-figures this year in her business. She gained several invaluable lessons from their debt struggles and her challenges with becoming a powerful money creator that will stay with her forever.

Leslie says her rules to live by are:

1. Be committed to transforming your situation.

2. Opportunities will present themselves to you during your journey as a result of your commitment. Many people won't begin a journey or declare a goal because they can't see the means to achieving it – so they give up. More often than not you won't see the means of accomplishing a goal until you make a commitment and bravely begin your "hero's journey."

3. Take full responsibility. Instead of blaming the economy or factors outside of yourself be willing to accept full responsibility for transforming your financial life; eliminating debt and investing money to learn how to increase your income, make a difference for your clients and achieve your financial goals

Leslie says her challenge was how to be a great mother while creating a successful coaching business. Her business took a dramatic leap forward after their son was born because she had established in herself a HUGE level of intention to being an amazing mother and a business owner who was committed to making a world famous difference for my clients.

Leslie Cunningham

Recipe for SUCCESS!

1. Create a clear work schedule. And if you have young children spend the money to pay for childcare. Otherwise you'll never be able to fully give your work OR your children the attention and time they deserve

2. Create both a monthly, weekly and daily to do list

3. In your weekly and daily to do list, identify your business tasks that must happen consistently (like writing your newsletter, or activities that grow your recipients list) and make sure those tasks are always given the highest priority and you always do those first before any other activity

4. Always integrate your fun and personal goals in your to do lists. Otherwise you will get off-balance and begin to resent how hard you work and how little personal time you have

5. Make sure you focus on these three business priorities every week: 1) enrolling clients in your programs 2) growing your list 3) serving your current clients to your fullest

6. Managing your business and personal cash flow, income and expenses is as ESSENTIAL as is getting on the same page with your spouse around money – you must get a handle on this because it will make or break your business and even make or break your marriage

7. Make a deep commitment to learning from mentors and doing whatever you can do to succeed in your business. Success doesn't always come over night -- but if you remain committed and continuously take the next step forward and invest money in learning from mentors who have succeeded, you will eventually succeed as well

About Leslie Cunningham

Leslie Cunningham is a certified money and business coach, internationally published author and leading expert in the field of personal financial growth, money and prosperity.

Leslie Cunningham
Live and Love Richly, LLC
7781 Nez Pierce Drive
Bozeman, MT 59715
Email: leslie@financialdating.com
Phone: 406-586-5561
Website: www.financialdating.com

Linda Adams

"Are you going to change your life or just sit there and change the channel?!"
My husband, Ronald Adams

The Clean Credit Queen Comes Clean

With a name like the Clean Credit Queen you would automatically assume that Linda has always had the best credit possible, well you would be wrong. She started learning about credit to obtain loans for her real estate business. She was so successful that within less than a year she was a credit millionaire.

Unfortunately, the collapse of the real estate market left her deeply in debt. After trying for nearly two years to climb out of that debt she was forced to declare bankruptcy. At that point instead of giving up, she used what she had learned about credit to start over. Only nine months after declaring bankruptcy Linda was able to bring her score up over 150 point. She did not find a magic bullet, she just applied the practical common sense tips and techniques she had gathered over the years to clean up her own credit report and start to rebuild her credit.

Linda says that declaring bankruptcy was the most difficult decision she ever had to make but it turned out to be a blessing in disguise. After years of trying to help others improve their credit, she was able to show that the techniques she had been sharing really worked. Linda now tells her story so that others can realize there is hope and good credit even after bankruptcy.

Linda's first challenge was moving from the stability of a steady job to working on her own business. Fortunately her leap of faith was justified and she and her husband were very successful.

Keeping up with paperwork and taxes was also a challenge for Linda. She finally realized it was essential to have a good business accountant on her team.

Linda's ongoing challenge is trying to help people realize that learning how to fix their own credit and maintain a good credit score is more important today than ever. It's just like the old story, she is trying to teach people how to help themselves, not do it for them.

Linda Adams

Recipe for SUCCESS!

1. Build a team

2. Keep up with your record keeping

3. Learn to ask for help when you need it

4. Focus your advertising on your target market

5. Read motivational books

6. Keep educational tapes in your car CD player

7. Stay positive

About Linda Adams

Linda Adams has been an educator for more than 20 years. She and her husband Ronald started LDRA Performance Consultants Inc. a home based business back in 2000. They have worked with a variety of clients from ATT to the Air Force, and from Maryland high schools to the Maryland State Department of Education. Linda and her husband analyze performance needs and design and implement training programs and other programs for audiences of all ages. Their specialty is helping people solve performance problems. Linda often found herself engaged in discussions with other real estate investors who were having credit related problems. She discovered that there was a need for credit education among not only the other real estate investors, who needed to maintain good credit in order to borrow money, but also among the general public who were having trouble qualifying for loans to buy houses. Linda and Ronald created the brand The Clean Credit Queen and developed seminars, a newsletter, and website, as well as a radio program to help people improve their credit performance

Linda Adams
LDRA Performance Consultants, Inc.
PO Box 12119
Baltimore, MD 21281

Email: linda@letschataboutcredit.com
Phone: 888-592-4512
Website: www.letschataboutcredit.com
Twitter: credittweet

Linda Howell Edwards

"You cannot fix that which you cannot face"
James Baldwin, American Author and Poet

My Journey, My Vision, My Terms!

14 years with the same company is a long time. When your skills are underutilized, the time seems even longer. Fearful of becoming a cog in the wheel, Linda set out on her journey to fulfill her passion of connecting with people. Ignoring naysayers, some of them close friends; she left her position as a diversity leader and struck out on her own. The first year was smoother than the second year. Her business contacts that she had amassed proved helpful, that is until she decided to move to North Carolina. She did not know anyone and found fitting into the new market was difficult. She described Charlotte, NC as a nice community but she found it somewhat closed. A popular comment from the locals, "Where are you from, oh you're not want of us," to be a barrier. Luckily, she had clients and potential clients all over the United States. Many of her clients came to her through word of mouth. While this kept the money coming in, she felt her impact in making a difference was somewhat limited; she found that she was doing more facilitation than consulting and developing leaders. Her passion is people and understanding the differences as complimentary rather than competitively. She soon realized that the market was becoming overrun with diversity consultants and the messaging of embracing differences became a catch-phrase for some companies. Linda made a decision to focus her energies on curriculum development, coaching for performance on a professional and/or personal basis. One of the largest setbacks that she faced was as a subcontractor for a large consulting firm. The firm went out of business owing Linda, and other consultants, thousands of dollars. She learned to trust her instincts as she had confided to several of her peers that she felt it was just a matter of time before the company would bankrupt. She allowed others to talk her into staying and ultimately she paid the price. She is taking more control of what companies she partners with ensuring that they match her values and beliefs about people and their contributions, on her terms.

Cash Flow. Business has slowed. During this downturn I changed my spending habits (expenditures) to reflect the changes in my income. To overcome anxiety, I focus on the positive

My ideal client is one that is interested in achieving optimum results based on organization needs. Clients that truly believe in people and the success of their people. Conversely, individual clients who really want to succeed and operate within their purpose.

Linda Howell Edwards

Recipe for SUCCESS!

1. Client Focused

2. Active Listening - pay attention to what is being said

3. Know your products and services and how they fit into the market

4. Be both tactical and strategic

5. Develop a Business Plan

6. Have a strong network of allies

7. Do what you have to do in order to do what you want to do!

About Linda Howell Edwards, MS

Linda Howell Edwards - as President and Chief Consultant of Edwards & Associates, she has more than 25 years' experience in both the public and private sectors. Linda has provided consulting and training services to the utility industry, manufacturing, city governments, educational institutions, not-for-profit agencies, and the hotel industry.

Experienced in the design and implementation of systems wide change initiatives, strategic planning, culture change, diversity and inclusion management, organizational analysis and assessment, human resource management, executive and life coaching, leadership development and facilitation.

Linda is co-author of the self-published book, In Black and White: Ten Reasons Organizations Fail At Race Relations. In this compelling look at race in the workplace, the authors address real-life, real-time, racial diversity concerns that organizations grapple with. Even more, the authors offer concrete strategies and insights for addressing issues before and after problems arise. Linda just completed her second book addressing issues confronting women in the workplace.

She has a Masters in Organization Leadership and Change from Pfeiffer University, Charlotte, NC; and BA from the University of Illinois, Springfield in Business Management.

Linda Howell Edwards
Edwards & Associates
PO Box 724051
Atlanta, GA 31139

Email: LEdwards@theedwardsgroup.org
Phone: 678-239-4479
Website: www.theedwardsgroup.org

Careers from the Kitchen Table Home Business Directory Second Edition

Lisabeth Saunders Medlock

"Once you label me, you negate me"
Kierkegaard

Changing people and organizations in the midst of personal change

Lisabeth has reinvented herself professionally over the past 18 years. She received a doctorate in Clinical/Community Psychology, focusing on child and family therapy and prevention programming for youth. For the past thirteen years, Lisabeth has worked with nonprofit and community based organizations in implementing outcome measurement and developing and implementing strategic and operational plans. She also worked with organizations to improve services through conducting needs and assets assessments and developing standards. Her transition into Life Coaching represents a blend of her training and work as a therapist with her focus helping organizations set and achieve goals. A Certified Life Coach through the ICF she provides individual and group coaching and delivers workshops. In July of 2010 Lisabeth became visually impaired and continued her work as a coach and consultant, as well as advocate for others with disabilities. She also does motivational speaking where she tells her story and what she learned by going through a traumatic, life changing event and how others can overcome any obstacles in their lives.

The first and somewhat ongoing challenge in business is establishing one's self as an expert and establishing credibility. Lisabeth has done this through consistently providing quality services and making good on any promises she makes. She also maintains her credibility through saying no to people and projects that have been beyond the scope of her expertise or that she could not complete in a desired timeline.

The second challenge Lisabeth has had to face is a recent one that has occurred as a result of an accident that left her visually impaired. Her challenge was to continue to provide services and run my business without sight. Lisabeth worked with the Commission for the Blind to get the low vision tools and technology she needed so that she could function on the computer and she hired an assistant to drive and co-facilitate meetings. Lisabeth also transitioned her clients from meeting at my office to meeting over the phone. Today it is business as usual.

Dr. Lisabeth Saunders Medlock

Recipe for SUCCESS!

1. Know your abilities and strengths, as well as your weaknesses and limits

2. Be willing to take risks. Playing it safe will not grow your business

3. Think out of the box as much as you can and take a creative approach. You will need good problem solving skills as well as the ability to make lemons into lemonade

4. Be honest and authentic about what you can provide or deliver. Do not overpromise

5. Don't be afraid to ask for help when you need it. This includes taking financial help like a small business loan

6. Market yourself with confidence and out yourself out there. Always remember that you are your business

7. Have faith and hope that you will be successful and maintain a positive attitude

About Lisabeth Saunders Medlock

In my professional life I have reinvented myself over the past 18 years. I received a doctorate in Clinical/Community Psychology and focused on child and family therapy and prevention programming for youth. For the past thirteen years, I have worked with nonprofit and community based organizations in implementing outcome measurement and developing and implementing strategic and operational plans. I have also worked with organizations to improve services through conducting needs and assets assessments and developing standards. My transition into Life Coaching represents a blend of my training and work as a therapist with my focus helping organizations set and achieve goals. I am a Certified Life Coach through the ICF and I provide individual and group coaching and deliver workshops.

In July of 2010 I became visually impaired and continue my work as a coach and consultant, as well as advocate for others with disabilities. I also do motivational speaking where I tell my story and what I learned by going through a traumatic, life changing event and how others can overcome any obstacles in their lives

Dr. Lisabeth Saunders Medlock
Life By Design Coaching/Results Consulting
4420 Mimosa Rd
Columbia, SC 29205

Email: lbdcoaching@aol.com
Phone: 803-960-1844
Website: www.lifebydesigncoaching.org
Facebook: http://www.facebook.com/#!/pages/Life-By-Design-Coaching/181753829028
LinkedIn: http://www.linkedin.com/pub/lisbeth-saunders-medlock/8/bb7/7b6
Twitter: http://twitter.com/#!/lbdcoaching

Careers from the Kitchen Table Home Business Directory Second Edition

Lorraine Edey

"You must do the things you think you cannot do"
Eleanor Roosevelt

From Practice to Performance

Are you a self-employed business owner or are you and entrepreneur?

This is a question that Lorraine should have asked herself a long time ago. However as a woman who wanted to serve and make a difference in people's lives this question never occurred to her.

According to a blog written by The Great Office Escape, "Entrepreneurs have a vision and an idea." On the other hand a self-employed individual is someone who relies on himself/herself to create his/her own income. Their pay comes from their clients.

Lorraine's role models were her paternal grandparents and foster mother. These individuals were her inspiration as she later ventured out into her own entrepreneurial adventure at the tender age of 12. Lorraine formed her own cleaning and child care business that ran successfully until she was 16 years old. This was the magical age when she received working papers and Lorraine shifted for a young budding entrepreneur to an employee.

After a variety of work experiences, marriages and two children, Lorraine felt restlessness. There was something more that she wanted and the more was education. And so Lorraine decided to return to school at the age of 28.

What was she thinking? Lorraine was divorced; the sole supporter for her two children and working two jobs to make ends meet. This was not the perfect environment for Lorraine to go back to school, it was 19 years since she laid eyes on a classroom and this decision filled her with anxiety, fear and doubt.

Through trials and tribulations Lorraine received her bachelor's degree and went on to complete a master's degree in social work at the age of 35. Now she was remarried with the pressure of taking care of a home, a new husband, adolescent children and a new career.

The passage from motherhood and employment took a paradigm shift for Lorraine. She vacillated between being an employee to self-employment until Lorraine's career took off and she created a six figure "psychotherapy practice." This practice lasted 15 years and with burnout setting in she was looking for something new.

Lorraine went from practice to performance. Two coaching businesses later Lorraine knows that there is a significant difference between practicing and building a business model that will thrive and perform for itself.

And so this has been a journey of developing a new mindset. Lorraine learns daily about marketing, business strategies, leveraging her business, goal setting, and having a business plan.

These are all key ingredients in building your dream business and moving from practicing being a business owner to performing as a successful woman.

Lori shares the following two business challenges:

Marketing was my biggest challenge. I felt as though I was "begging" customers for something when I discussed my business. I was stuck and unable to move forward. I knew that what I had to offer was of value I didn't know how to get my message across, and so I hired a coach, her specialty... marketing. I learned that marketing was really about building relationships, providing a service, understanding that what I have to offer to customers was of value and if I did not provide my customers with the opportunity to see what my services were about I would be doing them a disservice.

Treating my business as though it was a hobby. I love the work that I do, providing couples who have been married more than once with a full proof plans to avoid yet another divorce. I had no idea that I was treating my business like a hobby. A hobby is just that, we play with our business and look at it as something to come back to when we have time. I was just interested in my business not committed to my business. When I was committed to growing my business I put a plan in place for growth and success. I commit daily to take actions that support my business growth.

Lorraine Edey

Recipe for SUCCESS!

1. Hire a coach or mentor-we all need support and direction

2. Be able to answer the question "What Do You Do". This question is a way of people asking for help. Can you meet their need?

3. Develop your business plan- "when you fail to plan, you plan to fail"

4. Be an expert in your area-get all the knowledge you need to be considered an expert

5. Hire an assistant-sometimes we waste precious time trying to do task that we either do not like or are not good at. Time is money-use it wisely

6. Have your own what I call "Professional Committee". These are individuals that can support you. For example, Accountant, Lawyer, Bookkeeper, Financial Planner, etc. This committee is important for your business as well as advisors when you need the support.

7. Be patient with the process and savor small accomplishments. "Rome was not built in a day" and neither will your business

About Lorraine Edey

Dr. Lorraine Edey, known for her Extreme Money Makeover™ program, brings her wealth of experience to "married again" couples to help them find success in their new relationship.

Second marriages bring a unique set of challenges, and Dr. Edey draws upon her wealth of knowledge, expertise and practical advice to create "recipes for extraordinary relationships," helping couples achieve marriage success using tools she has used since the 1980s to help individuals overcome alcoholism, trauma, relationship problems and more.

Dr. Edey earned her Bachelor of Psychology at the College of New Rochelle in New York, and her Master of Social Work from New York University. She later received her Doctor of Philosophy from Westbrook University in Aztec, New Mexico.

Her experience includes more than 20 years of couples and relationship coaching as a psychotherapist.

An acclaimed author and speaker, Dr. Edey presented programs for the New York City Committee on Women and Alcoholism, the American College of Nurse-Midwives, the New York City Board of Education, Girl Scouts Council of Greater New York, Inc., Federal Emergency Management, Emory School of Business and Bank of America, among others.

Her articles have appeared in numerous publications including The Connection Magazine, Orlando Life Magazine and Natural Awakenings Magazine, and the book which she co-authored, "Wake Up Women: Be Happy, Healthy and Wealthy," has reached #7 on the Barnes & Noble Bestseller list.

She also can be heard as a guest on Blogtalk radio, where she shares advice on managing money and relationships.

Lorraine Edey, PhD, LCSW, ACC
Second Time Around
PO Box 1779
Jasper, GA 30143

Email: loridey@aol.com
Phone: 678-454-1272
Website: www.secondtimearoundlove.com
Facebook: http://www.facebook.com/lorraine.edey
LinkedIn: http://www.linkedin.com/in/lorraineedey

Lynn Doxon

"Every great dream begins with a dreamer"
Harriet Tubman

Redesigning Retirement

After working in a business she or her husband owned for most of her working life, Lynn felt trapped as a middle manager in a small business.

Since middle school people had come to her for help in clarifying their vision for their lives. Looking for ways to capitalize on that, she chose lifestyle coaching.

Because she was helping her daughters decide on careers she considered being a career coach. Her interest in the environment and alternative energy led her to consider being a green living coach. Then she discovered retirement coaching.

The challenge of creating a fresh vision for retirement excited her. Here was a generation she could connect with. While still working she completed the Retirement Coach Certification Program with Retirement Options.

Shortly after when she left her job she realized that she needed to know more about doing business on the internet. Those over 55 are the fastest growing segment of Facebook users.

She got a crash course in social media networking from her daughter, and then attended a weekend seminar on creating an online business. Armed with her new knowledge she created a website, a Facebook page and a twitter account.

She developed a series of courses, "Help, I'm About to Retire!" "I'm Retired, Now What Do I Do?" and "What Do You Do in the Fourth Quarter When You Have Already Won the Game?" Each course is designed to guide clients in the creation of a vision and plan for a different stage of retirement.

She is currently working on additional resources for those who retired and would like to go back to work and for those who are interested in relocating.

Besides coaching retirees she publishes an online magazine The Sustainable Desert Garden.

She started her business with almost no money, which meant getting started quickly and cheaply.

My three teenage daughters and one teenage grandson are in and out of the house all the time. Four teenagers and friends can be very distracting

Lynn Doxon   *Recipe for* SUCCESS!

1. Know yourself, what you are good at and what you enjoy then make that into a business

2. Evaluate any opportunity that comes along in terms of what it will do for your business

3. Focus on the task at hand

4. Take some action every day

5. Get organized —have a plan for keeping track of all the computer files and paper

6. If one day does not go well, start anew the next

7. Always let your customers know how much you appreciate them

About Lynn Doxon

Lynn has spent most of her life in the desert southwest, except for a brief but important time in Kansas where she owned her first business, got a Master's degree, a PhD and a Husband. Although her education was in horticulture she has owned a company that produced fuel alcohols stills, been Urban Horticulture Specialist for the New Mexico Cooperative Education Service, worked with her husband in his liturgical design firm, written three books, homeschooled her daughters, managed a native plant nursery and been Executive Director of a small private school. Her three published books are The Fuel Alcohol Handbook, High Desert Yards and Gardens and Rainbows from Heaven. Her husband had two sons when they married and they adopted three daughters from Ukraine. They also have three grandsons. Her retirement plans include building small, energy independent house, establishing a model urban farm and traveling, mostly in the southern hemisphere since she will be gardening in the northern hemisphere summer.

Lynn Doxon
Life Arena Coaching
4005 Tara NE
Albuquerque, NM 87111

Email: lynn@lifeareanacoaching.com
Phone: 505-459-3597
Website: www.lifearenacoach.com
Facebook: http://www.facebook.com/home.php#!/pages/Life-Arena-Retirement-Coaching/231602116866331
LinkedIn: https://www.linkedin.com/e/fpf/37456703
Twitter: @lynndoxon

Careers from the Kitchen Table Home Business Directory Second Edition

Lynn Hidy

"Opportunity is missed by most people because it is dressed in overalls and looks like work"
Thomas Edison

Your Own Success Definition

Lynn Hidy never imagined that career success would make her so unhappy! She had worked her way up from in inbound focused telesales rep, through territory sales, and into sales leadership. Now that she had achieved what everyone had told her was the goal – she didn't want it. In fact, she disliked the person she was playing the role.

The bright spot was her boss didn't have a cookie cutter approach to his leadership team. They discussed what Lynn was passionate about, it emerged that her training and coaching was what made the salespeople on her team successful. Together they developed a role where she would be a full time sales trainer and coach. The new role completely changed how Lynn felt about coming to work every day AND the people who worked with her increased their sales by 19% after working together.

Then the corporate winds of change blew in a different direction and that position disappeared. It was choice time; to play the corporate game or figure out a way to keep the dream alive.

UpYourTeleSales.com was born at the first annual Sales Shebang Sales Experts Summit. Jill Konrath, the creator of the event, along with Brooke Green, the Ultimate Sales Chick, was having drinks with Lynn one evening after the event. They started her thinking about what jumping out of the corporate world could look like. Jill expressed.... laser focus on your target market, you can expand later if you want, but at the start, laser focus on your target market. Then they talked about Lynn's experience and expertise. Brooke made an offhand comment.... that she thought Lynn was funny and liked her delivery. She may not have been the first person to say it, but she was the first one to remind Lynn that it was part of who she was as a presenter and to capitalize on it

Where do passion & excellence meet? - Lynn was good at a job she hated. She had been taught success is doing what you're good at; they forgot to mention making sure you WANTED to do it.

Researching what market to focus on – learning to focus on a very specific target market felt like excluding potential business to Lynn but she learned to overcome that and see the benefits of working within one's target market.

Lynn Hidy

Recipe for SUCCESS!

1. Just because a concept is simple, doesn't make it easy to implement

2. People buy from people – be yourself on the phone, not some imaginary recording of what you think a salesperson sounds like

3. Speak in the language of your target market – key words and phrases that your prospects use will make it easier for them to identify with you and your message

4. Practice makes permanent! Be sure you're practicing what you want to be – permanently

5. Have a purpose on every call, one that is all about the results that your prospects and customers will receive from working with you

6. Measure call success based on movement in the sales process – yes or no – both are good results! (of course we all prefer yes)

7. Inspiration combined with Perspiration = Magic, you'll be amazed at your own results.

About Lynn Hidy

Lynn Hidy founder and principal coach at UpYourTeleSales.com is the specialist at creating profitable telesales sales people and organizations. Lynn knows you can make six figures over the phone - she does!

Working together you will learn to create a phone experience where they will forget you aren't actually having a cup of coffee together.

Most of her clients will tell you that the work they do together is not rocket science, but all of it takes effort.

Lynn Hidy
UpYourTeleSales
PO Box 42
Paul Smiths, NY 12970

Email: lynn@upyourtelesales.com
Phone: 315-751-0146
Website: http://www.upyourtelesales.com
Facebook: https://www.facebook.com/pages/UpYourTeleSalescom/94567576544
LinkedIn: https://www.linkedin.com/in/lynnhidy
Twitter: http://twitter.com/#!/upyourtelesales

Careers from the Kitchen Table Home Business Directory Second Edition

Martha Lask

"Out beyond ideas of wrong doing and right doing there is a field. I'll meet you there."
Rumi, 13th century Persian, Sufi poet and theologian

"Being True to Yourself is Good Business"

The *shape* of her business is Martha's story. Martha chose to leave the hectic pace of international consulting, after 20 years of business travel. She had consulted in many kinds of organizations in many industries. She wanted to refocus her work and get off the road.

Two things she missed while traveling: dance and art. For her, dance and art bring beauty into the world and showcase innovative ideas. She wanted to integrate them into her consulting work.

But how? How to refocus her work? How not to travel? She needed time to think. She invested some of her savings to buy herself some time.

Taking time was invaluable. She reflected on the values that brought her to organization consulting. She cares profoundly about:

- Helping people at all levels of organizations to develop and speak their voices.
- Activating compassion between people in and out of the workplace.
- Promoting human dignity and respect.
- Developing partnerships across a variety of boundaries.
- Encouraging self-reflection and self-awareness.
- Creating meaningful connections by *really* listening to one another.

Based on these values, she developed a program for leaders in the nonprofit sector called *Executive Leadership Exchange (ELE)*. After a year or two she piloted this program and it took off! She has now developed variations of ELE for other organizations. All in her home location.

At the same time, she began to introduce art and dance activities to clients, conference attendees and colleagues and to use dance and art activities with coaching clients. For instance, she has invited certain coaching clients into the studio to explore emerging themes in a full bodied way.

The integration of dance and art and consulting is now occurring, to her great satisfaction. It offers many gifts:

- She is a stronger consultant, using the wisdom of her body as well as her mind.
- She is bringing her values more clearly and consistently to *all* of her work.
- She is developing exciting connections between different fields of study (consulting, coaching, dance and art).
- She is bringing her "best self" to her clients.

Two challenges in Martha's consulting business occurred 5 years apart. The first, when she felt disheartened about the approach she had been using to help organizations. Asking people: "What doesn't work here? How would you improve it?" left them feeling discouraged and depressed. She decided to leave consulting and applied for jobs as an executive director of a few nonprofit organizations. At the same time, she began to research other consulting approaches. After a couple of job interviews and many hours of research, she discovered a consulting approach called *Appreciative Inquiry* which asked people to focus on what worked in their organization rather than what was wrong! This made all the difference. The first time she tried using this approach, people were excited and energized. Martha transformed her consulting business, using this positive approach.

The second challenge occurred 5 years later. Martha developed a leadership development model, called *Executive Leadership Exchange*, for leaders of nonprofit organizations which included gathering leaders together to coach one another, a vehicle the private sector had been using very successfully for a long time. She spent many months meeting with various funding sources to determine who might fund such an effort, to no avail. People were interested but not willing to fund it. She let the idea rest for a while. Nine months later, over dinner, after making a conference presentation, an opportunity emerged. Someone was interested! It took a year and a half after that dinner to get the project going. Six years later *Executive Leadership Exchange* is going strong!

Martha Lask

Recipe for SUCCESS!

1. Keep learning

2. Persevere – stay with it!

3. Get up and move around – let the air blow through your head

4. Ask for help from people with different strengths than yours

5. Take a risk

6. Sort your priorities weekly and make sure that how you spend your time is in line with your priorities

7. Make a choice every day to do what you are doing

About Martha Lask

Martha Lask has over 30 years' experience in the private and non-profit sectors. She has provided consulting and executive coaching services and taught coaching skills in 28 organizations in both sectors.

Prior to starting her consulting practice, Martha was Senior Staff Development Specialist at Towers Perrin, global management consulting firm. She selected and implemented a new coaching and mentoring program that changed the company's approach to management.

Before Towers Perrin, Martha served as Executive Director of South Portland Neighborhood Housing Services, Inc. (SPNHS), South Portland Maine, where she created a private/public partnership and administered a revolving loan program which reversed housing decline in two neighborhoods.

Martha holds an MS in Organization Development (MSOD) from American University. She earned certification in the LeaderCOACH methodology of Perrone-Ambrose Associates, leaders in coaching and mentoring since 1985.

Martha also has over 30 years of experience and training in dance, and body work, and a certificate in Authentic Movement / Contemplative Dance.

Martha developed an innovative approach to enhance consulting and coaching skills, using Authentic Movement. She facilitated a seven-part series called "Presence and Attention at Work" for several groups and delivered workshops at La Salle University, and at three professional conferences.

Martha Lask
Martha Lask Consulting
120 West Mt. Airy Avenue
Philadelphia, PA 19119

Email: Martha@marthalask.com
Phone: 215-247-1740
Website: www.marthalask.com
Blog: http://www.marthalask-blog.com

Melanie McGhee

"Do you ever get the feeling that there's something going on we don't know about?"
Kevin Bacon in "The Diner"

Melanie McGhee, ~ a

Melanie received her master's degree in social work in 1984. After the birth of her first daughter in 1986, her boss told her she could come back to work full time or not at all. With a strong desire to work part time and take care of her young family, Melanie realized, "Well, I guess it's going to be not at all."

Embarking on a journey into private practice as a psychotherapist, Melanie picked up odd jobs to make ends meet while she learned the ins and outs of being a solo-preneur. That word did not even exist back then!

With the support of mentors and friends, Melanie discovered how to make it work --- with persistence and a commitment to providing stellar care, Melanie is among the few who have successfully maintained a private practice for close to thirty years.

Early in her career, Melanie discovered that she had a knack for facilitating learning and personal transformation experiences. Since the mid-1980's she has been designing and facilitating personal and spiritual growth retreats for both large and small groups.

More recently, Melanie has taken this gift to a new level by designing private individual and couples retreats for people who are ready to make a big leap forward in their relationships with themselves, others and Life.

Melanie insists that she stands on the shoulders of giants. She's been blessed to receive mentoring and training from some of the world's most sought after teachers. It's no secret that Melanie is committed to life-long learning. This commitment has served her well as she is now a recognized leader in the yoga of relationship.

Melanie's specialty is serving people who long to more fully integrate their spiritual beliefs and practices into their life. She is particularly adept at helping people release emotional pain so that they can step into emotional freedom. This freedom comes from an ease of being that is the true essence of yoga – which means union, ultimately union with God. It is Melanie's aim to support people in their quest to experience that kind of union in daily life

Melanie's first challenge was filling events. Taking the advice of my business mentors, Tory Johnson and Michelle Pippin, she adopted a practice of authentic personalized contact with my marketing list.

She found being her authentic self in a small community where what she offered was not the norm. She "came out of the closet" and business is booming.

Melanie McGhee

Recipe for SUCCESS!

1. Find a business mentor whose values match your own values

2. Commit to being a life-long learner. In this way, you advance your skills and become a master of your trade

3. Cultivate confidence that is grounded in experience

4. Learn and practice a daily centering routine to help relieve stress. Think of it as hygiene for your heart

5. Make exercise a priority. Many business women take better care of their cars than they do their bodies. Become a woman who values her body as the vehicle for her life

6. Start a small mastermind group with local like-minded business women

7. Learn the skills to maintain relationship harmony. This means learning to express your needs, wants, feelings. It also means listening to others with an open mind and soft heart

About Melanie McGhee

I have a foot in two worlds. I am an experienced psychotherapist and coach who specializes in the use spiritual technologies for spiritual and personal evolution. Listening deeply, I help people open their heart and come back to center. In that return to center, my clients learn to live a balanced life and develop a new lens through which to experience their inner world and their outer life.

I listen beneath the dramas and stories of life to what it is going to take to take you back to your heart, back to a space of equanimity.

In the sanctuary of our work together, you learn to live from a place of peace. It's a different way of BEING. It's about being the essence of what you are. It's about using life experiences to clear away old ways of being so you can finally BE who you are. You learn to practice the yoga of relationships. In practicing the yoga of relationships, you recognize points of being out of balance, feeling tension or rigidity and learn how to release into the Essence of what you are, ultimately liberating yourself from the pain at its root.

Melanie McGhee
Illuminated Life, LLC
718 Hickory Lane
Maryville, TN 37801

Email: Melanie@peacefruit.com
Phone: 865-384-4104
Website: http://www.peacefruit.com
Facebook: http://www.facebook.com/peacefruit
Twitter: http://www.twitter.com/melaniemcghee

Michelle Peavy

"I came to the fork in the road and chose the fearless route, and so my journey begins"
Michelle Peavy

The Freeway of Life

Once upon a time, Michelle was driving on the freeway and then all of a sudden life got in the way. She is a cancer thriver, followed by the tragedies of her two friends. Consider getting in your car and using it as a metaphor for life. You put your vehicle in the DRIVE mode, you move forward. As you begin to drive on the freeway, you usually start at the speed limit, but then as you look at your watch, you realize you are late. At the same time, your cell phone rings and as you answer it, you spill your coffee. You proceed to grab a pen to write down info from the caller on the phone. As you hang up the phone, you look at your watch, and realize you are late. You proceed to speed up, forget to signal as you move into the next lane. Not paying attention to the signs on the freeway, you get off and miss your exit. Then all of a sudden you get a flat tire. What happens to you when you get a flat tire? You start to think, you are at a complete stop, no one around to help, and have no idea how to change the tire. It sucks doesn't it? It's inconvenient, it gets in the way. Yes, that's what happened to Michelle. But what she realized was, she had to get a flat tire to learn how to live life. Her light switch was turned on, and now she could move forward everyday knowing to pay attention to the road signs and to know what to do when she get off at the wrong exit and got flat tires. They are just obstacles disguised as opportunities to discover so many wonderful things and blessings that others can give you or things you did not know about yourself. You are forced to get inside your head and think and find the answers, as they are always there.

As someone who runs three businesses in two countries, Michelle found that balancing her schedule was the toughest part. Delegating and teaching others in order to free her time up to work ON the business vs. IN the business was the toughest part.

As a firm believer that success is not given but rather earned, Michelle is often described as a Multi-Dimensional, Magnetic, but Universal woman. These talents go beyond business. As a singer, often singing the National Anthem for the NBA Houston Rockets, she has also performed as a warm up singer on Jimmy Kimmel LIVE, America's Got Talent, eWomen Got Talent, the Business of Bliss, Fearless Women Day, and expanding her repertoire as a Closing Keynote Speaker/Singer for corporate conventions and events. In addition, she has been the President/Owner of Rimi and Company, www.rimipv.com for the last 11 years, an executive recruiting firm for Houston, Calgary, and expanding into Toronto markets. Michelle is also a Certified Fitness Instructor and Healthy Coffee Distributor.

She was featured as a Back Page Cover Girl, as one of 40 Women (one of two Canadian Women) in a book called FEARLESS WOMEN – FEARLESS WISDOM, Cover of Today's Business Woman Magazine and recently authored her new CD, where she shares her fearless story about her journey on the FREEWAY OF LIFE and how she became THE FINAL NOTE™. Her last completed project was the 1st annual AllWomen Summit, which was a huge success in Toronto, Canada and the newest release of her song called The Final Note, along with continuing to expand further awareness of new upcoming projects.

Michelle Peavy
Rimi and Company
7251 Topping Rd
Mississauga, Ontario, Canada L4T 2Y6

Email: michelle@rimipv.com
Phone: 877-643-6254
Website: www.michellepeavy.com
Facebook: http://www.facebook.com/reqs.php?type=1#!/michelle.peavy
LinkedIn: http://www.linkedin.com/pub/michelle-peavy/0/23a/3b4
Twitter: @michellepeavy

Misa Leonessa Garavaglia

"Every event in life is an opportunity to choose love over fear"
Author Unknown

From Abuse Survivor to Thriving Professional

Misa grew up in a severely abusive environment and took on the self-limiting beliefs that she would never be enough to warrant love and acceptance. After studying Non-Profit Administration and Sociology in college, she worked as the Program Director for International Student Support Services at University of Santa Clara and then became the Executive Director of the Monterey Volunteer Bureau. She spent the next 22 years raising children and homeschooling while she walked a long a painful healing journey. She knows first-hand how challenging it is to recover from emotional, sexual, physical, and spiritual abuse. After graduating her last daughter from homeschool she embarked on her training as a Life Coach and Spiritual Director. She has gone from one controlled by fear to a professional woman, wife, mother and friend who is able to give from her passion to help others become the best they can be.

Misa Leonessa is a life transformation specialist. She believes that relationships have the power to heal and offers a safe, accepting, and courageous environment within which to learn and practice new skills and create personal growth. It is her passion to help you find the strength, resources, and courage to live a vibrant life. She believes that life is 10% circumstance and 90% what you do with it. You CAN find hope in the midst of life's challenges.

Misa is an infuser of hope and a carrier of courage. As a life coach, speech coach, spiritual director and speaker, she is committed to helping people find a new inheritance of life, love and joy. She works with individuals and groups who are committed to pursuing greater relational, emotional, and spiritual wholeness. As a survivor herself, Misa is an advocate for survivors of childhood abuse and a guide to those ready to move beyond survival and thrive.

Misa Leonessa Garavaglia

Recipe for SUCCESS!

1. Know who you are – find your passion and follow it

2. Don't try to do it alone – there are lots of options for support and assistance out there

3. Stay connected with your authentic self and give what you have from the center

4. Take your eyes off of you and put them on what other people need and how you can be a blessing to them

5. Find a coach or spiritual director to help you work through the spots where you WILL get stuck

6. Don't "market" yourself – BE yourself… a loving, giving person who genuinely cares about others, and you will attract business

7. Don't give up! Be committed to the long haul. It will take time and be a lot of work

About Misa Leonessa

Misa is a member of the International Coach Federation and Spiritual Director's International. She received her training at the Institute of Life Coach Training and the Mercy Center in Burlingame, California. She is a TEDx speaker trainer and a fund raiser and speaker for the Survivor's Healing Center of Santa Cruz.

Misa Leonessa Garavaglia
Misa Leonessa Life Coaching
6350 Wright St.
Felton, CA 95018

Email: inspire@misacoach.com
Phone: 831-335-1265
Website: http://www.misacoach.com
Facebook: http://www.facebook.com/pages/Misa-Leonessa-Life_coaching/196486313059
LinkedIn: http://www.linkedin.com/pub/misa-garavaglia/b/582/259
Twitter: http://twitter.com/#!/misaleonessa

Nancy Alert

"Do What You Have To, So You Can Do What You Want To!"
James Farmer, Sr.

Making It Happen

In 1996 Nancy decided she wanted to get into the Real Estate Industry, Nancy always loved meeting new people from all over the world and she wanted to run my own business. So in September 1996 her Real Estate career began. At that time Nancy was a paralegal and was about to embark on her new career as a part time Realtor which quickly turned into full time position. Nancy was first licensed in Virginia and affiliated with Weichert Realtors. For 5 years she worked as a Paralegal full time and as a Real Estate Agent.

In 2005, 5 years into her career as a Realtor and the upward shift in the Real Estate Market she quit her job as a paralegal and decided to focus all her time and energy on Real Estate. Nancy's plan was always that she would quit her job as a Paralegal once she made $300,000 in one year. In 2005 Nancy made $386,000 and even though sge was very nervous about quitting her job as a Paralegal since it included giving up paid medical, 401k and salary she quit the job. In addition, the Real Estate Market was similar to the current real estate market (declining) yet she did quit the legal industry and went full speed ahead in the Real Estate Industry. Very soon after Nancy created her own LLC and became affiliated with RE/MAX Allegiance and the business took off. In 2011 95% of her business is by referral. Because she stuck with it and provided outstanding service her business went to the next level.

Nancy knew she needed to build my list and get prospect without spending a lot of money so she pushed through and explored all the different free avenues to get new clients (cold calling, agent of the day, open house, networking etc.) and provided outstanding service for her clients and most importantly she "Did What She Said She Would Do". Not long after the referrals started to roll in. Referrals are an excellent source of validation that one is doing a good job. Nancy kept providing excellent service, treated her clients honestly while giving them what they wanted. Be honest in all your dealings, work hard, play hard and live "A Life By Design Not By Default", it is simple, hard work pays off! Nancy is living her dream, doing what she loves which makes it easy every day to go to work because she loves her job.

Nancy says her current challenges are related to today's economy. Currently it is very difficult for buyers to obtain a loan and a good appraisal in the real estate industry because of all the mortgage fraud; my solution to this is to sell to more investors and buyers who are purchasing second homes.

The real estate market is going through a major shift, prices are lower, and lots of short sales and foreclosures- I have become a short sale and foreclosures specialist so I can move with the industry and focus on selling short sales and foreclosures. I have lots of investors and first time home buyers who are purchasing the short sales and foreclosures.

Nancy Alert

Recipe for SUCCESS!

1. Do What You Say You Will Do

2. Give Your Clients What They Ask For

3. under promise and over deliver

4. All sales people/entrepreneurs must remember your most important job every day is Lead Generation

5. Social Media is one of the best and least expensive ways to promote your business

6. Be honest and true with all your clients

7. A Positive Attitude is required for a positive and healthy personal and business life

About Nancy Alert

Nancy Alert, licensed Realtor in Virginia, Washington DC and Maryland for the over 15 years. Nancy is known in the Washington DC Metro Area as the go to Realtor® for all of your real estate needs locally & internationally. Nancy assists clients in purchasing and selling real estate with a focus on Luxury homes, 2nd homes and investment properties within the United States and Internationally.

Nancy is one of the few agents in the area who literally list your home in the specific city, state and or countries where the buyers for your home are. We live and do business in a global economy; it's NOW time for you to hire a global agent with the personal touch, NOT just a local agent!

Nancy is the owner of Nancy Alert & Associates, a real estate consulting company affiliated with RE/MAX Allegiance.

Nancy Alert
Nancy Alert & Associates, LLC
6226 Old Dominion Dr.
McLean, VA 22101

Email: nancy@nancyalert.com
Phone: 703-861-7355
Website: http://www.nancyalert.com
Facebook: www.facebook.com/AllAboutArlington
LinkedIn: www.linkedin.com/in/NancyAlert
Twitter: www.Twitter.com/NancyAlert

Careers from the Kitchen Table Home Business Directory Second Edition

Patricia Clason

"If you have built castles in the air, your work need not be lost; that is where they should be. Now put the foundations under them"
Henry David Thoreau

Courage, Confidence and Passion

It really did start at the kitchen table where Patricia (age 22) explored the business of promoting and producing events for workshop leaders, especially her Tai Chi instructor, Fredric Lehrman. One day Fredric told someone about Patricia's skills as an organizer and she was invited to San Francisco to do a seminar on how to organize seminars. "I loved it and I got to expense on my taxes what felt like a great California vacation!" That was the beginning of Genesis, a seminar business that is now the Center for Creative Learning. From the table to the traditional office, she maintained the feeling of a permanent vacation by being in charge of her own schedule and doing what she absolutely loves to do.

Almost forty years later, Patricia's work involves coaching, teaching/training, and consulting, with one-person businesses to Fortune 50 companies and executives. The theme in all of her work is about Emotional Intelligence, because it was learning about healthy emotions that saved her life many times over the years.

Major crises in her life included divorce, being a solo-mom, purchasing an office building that turned out to have oil in the soil (undisclosed by the former owner), a resulting bankruptcy, her mother's suicide, several business partners gone bad, and healing the impact of childhood sexual abuse. Using every tool she could learn for emotional release, stress management, healthy communication, boundaries and self-care was what got her through these challenges without giving up or giving in to fears.

"No matter what happened, I moved forward. 'So What! Now What?" is still her motto. She faces the challenges life brings with a deep breath and gratitude which helps her to focus on the Now and the next step. And above all, it is love, of God, of family, of her work, that permeates everything and gives her passion and courage.

So when Patricia says, "I can be your guide/coach," you can trust that her real life experience and wisdom will light your path to help you build the confidence, courage and passion that will take you to the success you seek.

When asked to name her greatest challenges, Patricia named two. Maintaining her priorities – as a single mom and a business owner – After 15 years of building her business, a divorce resulted in a necessary re-prioritization so Patricia could raise her then 3 year old daughter, Secily. Working quarter-time to keep her name in the game, Patricia spent the next 12 years putting her daughter first. In Secily's last few years of high school, Patricia ramped up her schedule and returned to full-time speaking and coaching. Letting go of judgment ('I should have done more by now, be making more money, etc.) and being satisfied required frequent re-direction of her thoughts and constant appreciation for the gift of her daughter!

Building her business with a commitment to staying debt free – Patricia has a strong prosperity consciousness and commitment to staying debt free. This presented a significant challenge, requiring a creative approach to obtaining the guidance, tools and capital needed to grow her business. As a result, she knows how to make it happen and can help you manifest your dreams, without breaking your budget.

Patricia Clason

Recipe for SUCCESS!

1. Own It! - Personal Responsibility = no blame, reasons or justification.

2. Remember it's about the process/journey, not a destination

3. Choose – not making a decision is a decision for others to run your life

4. Take Action – which means taking the risk that the results may be not be perfect. Remember, it doesn't have to be perfect; it just has to be your best!

5. Be accountable for what you did and did not do. Mend your mistakes, celebrate your accomplishments

6. Include others: Get support, Give support, and Make it happen together. We live in an inter-dependent world

7. Review, Refine, Repeat 1 through 6 and enjoy!!

About Patricia Clason

For almost forty years, Patricia Clason has traveled the continent doing speeches, workshops and media appearances as a professional speaker, trainer, consultant, writer, and coach giving over 4,000 presentations. Now the Director of the Center for Creative Learning (www.lightly.com/faith) which offers programs for personal and professional development in Milwaukee, Madison, and Detroit, Patricia has written many articles, training programs and personal growth seminars and is a sought-after guest for radio and television.

She also leads Accountability Coaching Associates. As a consultant and business coach she works with large and small companies, including executives in Fortune 50 companies, managers and supervisors, business owners, management teams, and solo entrepreneurs.

Patricia was the first to receive the Registered Corporate Coach designation from the Worldwide Association of Business Coaches. Founder of the Business Coaching Certificate program at the University of Wisconsin Milwaukee, she now teaches Emotional Intelligence classes for their Management Certificate program. Patricia also taught coaching in the Alverno College Telesis Institute Management Certificate program and is adjunct faculty at several Milwaukee universities.

Patricia is the author of Claim Your Unlimited Potential, a 12 workbook course for Building the Life You Want http://claimyourpotential.wordpress.com and co-author of Speaking of Success and Faith's Journey (www.lightly.com/faith).

Patricia Clason, RCC
Your Everyday Emotional Intelligence Coach
2437 N Booth St.
Milwaukee, WI 53212

Email: patricia@patriciaclason.com
Phone: 414-374-5433 / 800-236-4692
Website: http://www.patriciaclason.com
Facebook: www.facebook.com/patricia.clason
Linkedin: http://www.linkedin.com/in/patriciaclason
Twitter: http://twitter.com/EQCoachClason

Rayna Bergerman

"Character is higher than intellect. A great soul will be strong to live as well as think."
Ralph Waldo Emerson

From Failure to Success...You're Child CAN DO IT!

Rayna's journey into helping youth in academics and personal growth started while completing her first University degree. Her prof at the time was the first instructor she had ever had that took the time to ask her how she liked to learn. It was obvious to Rayna that for years, while cooped up in a traditional classroom her interests were always about the outdoors, athletic pursuits and music. Whenever these 3 elements were infused into lessons Rayna found success. This was not the norm and Rayna fell into the belief that she was stupid and incompetent in many subject areas. This prof invited her to participate in a field school in the thick, bug-infested, culturally rich rainforests of Belize, Central America to study the Black Howler Monkeys. This adventure of a lifetime changed Rayna's whole perspective on learning and she realized that she could indeed learn and that she LOVED learning, but it was just in a different way than everybody else.

This realization helped her through her next degree where she advocated for herself and her preferred ways of learning and presenting information. She earned the Gold Medal and graduated at the top of her class.

Rayna now shares these methods to success through her business and signature system, The Inspire More Students Good Grades Solution. Students that have been working with Rayna and her certified team of tutors and subject experts have seen grades skyrocket upwards of 40% in one term, confidence shoot through the roof and laughter become part of learning again. Students all over North America can benefit from Rayna's coaching as her practice is available online as well as in-person.

When there are other issues with organization and thinking skills, Rayna coaches through an executive functioning skills model, allowing youth to learn vital skills needed to succeed in both life and school.

Rayna's believes to her core that it is our responsibility as adults to better understand our children's needs. It is completely unacceptable for any child to feel stupid or "less than" when we have the tools to serve them better.

When Rayna isn't reading, working or hiking she is playing out in nature with her family and friends.

Her challenges in building her business revolved around marketing. She hired a coach and it was a disaster. She felt completely inauthentic and insulting. She took everything good that he had to offer and scrapped the rest including him! Now she has a coach that has guided her in really seeing her client, how she can best serve them and what that means to THEM.

Rayna Bergerman — Recipe for SUCCESS!

1. Start your day before you usually do

2. Make a plan for what you need to accomplish today

3. Ensure that the elements of that plan are money-making

4. Delegate tasks that are too time consuming or that you don't enjoy

5. Use social media wisely and to your advantage, not as a distraction

6. Talk to people, open dialogues everywhere about how you serve your clients

7. Always remember that your client's needs are what matter, not yours

About Rayna Bergerman

Rayna Bergerman, Kidterpreter & Learning/Life Skills Consultant is a Master Teacher and expert when it comes to, understanding kids, interpreting who they are, and then making learning and life easier and more engaging for them.

Having won the Clarence Sansom Gold Medal for Academic Mastery at the University of Calgary, she herself has used the techniques that she now teaches to quickly "get to the head of the class." Students using the Inspire More Students System have seen grade level increases from c's to a's and up to 30 percentage points in less than 4 months. When our youth feel understood and valued, their confidence soars and the cycle repeats. Parents walk tall, empowered with the tools they need to coach their children through the tough stuff, and rest easy knowing that the investment that they have made in their child's development will reap lifelong rewards.

Being a lifelong learner herself, last year Rayna studied the Child Coaching for Life Skills Certification program through Oxford College, which gives her the edge in coaching kids, and their parents, through life challenges that can stand in the way of academic achievement. This year, she has been invited to attend the Gurian Institute Summer Session regarding gender differences in learning.

Rayna Bergerman
Inspired Learning Centers Canada Inc
56 Deermoss Cres. SE
Calgary, AB, Canada T2J 6P4

Email: Rayna@inspiremorestudents.com
Phone: 403-863-1939
Website: www.inspiremorestudents.com
Facebook: www.facebook.com/rayna.bergerman
LinkedIn: http://ca.linkedin.com/pub/rayna-bergerman/30/b7b/965
Twitter: www.twitter.com/raynabergerman

Careers from the Kitchen Table Home Business Directory Second Edition

Sandra Tucker Jones

"If one advances confidently in the direction of his dreams, and endeavors to live the life which he as imagined, he will meet with unexpected success in common hours. He will put something behind, will pass an invisible boundary; new, universal, and more liberal laws will begin to establish themselves around and within him, or the old laws will be expanded and interpreted in his favor in a more liberal sense; and he will live with the license of a higher order of beings."

Henry David Thoreau

The Journey to Lightworking

Sandy Jones, founder of *Synergy Breakthroughs*, spent much of her working life in technology as an IT consultant. But her real journey started when she was diagnosed with uterine fibroids and was told she had to have a hysterectomy. Although knowing little about healing at the time, she was able to reverse the situation with fasting, raw juices, herbs, and other approaches, and never did have a hysterectomy.

This experience amazed her, and became the catalyst for a strong interest in healing modalities! While working the office/corporate gig during the day, eventually becoming an IT consultant, Sandy "moonlighted" as a student of healing during off hours, studying a variety of healing approaches over the years from Barbara Brennan, Robert Jaffe, Kam Yuen, Stephen Ko (Master Cho), Bruno Gröning Circle of Friends, Radionics teachers, hypnotherapist Dolores Cannon, Alex Loyd, and others. Sandy's greatest lesson from all of this was that we are all students of healing. We learn these lessons each day, and we have a choice every day: to heal, or to harm. But, as students of healing, we all came here to help each other.

While having profound respect for alternative approaches, she also encountered situations that were all too similar to what is problematic about mainstream health practices: Limited access to practitioners, expensive treatments, and lack of interest in the self-empowerment of the client to learn about and effect his or her own healing. This led her on a search for self-healing modalities. She learned that, as we heal ourselves and help others to heal, nothing should be a struggle, and no one should have more to give than anyone else. Inequality is an illusion; we are all unique, but equal in the gifts we have to share.

Sandy currently works with clients as an intuitive life coach and hypnotherapist. In addition, having experienced from a family tragedy that there is a great deal of public misunderstanding and ignorance regarding heavy drinking and alcoholism, she is also working on a book and teleconference entitled, Intervene! An Emergency Guide to Heavy Drinking and Alcoholism.

One challenge was what I feel the majority of us experience: Getting from where I was, to where I wanted to be. After experiencing my own struggles and observing the struggles of others, I became a life coach to help people grow into what they came here to be. Life is way too short and way too precious to be lost on years that have no meaning for you. At the same time, no matter where you may be in life, every experience is a stepping stone to where you want to be. The fluidity of life is a gift that allows you to keep changing, and to keep changing your goals as *you* change. But the most important thing is to just keep dreaming, keep moving forward, and keep trusting the process (even if you don't understand it in the present).

A second challenge was to sort out the facets of myself that were unfolding in my life, not just professionally, but also personally. The field of psychology has established that we are not tabula rasas; we come with quite an assortment of characteristics, and from the time we are born, this foundation is built upon by the conditioning of our families, our environments, and our experiences. Maya Angelou once wrote, "There are words in the walls." The words are not just in the walls – they are deeply embedded in our bodies, as mind-body science has established. We are vibrating data fields that are constantly attracting or repelling the people, places and events in our resonant universe. Just becoming aware of this and stepping with courage into the unknown is a movement away from victimhood and a start to a happier, more self-empowered life.

Sandra Tucker Jones

Recipe for SUCCESS!

1. Get to know yourself, and make friends with yourself

2. Discover, and most importantly, *share*, your gifts

3. Yesterday is history and tomorrow is a mystery, but "the present" is a gift

4. Not taking a risk often entails greater loss than taking a risk

5. Listening to others often entails greater loss than not listening to others

6. Ask the right people for help, encouragement, and support

7. Find environments and people that you resonate with, dream, and thrive!

About Sandy Jones

Sandy Jones was born in the Washington, D.C. area, and received her undergraduate and Master's degrees in Psychology and Education from the University of Virginia. Later, she went on to graduate with a Master's in Organizational Behavior. After working in organization development, she transitioned into information technology and spent a number of years as an IT consultant. She worked in many different capacities (technical and nontechnical training, instructional design, technical writing, business analysis, process analysis and improvement, etc.), in a variety of different industries and environments (publishing, finance, hardware, software, etc.), and for many different kinds of companies, from small companies to Fortune 500 companies. However, her true interests lay in business and life coaching, and the study of healing modalities. She currently lives in the Las Vegas, Nevada area, where she works with clients as a life coach and practitioner of the hypnotherapy techniques of world-famous author and hypnotherapist, Dolores Cannon.

Sandra Tucker Jones
Synergy Breakthroughs
1660 Liege Dr.
Henderson, NV 89012

Email: synergybreakthroughs@gmail.com
Phone: 303-400-8875
Website: www.synergybreakthroughs.com
Facebook: http://www.facebook.com/sandytjones
LinkedIn: http://www.linkedin.com/pubs/sandy-jones/4/231/206

Saskia Jennings- de Quaasteniet

"You Deserve The Best"
Susan Polis Schutz

Challenge yourself: find & become you!

Saskia was born and raised overseas in Holland. Her career journey includes working as an Executive Secretary/Office Manager in Human Resources, Sales and Marketing in a variety of offices. While sick in 1999 she tried Natural Healing Therapies with great results. That was a turning point in her life: feeling better, inspired, happy and empowered!

She took her first visit to Canada in 1999 and faced a big AHA-moment: "here's where I belong!" When she came back to Holland she followed her 'gut feeling' and completed training in alternative medicine like Shiatsu, Reflexology and CranioSacral Therapy.

After many visits to Canada, she quit her job, put her apartment up for sale and moved to Canada in 2005. Married 4 months later and landed deep in the Canadian woods. Saskia faced numerous challenges: not allowed to work yet, no car for over a year, no high speed internet, no neighbors and a small town half an hour away. In this learning process she relied a lot on her husband.

In the fall of 2006 she became a Permanent Resident and started working as a Personal Support Worker.

However, her true nature kept calling and she got the idea of starting her own business in Natural Healing Therapies. Unfortunately her Dutch diplomas were not recognized so she retrained for Reflexology and CranioSacral Therapy and became a Karuna Reiki Master. Finally she founded her own business, Creating Being Well, May 2009, offering Holistic Health Support through Reflexology, Reiki, CranioSacral Therapy and soon to come: Life Coaching! She made (what seemed) a difficult decision to step out of her marriage and went on her own again.

From here on Saskia is going full speed ahead, both personally and in business! Her Business is her passion: motivating, supporting others to create a fulfilling life.
Saskia is able to encourage and stimulate others, mostly women that are looking to find their

purpose & happiness in life and want to feel better & inspired. Saskia's dynamic energy and spirit is a huge stimulant for everyone who meets and connects with her. "Believe in yourself" is on top of her list!

She found her biggest challenge as an immigrant eager to build credit history and learned to apply for different credit cards with small credit limits, pay in full always, then increase your flow = increasing possibilities. She also says letting go of fear to move forward: listening to your heart and your coaches and practice, practice is key to improving and to always keep believing in yourself.

Saskia Jennings - de Quaasteniet

Recipe for SUCCESS!

1. Believe, be passionate and create!

2. Share life, laughter and tears with loved ones

3. Work with coaches: they help you focus

4. Let go of fear and limiting beliefs

5. Be Professional

6. Take time to listen to your intuition and inner guidance: meditate, sing, dance

7. Work your body: exercise and enjoy nature

About Saskia Jennings-de Quaasteniet

Saskia Jennings-de Quaasteniet was born and raised overseas, in Holland. She had a long time career in an office, and lived in Rotterdam.

While sick and 'burned-out' in 1999, she tried natural healing therapies to recover and that worked really well for her. Because it was such an eye opener, she started studying those therapies like Reflexology, Reiki and CranioSacral Therapy.

For some reason she also started exploring Canada and all this turned out to be a life changing experience for her. In May 2005 she moved to Canada (Parry Sound/Muskoka, ON) and challenged herself to adjust from 'City Girl' into her new life in the woods.

The peace & beauty of nature inspires her to move forward on her spiritual path. Saskia reviewed Reiki, Reflexology and CranioSacral Therapy in Canada.

In 2009 she founded her own business: Creating Being Well, offering holistic health support. Location: Parry Sound area, ON, Canada.

Saskia is a Registered Certified Reflexology Therapist and Karuna Reiki Master. She is also a CranioSacral Therapy Practitioner. Next step on her path is to become Your Ultimate Life Coach! Saskia is a well appreciated member of her community through her work and volunteering activities.

Saskia Jennings-de Quaasteniet
Creating Being Well
37 Silver Point Drive
Parry Sound, ON, Canada P2A 2W8

Email: Saskia@creatingbeingwell.com
Phone: 705-773-8411
Website: www.creatingbeingwell.com

Sheila McClain

"Be a life enhancer and surround yourself with life enhancers"
Walt Disney

Passion to make a difference!

Sheila for many years has worked in customer service industries and enjoys working with people to get what they want out of life. Throughout her life, she would be finding ways to assist friends and co-workers solutions to problems.

Sheila has experienced the issues of the "trip ups" while working in many different locations and learned that staying focused on what is really important in her life was the way to go, not to spend time on individuals who desired to step on her to get to the top, she has stepped aside and saw there was a purpose in the lesson. She believes in prayer gets you further in this world that has its good and bad. Sheila holds her head up, smiles, and seeks life enhancers to surround her and in turn will be genuine to build another person up even when she is in tough challenges in her life.

Determination and inspiration comes from this lady, her passion for the wellness and health of family and friends has guided her on a journey to find her true passion of helping others through life and business coaching.

Sheila McClain   *Recipe for* SUCCESS!

1. Clarity
2. Focus
3. Prioritize what is important
4. Desire
5. Belief in oneself
6. Determination
7. Consistency

About Sheila McClain

Sheila McClain is the proud owner of Fyntoon Solutions, offering coaching on life and business challenges. Sheila is passionate about assisting individuals and teams to exceed their own expectations. Sheila has given numerous inspirational and motivational speeches for several groups including Herald College. She completed her coaching certification program with the Institute for Professional Empowerment Coaching. She is very active in her community where she is a member of Soroptimist of Lodi Sunrise and BNI clubs. Sheila currently lives in Stockton, CA with her four beautiful children. She enjoys spending time with her children, working out in her home gym, riding her bike out in the orchards and walking her dogs. She enjoys spending quality time with friends and seeing a great movie.

Sheila McClain
Fyntoon Solutions
2000 W. Kettleman Lane Ste 201A
Lodi, CA 95242

Email: fyntoon@yahoo.com
Phone: 209-712-2073
Website: www.fyntoonsolutions.com
Facebook: http://facebook.com/Sheila.McClain.CertifiedLifeCoach

Sherry Prindle

"Humans cannot do projects, only tasks: to get big things accomplished, break them down into doable steps."
Takashi Yamada

Do as You Are, Not as They Say

An only child surrounded by adults, Sherry Prindle's answer to, "What do you want to be when you grow up?" often changed but always involved travel, adventure, and performing before an audience. She listened to the adults and avoided what they warned against—drugs, fights, young lust, slacking off, causing trouble. She also watched adults and noticed what made them happy—getting involved, playing games, debating controversial subjects.

What she never understood was people trying to persuade her to do the opposite of what gave them happiness—"Get a job," "Get married and have children," "Don't drink," "Save money for retirement," "Buy a house and keep it nice like the neighbors'" they admonished her to play it safe while they craved excitement.

As a college exchange student, she saw how big the world was and grew into it. Graduating and moving back to Japan, she ceased the opportunity to star in a prime-time documentary. A local celebrity in four years, she decided to start over in another country to see if she could do it again.

Studying in a Moscow, Russia dormitory of language learners from every country and finding her calling as the host of Radio 7's Morning Zoo, she found the same local celebrity status three years later. Her goodbye party made the front page of the Moscow Tribune newspaper.

All this she did without a job or family, finding amazing friends in bars, at parties, playing games, and getting involved in community events while debating controversial subjects—the travel, the adventures, making plenty of money to pay for the next day.

A Master's Degree and a successful 15-year speaking career later, Sherry is still traveling every week, still unattached, still debating—and ecstatically happy. Known as the Motivational Mastermind, she leads others who want to change the world and be present in the passion of doing it through the process of finally becoming what you want to be when you grow up. It's not too late, the key is to do what you are and not what they say you should be

Not wanting to narrow my focus and give up any areas of expertise, I found a universal "umbrella" concept under which all my offerings could co-exist.

I couldn't afford an assistant, so I bartered my service with several people and got really savvy at having a different assistant every few weeks.

Sherry Prindle

Recipe for SUCCESS!

1. Whatever you are doing right now, immerse yourself in it entirely

2. Is our purpose on this planet really to work a job? Experience life as you live it

3. Stop to right the wrongs you notice in your path, pick up trash, return a shopping cart, even if it was not yours

4. Let people know the nice thoughts you are having about them

5. Your conscious mind doesn't have to understand everything; let it be okay just to know it's right and what you want

6. Have fewer rules for yourself and others, so you can enforce them regularly

7. Be the person you would have thought as a kid was cool

About Sherry Prindle

Sherry Prindle, the Motivational Mastermind, provides the perfect middle ground for creating a life-change business. Between paying others to create a viable business and doing it all yourself emerges the Motivational Mastermind membership group. Leveraging the group dynamic, Mastermind members get hand-held, step-by-step, done-for-you resources that create immediate avenues of growth and streams of income.

A respected corporate consultant and coach, Sherry conducts Life Coach Certification classes for the Certified Coaches Federation and trains all new Seminar Leaders for Fred Pryor Seminars. She has delivered over 3,000 training seminars and 400 keynotes in 40 topics over 12 years across all 50 states and 6 countries in 3 languages.

Co-author of the 15 Winning Ways to Better Living, she has an M.A. in Business and Linguistics from the University of Texas at Arlington and a B.A. in Communications and International Relations from William Jewell College in Liberty, Missouri.

She lived in Fukuoka, Japan for four years working as a television news reporter for RKB-Mainichi Television and in Moscow, Russia for three years hosting the successful Morning Zoo morning drive show on Radio Seven.

Sherry Prindle
Motivational Mastermind
601 E Highland Ave
St. Joseph, MO 64505

Email: sherry@motivationalmastermind.com
Phone: 817-657-5301
Website: www.motivationalmastermind.com
Facebook: http://www.facebook.com/MotivationalMastermind
LinkedIn: www.linkedin.com/in/SherryPrindle
Twitter: www.twitter.com/sherryprindle

Susan Bock

"Whether you believe you can, or believe you can't, you're right!"
Henry Ford

Choosing Thrive over Survive

A true survivor of having her life turned upside down more than once, Susan had to embrace change and connect with her inner strength, or she would not have survived. Survival can be a powerful motivator and it gave her the courage to discover who she really was and what she had to offer.

Was it easy? Absolutely not. What is worthwhile? More than she could have imagined. The joy of sharing her discoveries makes your journey much easier – she can give you the shortcuts! Today, Susan is the CEO of her life. How did that happen? By believing in her potential, discovering her purpose and stepping into her power....call it the Power of 3 P's.

Whether talking one-on-one with a client or speaking to an audience, Susan's goal is this: "At the conclusion of our time together, you will have a new way of thinking about yourself, your business and your life."

Her foremost challenge was to determine priorities. There were so many components to starting her business; www.SCORE.com was the solution.

Success brought the next challenge - demands of 'running a business' left little time for 'doing the business', which is where she excelled. Selective hiring was the solution.

Susan Bock

Recipe for SUCCESS!

1. Tuesday - Thursday are the high-energy days - appointments, networking, visible

2. Monday and Friday are office days - booking appointments, personal tasks, creative thinking

3. Read the 12-week Year

4. Use a 12-week year plan. See http://www.pdfcalendar.com/12-weeks/

5. Schedule vacations and make the reservations in January - 2 'vacations' a year

6. Join a group for fun - not just for business

7. Be an expert in your industry - read books, attend webinars and seminars - always expanding your knowledge and your contacts

About Susan Bock

After entering the entrepreneurial realm in 2000 as a Master Certified Executive Coach (MCEC), Susan's firm launched into immediate demand and success. She learned early on that her corporate experience served her well, AND she needed to quickly expand her resources and tool kit! Making mistakes, and learning at Mach speed, she has emerged as a professional speaker and is delighting her audiences with her message of transforming your way of thinking, your business and your life from the inside out!

Susan Bock's career began with American Express and she concluded her 'corporate' life after 15 years with multi-national advertising and communication firms. She is known for her creative thinking, thought-provoking conversations and inspiring spirit.

Susan has a PhD. - Business Management, is a Master Certified Executive Coach – College of Executive Coaching and received her Master's Degree in Organizational Management.

Susan Bock
SBS
8201 Newman Ave. Ste 102
Huntington Beach, CA 92647

Email: susan@susanbock.com
Phone: 714-847-1566
Website: www.susanbock.com
Facebook: http://www.facebook.com/susanbock.coach.speaker
LinkedIn: www.linkedin.com/in/susanbockcoachandspeaker
Twitter: www.twitter.com/susanbockspeaks

Tami Gulland

**"What lies behind us and what lies ahead of us are tiny matters
compared to what lives within us."**
Henry David Thoreau

From the Perfect Storm to Divine Transformation™

Three major events in Tami's life created the perfect storm. By utilizing the lessons learned from these challenges and receiving them as gifts, they provoked Tami to make big changes. The changes propelled her on the path to the successful business she has today.

Tami was very intuitive, but hadn't fully accepted and embraced her gifts. In fact, she hid them. When she responded to "the call" to launch her coaching business it meant that she had to leave the familiarity of her corporate job and begin to really trust her intuition. This leap of faith triggered a deeper awareness of her gifts and nudged her to share them with others. Through her own experiences and in working with clients, she developed the process of Divine Transformation™, which she now teaches her clients.

Divine Transformation™ is a systematic approach to turn confusion, overwhelm and fear into clarity, and activate inspired action with the help of Angels. It includes step-by-step methods to help women:

- Identify, trust, and follow Divine Guidance.

- Confidently make decisions true to personal values and priorities.

- Understand and utilize their unique energy and gifts to dissolve struggle and be in 'the flow'.

How does Divine Guidance Really Make a Difference?

Rachel, one of Tami's clients, was making a major life transition. She wanted to invest in a program to build her business, but also needed resources to move.

She actually didn't have the money for either. Without being aware of way, she asked her Angels for guidance to do both. She stopped and listened. She didn't have to wait long to receive an insight. She took action based on the guidance she received and stayed receptive. She repeated this each step of the way.

To her delight she received the money and resources needed to take the program and move.

For years Jennette wanted to up level her status in her network marketing company. Immediately after Tami began working with her, Jennette was regularly connecting with and following her Divine Guidance. Within a couple of months she received the promotion she desired.

Tami Gulland

Recipe for SUCCESS!

1. Bring the dream that lives in your heart into the world by first holding a picture in your mind for your ultimate business experience and connecting emotionally to it. (Note: This process is also important for each step of the business building process.)

2. Clarify your intention by identifying why you want it and how it ultimately will serve others

3. Feel gratitude, in advance, for being able to bring your gifts out into the world and make a difference in a way only you can uniquely contribute

4. Ask for support from your Angels, your Divine Team and Source to guide you every step of the way, helping to orchestrate your dream into reality. Trust you deserve this support and be willing to receive it.

5. Be observant of people in your life and those you meet who show up with a certain piece of information, the ideal connection, or insight to help support you to manifest your dreams

6. Believe you can do it, despite what others may say and even if you don't know how to do it right now. Never give up. Allow your Angels to show you the way. Be open to listening and receiving ideas, information and guidance every step of the way

7. Pay attention to what shows up as internal impressions and external cues to act upon. Take action on the inspirations you receive. Celebrate each success no matter how small or large

About Tami Gulland

Tami Gulland, Founder of Angels ForSuccess.com teaches high-achieving, spiritually-oriented professional women and entrepreneurs how to easily access their Angels, Divine Guidance and find their own authentic answers. She specializes in coaching women who feel overwhelmed, disconnected and exhausted to dissolve the blocks that have kept them stuck and struggling.

She helps women to tap into the Divine support system available 24/7, so they feel empowered, joyful and spiritually connected, whether at work or in everyday life.

Tami has learned both through her personal experience and in working with clients, when people listen to their Angels, they significantly reduce anxiety, overwhelm and stress in health, relationships, and business and even with money. By identifying, trusting and following their Divine Guidance they find the clearest, most direct path to success.

Tami is a Certified Coach, Angel Therapy Practitioner and Medium. She is the author of **"Conversations with Angels: Divine Inspirations to Uplift Your Heart" and "Embracing Your Spirited Child."** Tami I also the contributing author to **"Pearls of Wisdom: 30 Inspirational Ideas to Live Your Best Life Now**" with leading author Jack Canfield and several other books. She shares inspirational channeled messages from Angels, Masters, Saints and Guides and insights through her ezine at www.AnglesForSuccess.com.

Tami Gulland, ATP, CM
Your Angel Guide for Success
5133 Caton Lane
Waunakee, WI 53597

Email: tami@angelsforsuccess.com
Phone: 608-850-6437
Website: www.angelsforsuccess.com
Facebook: http://www.facebook.com/tamigulland
LinkedIn: www.linkedin.com/in/tamigulland
Twitter: www.twitter.com/tamigulland

Careers from the Kitchen Table Home Business Directory Second Edition

Tanya Jones MD

"We are the Ones we have been waiting For"
Dr. Tanya Jones, MD

Tanya's Grandmother saved my life with tar and sulfur... her mother almost died when she was 10 and she vowed never to let anyone she knew be at the mercy of uncaring or incompetent people. She loves to travel and began in International Relations... became a psychologist... became a Doctor... became a national leader... became an Intuitive... became a Healer. She bridges dimensions now and helps people recognize their strength, their connection to powers greater than they can imagine... She is a cosmic catalyst and world changer.

The journey was not without pain... she flunked out of the University of California... reentered and began her PH.D there. She had a brother murdered and a Sister who disappeared. There was domestic violence in her birth home and undiagnosed bipolar disorder. Tanya's Father received the Distinguished Flying Cross for flying around the world nonstop in the B-52 bombers. He was a Tuskegee Airman and began as a coalminer genius. Her mother was one of 12 children on a farm and a master teacher in the end. Tanya learned to persevere despite odds, she would creative curiosity and the ability to move quickly and adapt to different cultures and environments. She is a Psychic and medium yet was late to accept these gifts. She loves life and after raising two sons, surviving two divorces, four grandchildren finds that life loves her! She is fierce, gentle, loving, intellectual, fun loving, eccentric, and much more. She is becoming all that she was meant to be. She strives to be "Oneness" personified, she is Spirit in Action!

Tanya found integrating the analytic approach to business with the intuitive approach to be her biggest challenge. As with most things, she found that continued "practice" proved to be the key to success.

Tanya Jones

Recipe for SUCCESS!

1. Develop and maintain relationships with people you find interesting (via social media, skype, email and phone

2. Give away your services at least once a month... will lead to new contacts and new business and generate good will that will come back to you

3. Look for synergy possibilities in the people you meet and work with by using your imagination to "think" out of the box

4. Never burn your bridges even with people who didn't treat you fairly...treat them as you would be treated...

5. Read "Getting to Yes" – How to negotiate without giving in

6. Honor your "intuitive" or "Gut" feelings even when you analytical mind questions

7. Stay connected to a Power and Mission Greater than yourself... Be Living Spirit in Action

About Tanya Jones

I am a Healer and Intuitive Physician I began teaching Psychology and heading counseling departments. Later I transitioned to Medicine when I identified how emotional Health impacted Physical Health. I became a Professor, national leader of Family Medicine and international Speaker. I believe the "Art" of medicine embraces the best of alternative, energetic, and ethnic healing practices. I now "bridge Dimensions" & promote Healing at the individual, family, corporate, national and international level. I believe in "Oneness" and our interconnectedness.

Tanya Jones
New World Visions International
5 Ariel Court
Placitas, New Mexico

Email: drtanyaheals@gmail.com
Phone: 404-895-9552 or 505-895-9552
Website: www.tanyajonesmd.com
Facebook: https://www.facebook.com/#!/profile.php?id=690708895
LinkedIn: http://www.linkedin.com/pub/tanya-jones-md/3/114/549
Twitter: www.twitter.com/#!/DrTanya

Timi Gleason

"In every job there is to be done, there is an element of fun. Find the fun,
and the job becomes a game!"
Mary Poppins

Developing Star Power

For Timi health coaching was just a side line in 2009-2010. She was a dabbler and stretched thin by my full-time corporate job and side-efforts as a health blogger.

A coaching friend mentioned a client of his: "He positions himself as a guru. He has poise, confidence, and a specific approach. He commands more money and attention as a star."

It got Timi thinking. She already knew she had "followers." Did she have star power? If so, what was the evidence?

Timi was surprised by her own clarity:

- My friends seek out my perspectives about health issues

- They think of me as well-read and strategic about the root cause of health

- Many turn to me for a bigger picture of what might cause an illness at its root

- Before their doctor appointments they consult with me on questions to ask and data to request from their doctor

- They give my phone number to complete strangers who call me to brainstorm and sort through their health issues

- Colleagues ask me to recommend M.D.s and health specialists and practitioners

- One friend teasingly calls me Dr. Gleason!

How much evidence did she need that she had budding star power?!

Gurus are teachers, coaches, and leaders who stand out for their individualistic wisdom and approach. Frequently, they fulfill an unmet need in the hearts and minds of their audience.

Was Timi willing to step up to fill an unmet need?

Maybe she was. If you have seen the 2011 movie The King's Speech, think about the tremendous leap in self-confidence that was required of Lionel, the tutor. He knew he could help Prince Albert, and together they overcame overwhelming, embarrassing psychological and social obstacles on Prince Albert's behalf.

Around the world, audiences are searching for the "star quality" in others.

Check out this gutsy car washer on America's Got Talent: http://www.youtube.com/watch?v=rVflKxMN7wk Do you have his courage?

Ultimately, Timi joined a publically-held wellness group committed to changing the way America perceives obesity and illness. They are corporate like Timi. They are committed to helping people get off prescription meds. Timi found her "peeps"!

Timi notes her two biggest business challenges so far have been:

1) Getting off track…not spending enough time on business development To combat making sure her daily marketing occurs, Timi schedules up to five business contacts a day. Sometimes, at meetings, she can make up to ten personal contacts. Timi has found that she doesn't plan ahead, her marketing gets put off by other interruptions and priorities. "I make sure all the contacts have been made before I turn off the lights at night!"

2) Battling paper organization. Timi joined a group called *Clutterology.com*. Nancy Miller is her mentor. Nancy specializes in teaching people how to manage and file paper and projects. If you have a clutter problem, please tell Nancy that "Timi Gleason in San Diego" sent you.

She looks for her ideal clients in Chiropractors and M.D.'s who are looking for a way to help their patients slim down quickly and get off of prescription medication. HBB Entrepreneurs who want to join my team and learn how to help people heal themselves. "Ready" friends and family, who want to lose weight, improve their blood chemistry and who secretly dream of their bodies looking like they did when they were much, much younger! It's ALL possible.

Timi Gleason

Recipe for SUCCESS!

1. **Pay attention to what makes you choke up or feel protective.** Those physical reactions are your subconscious screaming at you to pay attention to something you are passionate about! Make a list of those trigger points. Learn about them and pinpoint your passion. Pay attention to how people respond to you when you speak passionately

2. **Believe in your own gift.** If there is even the slightest feeling of "con artist" in you, clean that up and keep it cleaned up. Practice peeling away your fear and self-doubt and learn to speak only from your authenticity and heart. Spread positive energy and you will make lots of money

3. **Come from your heart, not your pocket book.** This is not easy to do when you also need to make a living. The Universe will support you financially when you have mastered this

4. **Share your loving message with others.** How can you serve them? How can mankind be uplifted by your services? Speak to others respectfully no matter how annoying they are. Listen to their needs first. Develop your ideas from the voice of your customer

5. **Be willing to step up with courage and flair.** A star has presence and confidence. Often they are "characters", and do not fit easily into their own tribe. With a pragmatic heart, start your own tribe

6. **Graciously invite "followers".** In today's world of social media "follow me" is a common invitation. Stars always have fans and followers. Graciously welcome others into your tribe

7. **Be thankful** for your followers, for your star power and for the great services you have been blessed to share with the world. Practice showing great humility as a leader. And for every person who serves your needs, pass it forward generously. Start a gratitude journal

About Timi Gleason

In Timi's grammar school, they studied stories of the self-made men (and women) that made our country what it is today. Fortunately, it didn't occur to this little girl that she couldn't grow up to be self-made. The stories of immigrants like Rockefeller and Carnegie and courageous black men like Frederick Douglas and the female author George Sand inspired her to march to her own drum. As a child, her family life was difficult, and she thought that reinventing her destiny was going to be her best bet. She left home at 17 and learned quickly that she had to support herself. Her first direct sales group was Amway where she began to learn how to be entrepreneurial. For her, learning to be entrepreneurial has taken repetitious learning and tenacity. Today, Timi is the mother of two; lives in Californian, and has a Bachelor of Science degree that ultimately lead to her specializing in strategic thinking and becoming a leadership coach. As a senior wellness and weight loss coach with Take Shape for Life, she draws on her strategic skills to help clients lose weight, regain optimum health and quickly reach their goals.

Timi Gleason
The Natural Executive

Email: timi.gleason@gmail.com
Phone: 619-333-6945 (google voice)
Website: www.fatandthirstyradio.com   www.thenaturalexecutive.com

Tina Forsyth

"If I only see the solution, the obstacle must give way."
Napoleon

No turning back

Tina Forsyth never planned on becoming an entrepreneur. After graduating from business school she spent a few years in various administrative and marketing roles in the corporate world – quickly realizing that having a J-O-B was not all it is cracked up to be.

When she was offered a consulting position with a friend's new start-up in 1999 she jumped at the chance – quitting her job and diving headfirst into the crazy world of new media. Alas this company didn't make it (a HUGE lesson in how not to run a biz, hehe) but it was too late – Tina was bitten by the entrepreneurship bug and there was no turning back.

After a couple of consulting gigs she had the opportunity to work with Thomas Leonard, the founder of the coaching industry, as part of his business management team at Coach Ville. It was there that she fell in love with what it takes to grow a business online, and she coined the phrase Online Business Manager (OBM) to describe this new line of work.

In her work as an OBM she continually had business owners asking her "where can I find someone who does what you do?" Taking a look around she could see that there weren't many other OBMs, and yet there was a huge opportunity for those who wanted to pursue this line of work. And so she decided to write her book "Becoming an Online Business Manager: Playing a Bigger Game with Your Clients (and Yourself)" which was released in September 2008. The book quickly hit home for administrative and virtual support professionals who were looking to create a solid business that allowed them the flexibility to work from home while also making a great income.

Tina launched the Online Business Manager Certification and Training program in 2010 to help people create the same success and freedom that she enjoyed, and she continues to provide training, mentoring and support to people on their own OBM journey.

Her proudest achievement is the fact that she has grown a multi 6-figure business from home and is able to be an example for her two girls – age 3 and 5 – that anything is possible.

Tina says "one of my biggest challenges was realizing that it was time to shift my business from BEING an Online Business Manager for clients to TEACHING people how to become OBMs. This was a huge shift in my business model; it was a big risk and was mostly an internal struggle. Was I willing to take the risk? How do I make it work? I decided to hire a coach to help me through this transition - best decision of my life."

"Another big challenge was having a live event booked in Phoenix AZ and then realizing that I might not be able to get there due to some border crossing issues (I live in Canada.) I had people registered for the event already and decided that we had to cancel it - wasn't worth risking my not being able to be there! What we did was turn it into a virtual event instead, using some great webinar technology. We were open and honest with folks re: what happened, we reimbursed them for any out of pocket travel expenses and ultimately only had one person leave the event. At the time this truly felt like a challenge that could end my business - had we not come up with a solution and had to refund/pay expenses. It was a doozy!"

Tina Forsyth

Recipe for SUCCESS!

1. Get clear on what YOU really want (not what others want for you)

2. Quit trying to do it all alone

3. Making a decision is the first step

4. You can't please everyone - especially as your business grows

5. As great as working from home is, you NEED to get out and see people face-to-face as well

6. Don't try to work from home with kids - get help if need be to have dedicated working time

7. Do one business task/activity each morning before you open up your email

About Tina Forsyth

Tina Forsyth is a leading authority on establishing key systems and building virtual teams to help your business thrive. As the author of "Becoming an Online Business Manager and the CEO of the International Association of Online Business Managers she specializes in maximizing business growth potential by coaching business owners and virtual teams on revenue streams, operations management and team development. Having built and managed several six and seven-figure businesses since 2002, Tina knows firsthand how to implement a strong business foundation and the team to support it. Through her Online Business Manager Training & Certification she is teaching this process to other virtual support professionals who want to play a bigger game and become OBMs for their clients. She also launched the THRIVE Hiring System in summer 2010 as a one-stop-shop resource to connect business owners with the right virtual support team to support the growth of their business.

Tina Forsyth
OnlineBusinessManager.com
Box 29016
2515 Highlands Rd W.
Lethbridge, AB, Canada T1J 4Y2

Email: tina@onlinebusinessmanager.com
Phone: 877-576-2229
Website: www.onlinebusinessmanager.com
Facebook: www.facebook.com/tinaobm
LinkedIn: http://www.linkedin.com/in/tinaforsyth
Twitter: www.twitter.com/tinaforsyth

Careers from the Kitchen Table Home Business Directory Second Edition

Tom 2 tall Cunningham

"It's not what happens to you, it's what you do about it that counts"
W Mitchell

Living Positively With Chronic Pain and Disability

Tom started his entrepreneurial life by selling Napoleon Hill's single edition, leather bound, Law of Success door to door to businesses in Ottawa. His work promoting seminars and courses has brought him into contact with Tony Robbins, Zig Ziglar, Jim Rohn, Brian Tracy and Tom Hopkins to name a few. His greatest joy was becoming a Napoleon Hill Foundation Certified Instructor. He also introduced Jim Rohn to a crowd of about 1000 people and met the Prime Minister of Canada. He accomplished that goal and met with him by appointment with his friend Shane Morand, Co-Founder of Organo Gold. He and Shane Morand and Derrick Sweet also brought Mark Victor Hansen to Ottawa before the publication of his 'Chicken Soup For The Soul' book series. He has been featured in several newspaper articles, including the Ottawa Citizen for the way he lives so positively with such a debilitating disability. He has completed the Firewalk, walking about 25 feet over 1900 degree Fahrenheit coals. Working with Peak Performance Systems, Peak Performers Network and Success Source, he sold courses and seminar tickets for Zig Ziglar, Brian Tracy, Jim Rohn, David Chilton (The Wealthy Barber), Tom Hopkins, Tony Robbins and Mark Tewksbury (Canadian Olympic Gold medal swimmer) among others.

The biggest business challenge I had to face was finding a career suitable for someone with rheumatoid arthritis.

Tom 2 tall Cunningham

Recipe for SUCCESS!

1. Show up early to work every day and leave late

2. EVERY executive can be reached on the telephone given enough time and persistence

3. Answer Amazing! Every time you are asked how you are doing and people will remember you

4. God gave man 100% control over just one thing and that is his mind, so focus on the good, clean and positive and off the perceived negative things in your life

5. Be an encourager and good finder

6. Take a speed reading course and read as many non-fiction books as you possibly can

7. Do what you say you are going to do

About Tom Cunningham

Tom Cunningham was diagnosed with rheumatoid at the age of 5. It affects every joint in his body from his jaw to toes. In the 43 years since then, he has had 4 hips, 4 knees and 2 shoulders replaced and been hospitalized about 40 times. He always answers Amazing when asked how he is doing. He has made over 500,000 B2B telephone calls and spoken to well over 5000 owners, Presidents and senior executives.

Tom 2 tall Cunningham
34 Arizona Dr.
Brampton, ON, Canada L6Y 0R6

Email: tom@tom2tall.com
Phone: 416-414-9620
Website: http://www.tom2tall.com
Facebook: http://www.facebook.com/pages/Tom2Tall/121083711291696
LinkedIn: http://www.linkedin.com/company/tom2tall
Twitter: www.twitter.com/#!/tom2tall

Dr. Venus Opal Reese

"Your net-worth will NEVER exceed your self-worth."
Dr. Venus Opal Reese

When Venus was 16 years old she was living on the streets of Baltimore. One night, she was sitting on the corner of Monument Street and Jefferson Street with the stench of beer and urine wrapping their arms around her like to unwanted companions and she had the thought, "God, there's got to be more to life than this." She went to school smelling un-kept and the students teased her and the teachers turned their head. Except one. Mrs. Francis, her ninth-grade math teacher helped her get cleaned up, took her to get a warm meal, and dropped her off at Monument and Jefferson so she did not have to explain her situation. This went on for a while.

For a 6-month period she did not talk at all, because it hurt too much. And where she came from, you never tell. One day, Mrs. Francis marched to the back of the classroom where Venus was sitting in silence and barked, "if you are not going to talk then write!" as she shoved a pencil and a pad into my hands. Venus began to write down her thoughts. Her thoughts came out as poetry. Mrs. Francis read them, typed them, and sent them off to the NAACP-ACTSO poetry competition—Venus won.

When Venus understood what Mrs. Francis had done for her, she realized that the way she saw her was very different than the way she saw herself. Venus saw herself as worthless; Mrs. Francis saw her as valuable enough to take all these actions on her behalf that she did not earn or have to pay for with her body. Mrs. Francis actions told her something she had never heard and experience in her life: she mattered. She had intrinsic value. She had worth. The moment Venus realized she mattered, she had the thought that maybe she could do something with her life; something that went against all the evidence that said she was worthless. And she did. 14 years later she graduated from Stanford University with a 2nd master's degree and a Ph.D.

Venus has performed and closed a show Off-Broadway, presented research at the Sorbonne in Paris, traveled to Italy and Africa, as well as served her country as a Coastie. She has consulted with "O" Magazine, been featured in Glamour Magazine, on ABC News, NBC News, Diversity Inc., and the Associated Press. She has been featured in Glamour Magazine, on ABC NEWS, NBC News, and the Associated Press. Venus is a published academic and a tenured university professor. The list goes on. Her life's purpose and passion is, like Mrs. Francis did for me, to give people the tools to know they matter. When you know you matter, when you really comprehend and live your intrinsic worth, you empower yourself to defy the impossible in your life. You break through your inner glass ceilings just like she did. If she can do it so can you. Let her show you how.

Dr. Venus Opal Reese

Recipe for SUCCESS!

1. Know your worth

2. Take actions consistent with where you are going instead of where you are

3. Learn something new that will forward your commitment

4. Hire experts

5. Tend to what people value instead of what they say

6. Get a virtual mentor and do what they do

7. Identify your Angels, Ambassadors and Advocates

About Dr. Venus Opal Reese

Dr. Venus Opal Reese delivers authentic, high-impact trainings, programs, and keynotes for service professionals, executives, entrepreneurs, associations, corporations, and business owners. Dr. Reese's strategies, systems and services unleash an individual's heart-center to go further, faster while being fulfilled!

Once upon a time, Dr. Reese was a walking statistic. She was living on the streets by the age of 16 amidst violence, drugs, and prostitution. The predictable outcome was welfare, addiction, and ultimately death. However, 14 years later she graduated with a 2nd Master's Degree and a Ph.D. from Stanford University. Dr. Reese knows what it takes to breakthrough through inner barriers. She teaches her global audiences and high-powered professionals how to defy the impossible in professional and personal life.

Dr. Venus Opal Reese is a tenured professor, a published per formative scholar, and an award-winning theatre artist. She has consulted "O" Magazine, as well as been featured on ABC News, CBS News, in Glamour magazine, Diversity Inc. and the Associated Press. Her award-nominated solo performance work was produced off-Broadway in New York City. She is an expert in identity formation through language and strategic visioning. Her strategies, services, and systems are based on 20 years of research, teaching, personal experience, and multiple branches of philosophical training.

Dr. Venus Opal Reese
Creation Consulting Practice
10220 Nantucket Dr.
Providence, TX 76227

Email: dr.vor@drvenusopalreese.com
Phone: 214-551-9233
Website: http://www.drvenusopalreese.com or www.defyimpossible.com
Facebook: http://www.facebook.com/drvenusopalreese
LinkedIn: http://www.linkedin.com/in/drvenusoreese
Twitter: www.twitter.com/dr_venusoreese

Careers from the Kitchen Table Home Business Directory Second Edition

Vicki Garcia

"The greatest mistake you can make in life is to be continually fearing you will make one."
Elbert Hubbard

Your Past Doesn't Have To Dictate Your Future

Vicki's childhood wasn't pretty by most standards but it was all that she knew. Both of her parents were alcoholics and they were too caught up in their own disease and world of fear to notice her, let alone nurture and teach her. She also experienced physical abuse when her father was particularly angry and intoxicated. She grew up feeling invisible and unimportant. She appeared to have it all together on the outside but on the inside she was an emotional wreck.

Maybe your situation didn't involve alcoholism. Maybe it was drug abuse, or infidelity, or physical and/or sexual abuse, domestic violence. Maybe it was absent parents (either literally or figuratively). The point is most of us did not grow up in ideal circumstances.

These experiences shaped her in both positive and negative ways. She developed very clever ways of getting through the fear and dealing with the emotional pain and self-doubt that it caused. Unfortunately, these clever ways did not serve her well as an adult.

Discovering Life Coaching changed Vicki's life. Starting this process of working with a coach and learning how to coach others, absolutely and permanently changed her as a person.

She is now the confident person that everyone thought she was so long ago. She believes in herself and knows what her talents and gifts are. She still experiences fear and doubt sometimes. The difference is now she has some very powerful tools to use when fear and doubt creep in.

Vicki's wish is for you to have peace of mind, confidence, joy and happiness in your life and stop pretending that everything is ok. Stop going through the motions and really begin to enjoy who you are. It is possible and she is living proof. She says, 'If I can do it, you can do it'. Take the step and reach out to someone who can help get your started.

Vicki says her biggest challenge was that she used to believe what she thought! Vicki used to believe that she was unlucky. She said it all the time. If there was a contest, raffle or any opportunity, she wouldn't even bother with them because she was "unlucky". Vicki was a walking testament to the fact that your thoughts determine your outcomes. She believed and thought she was unlucky and so she was.

She began to practice a different way of thinking. Vicki managed her thoughts. She chose thoughts that made her feel good. Instead of thinking, 'I'm unlucky', she chose to think, 'I attract abundance easily'. Vicki said this to herself over and over during the course of the day. Vicki did this for weeks and something began to change. If she found a quarter on the ground, she took it as proof that she attracted abundance. Eventually, Vicki began to receive money from random places. She would find money; someone would pay up on a loan she had forgotten about, she got a check in the mail from the phone company saying she had overpaid one month. Suddenly, Vicki really was attracting abundance easily.

Every raffle Vicki entered; she won at least one prize. Sometimes she won three or four. Everyone was surprised and started telling her she was one of the most 'lucky' people they know. That experience changed Vicki. She now knows that her thoughts absolutely create her reality. By the way, they create yours too!

If you aren't getting the outcomes you desire, take a good look at what your thought patterns are. Chances are, they are based in fear and not serving you. Change your thinking; change your life. Give it a try and see what happens.

Vicki Garcia

Recipe for SUCCESS!

1. Take 100% responsibility for your life. Know that you created your current situation through thoughts and decisions made in the past and you can create a new situation by making changing your thoughts and choices

2. Commit yourself to what Anthony Robbins calls, CANI. Constant and never-ending improvement. You'll never be "done"

3. Feel your feelings and the fear. They will be there whether you try to avoid them or not. Feel them and then make decisions based on what your goals and priorities are. Never make decisions based on how you feel. Feelings lie!

4. Practice Thought Management. Your thoughts determine everything. Choose thoughts that make you feel good and empower you. Purposefully do away with the ones that don't

5. Change how you talk to yourself. Speak to yourself the same way you would speak to and encourage a child that you love dearly. Speak only positive, encouraging, uplifting and empowering words to yourself. Your words have more power than you know

6. Know that the things you believe are your faults are really your most powerful traits. They are like superpowers you don't know how to use. Acknowledge them, get to know them, hone them and use them as a force for good

About Vicki Garcia

A corporate refugee who spent over a decade in the bio-tech industry, and armed with a BA in Biology, Vicki is an entrepreneur who thinks like a scientist. She brings analytical thinking, intuition and a sharp sense of humor into her coaching. She's a real person who deals with many of the same challenges you do – kids, spouses, pets and a busy household – and she's constantly striving to 'up-level' her life and help you do the same with yours. Vicki is so confident you will get value from her coaching; she even offers a 100% Happiness Guarantee

Vicki Garcia
My Kick Ass Coach
1726 Hogar Dr.
San Jose, CA 95124

Email: Vicki@mykickasscoach.com
Phone: 408-723-5290
Website: http://www.mykickasscoach.com
Facebook: http://www.facebook.com/mykickasscoach
LinkedIn: http://www.linkedin.com/profile/view?id=18437827&trk=tab_pro
Twitter: www.twitter.com/mykickasscoach

Careers from the Kitchen Table Home Business Directory Second Edition

Yvonne Silver

"Be more concerned with your character than your reputation, because your character is what you really are, while your reputation is merely what others think you are"
John Wooden

You can be successful - no matter what anyone else says!

Growing up in "middle-class" England, Yvonne should not have turned out to be a successful entrepreneur today! Her family of 4 often ran low on food towards pay-day, and her father was very stringent with the housekeeping money (while her mother stayed home to raise Yvonne and her sister). It was not an easy life...she has always personally been very determined.

This was triggered by an event way back when she was living in England. Her father was a very insensitive person, negatively impacted by being in the 2nd world war, who told her that "You will never be successful in life", when she was 11. She missed passing her high-school exam by 2 marks, unlike her studious sister! Thanks for the encouragement Dad! From that day onwards, Yvonne set out to prove him wrong! That led to starting work at age 12 delivering newspapers. At 15 managing a retail store, by 17 having her first 2 self-employed business ventures, both in multi-level marketing sales.

Today, her coaching company - "The Shattered Ceiling" really speaks to her – as a woman that believes that we can "breakthrough" whatever barriers are put in front of us. Personally she has survived a few (moving from England by herself without friends or family at age 23), raising a delightful handful of a son who is a "special-needs" boy who is now 16, married and divorced then remarried and integrated 2 families with 3 step-teenagers, bought and managed - then sold - multiple revenue properties and homes, to name a few). As an employee, a business owner and entrepreneur, a VP and Leader - her life success adds to a rich experience that she brings to her coaching work. Yvonne says to be authentic as a Professional Coach you need to have been challenged (and survived) in life, in order to bring richness to your ability to help others. Attending Royal Roads University (back to school) recently to obtain her Certified Executive Coach designation was one more verification that success awaits - if you are clear in your intention and willing to work towards your goal.

Having had 6 businesses now, and been involved in 2 significant "high-tech" start-ups, challenges are frequent.

One of the most challenging parts of her life was with a past business - a construction company her ex-husband and she started together. It was ultimately not profitable; however, meanwhile he had hired his two elder brothers to work for him. When the business could not be sustained after 2 years of trying to make it work, it was extremely painful and emotional to let the entire family down by "letting go" of our 2 family employees, on top of almost losing our house in the debt process. Sometimes the biggest lessons are when you don't succeed - knowing when to quit, and NOT mixing business with family... To manage this dilemma, she used her many years of HR experience coaching managers with difficult employees to coach her husband to have those conversations, laid out the options for the brothers impacted, managed the inter-family relational issues in a compassionate manner.

Yvonne Silver

Recipe for SUCCESS!

1. Know your core values and the biggest "defining moment" that has contributed to who you are as a person today

2. Be Deliberate in your intentions: Deliberate, Positive Intention is my mantra

3. Find ways to maintain positive energy - when you are already "up", ready for when you need them next.

4. Eliminate negative words from your vocabulary! (Words include: "No, Don't, Won't, Can't, Shouldn't, BUT, and WHY")

5. Do what you say you will do – your reputation is priceless (it is earned not bought)

6. There are NO MISTAKES in life - only lessons (when you hit a roadblock, ask yourself "what is the learning experience here?")

7. Have a "success journal" and note your successes each day, monitoring what amazing things show up when you believe in yourself!

About Yvonne Silver

Yvonne Silver is a vibrant Certified Executive Coach, with over 20 years of business success personally – and a passion for stimulating positive change. A serial entrepreneur and business owner, previous corporate VP and mother of 4 - Yvonne founded The Shattered Ceiling Corp., focusing on Leadership Coaching, in particular to support performance acceleration for Leaders and Women professionals. She accelerates productivity (individual, team and business), converts positive insight into action, and helps individuals reach their maximum potential - while staying true to their "authentic self". After all, hiring a coach is about seeing results and personal growth – however, staying true to your own values. Credentials are valuable, however, a positive attitude and a wealth of life experience has shaped her values of deliberate and positive intention, and a keen desire to help others reach their maximum potential. Professionally Yvonne holds Certified HR status, combined with an Executive Coaching Certificate (from the internationally renowned Royal Roads University graduate program) and a General Management Certificate from the University of Calgary. Her own extensive personal development comes through following Tony Robbins, Brian Tracey, participating in various outdoor adventure courses held across North America, and being an avid reader.

Yvonne Silver
The Shattered Ceiling Corp
24 Evansdale Landing NW
Calgary, Alb, Canada

Email: Yvonne@theshatteredceiling.com
Phone: 403-999-4749
Website: www.theshatteredceiling.com
LinkedIn: http://ca.linkedin.com/in/yvonnesilver
Twitter: www.twitter.com/shatteredsilver

Careers from the Kitchen Table Home Business Directory Second Edition

Quick and Easy Recipes for the Busy Entrepreneur

Even when we have the opportunity to work from home, the time flies by and before we know it, it's time to fix a meal.

On the following pages, you'll find an eclectic selection of recipes from those contributing to the book.

Most are quick and easy making it possible for all of us, to sit back and enjoy a good meal.

Let's Get Cookin!
Bon Appetite!

Alanna Levenson

Baked Spinach and Artichoke Dip

2 cans of un-marinated artichokes, chopped

1/2 bag of frozen spinach, defrosted

1 cup of grated Parmesan

1/3 cup breadcrumbs

1 Tbsp. of crushed garlic

1 cup of mayonnaise

1 small can of diced fire roasted green chiles (Ortega)

2 cups of 2 different kinds of white cheeses, grated (1 cup of each: i.e. Swiss & cheddar)

Preparation: Once everything is chopped, grated and measured, just pour everything in a bowl and mix together. Put in a low casserole dish and flatten out so it's even. Sprinkle the top lightly with breadcrumbs. Cover with aluminum foil. Bake at 350F for 30 min. Check to see if cheese is melting or bubbling. Once it is, take aluminum foil off and bake for an additional 10-15 min. to lightly brown breadcrumbs on top.

Let cool for 15 min. and serve.

Serve with 1 bag of tortilla chips (or 1 box of crackers of your choice)

Angie Monko

FAUX MASHED POTATOES (Delicious!)

1 head cauliflower

1/4 cup organic half and half

1/4 cup butter

salt and pepper

Directions: Steam cauliflower. Add steamed cauliflower to food processor and add remaining ingredients and chop until smooth. Season to taste with salt and pepper.

Anne Duffy

Recipe for best Margarita

1 cans 6 oz. frozen lime juice
Fill empty juice can with beer
Fill empty juice can with tequila
Pour in blender
Fill blender with ice
Let it rip!

Anne Gordon

Easy Stir-Fry with Buckwheat Noodles

1 tablespoon olive oil

2 cloves garlic

1/4 chopped onions

1 baby bok choy

1 package sliced mushrooms

2 cups broccoli florets

1 chicken breast, cooked, sliced

1 package buckwheat noodles

1/2 cup halved cashews

1/4 cup shoyu, soy sauce or teriyaki

Cook noodles according to package's instructions. Heat large stir fry pan to med./high heat. Heat oil, garlic and onions with broccoli and mushrooms. Add 1/4 water and cover with lid for 5 min. or until broccoli is al dente. Stir frequently. Add bok choy, chicken, noodles and shoyu. Toss together in pan for 2-3 minutes. Serve in bowls, sprinkling cashews on top for garnish. Serves two people

---

Anita Kirkman

Heavenly Spaghetti Casserole

8 oz. Thin Spaghetti or Angel Hair Pasta
3 cups of Prego Spaghetti sauce
1.5 lbs. of seasoned ground beef
8 oz. cottage cheese
4 oz. sour cream
1 cup shredded mozzarella cheese

1. Preheat oven to 350 degrees. Cook spaghetti as directed on package and drain.
2. Combine sauce and cooked beef.
3. Combine cottage cheese and sour cream.
4. In 9x13 pan, layer bottom pasta, then with mixture, next with meat mixture, and sprinkle with cheese on top. Bake for 30-40 minutes.

Annie Kirschenmann

Easy Fried Rice

The most delicious rice dish I know --
Based on Graham Kerr's original recipe

1 and ¼ cup rice (basmati is best – you can use brown rice and you will need to cook the dish for much longer)
One small onion
4 Tablespoons butter (yes butter – indulge yourself with this – it helps to make the dish really special!)
2 cups broth (beef, chicken, fish, vegetable – depends upon your taste and what you are serving with the rice. You can also use water.)
Herbs – your favorite
Salt and pepper

Rinse drain and let the rice dry.
Preheat the oven to 450 degrees.
Melt the butter in an ovenproof pan on the stovetop. Chop the onion and sauté until golden and soft. Add the rice and cook for about 3 minutes, stirring frequently. Add the herbs to taste. Add the broth, salt and pepper to taste – stir.
Cook in the oven, uncovered, for 20 minutes.

You can serve this rice as a side dish to whatever main you are preparing. You can also add cooked vegetables, chicken, beef, seafood or pork!

Arris Turner Charles

The Three-Country Breakfast

From The Abs Diet Eat Right Every Time Guide
by David Zinczenko

1 microwaved egg
1 slice Canadian bacon
1 slice tomato
1 toasted whole-wheat English muffin
1 tablespoon shredded reduced-fat Mexican cheese blend
Arrange egg, bacon, and tomato on one half of muffin. Top with cheese. Toast in a toaster oven until cheese melts

---

Ashley Dais

Sausage, Rice, Green Bean Meal

White/Brown Rice
Green Beans
Chopped onions
Hillshire Smoked Sausage or Turkey Sausage
Vegetable oil/Olive oil Cook or steam green beans to liking
Cook rice until fluffy
Cut sausage into small pieces
Cook sausage until brown
Add Chopped onions and sauté with sausage until tender

Serve sausage over rice and green beans on the side! Enjoy!

Carmen Chandler

Spicy Thai Beef and Rice

1 pound lean ground beef
¾ cup Jasmine Rice
1 medium onion, chopped
2 tablespoons Soy Sauce
1 clove garlic, minced
1 ½ cups water
½ teaspoon red pepper
¼ cup chopped fresh mint leaves
2 carrots, thinly sliced
¼ cup chopped cilantro

Heat large frying pan over high heat. Add beef, stir fry for 4-5 minutes or until browned. Add onion, garlic and red pepper; stir for 1 minute longer. Mix in carrots, rice, soy sauce and water. Bring to a boil. Reduce heat to low. Cover and simmer 20 minutes, or until liquid is absorbed. Mix in mint and cilantro. Remove from heat and let stand covered 10 minutes before serving. Makes 4, 1-1/4 cups servings.

Note: Salt and pepper was not added when cooking this dish as soy sauce is salty and the red pepper adds the heat! But, may be added to suite one's individual taste!

Carol Mazur

Seattle Clams - C.A.T. Mazur

2 dozen fresh little neck clams
1 can beer
1 stick salted butter
¼ c fresh parsley chopped
¼ c parmesan cheese
½ tsp. garlic powder
1 tbsp. flour

Open the beer. Do not drink it. Wash the clams. Cover the clams with water in a large bowl. Add 1 tbsp. flour. Let clams filter for at least one hour in the refrigerator. Add beer, stick of butter, garlic powder, chopped parsley and parmesan cheese to a large pot. Melt the butter in the beer. Place clams in the pot. Be careful not to get any of the filtered water or sand in the pot. Cover; steam clams until they open. Remove the clams and arrange on a large platter. Pour most of the garlic-beer-butter-clam sauce over the clams, leaving the last part that might contain sand in the pot. Serve with fresh crusty bread.

Chris Barnett

Hummus.. high in protein, low in calories

Drain and rinse 1 can of chickpeas. Combine in a food processor with 1 tablespoon tahini, a drizzle of honey, 1 tsp. lemon juice (fresh is better, but come on, we're busy entrepreneurs), and, if you like, a sprinkle of cayenne. Blend to form a thick paste, continue to let processor run while pouring in extra-virgin olive oil until you get the consistency you want.

Put half in the fridge immediately so you don't eat it all at once!

Great with veggies, pita, or baked pita chips.

Christal Mercier

Classic Chili Pie

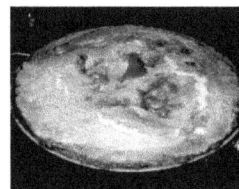

2 cans (15 oz.) of chili, divided
4 cups corn chips, divided
1 1/2 cups shredded cheddar cheese
3/4 cup chopped onion

Preheat oven to 350 F

Heat chili on stovetop until cooked to your satisfaction

In a 2-quart casserole dish, layer 2 cups of the corn chips, half of the chili, and 1 cup of the cheese and onions
Top with remaining chili

Bake 25 minutes

Top with remaining chips and cheese
Bake an additional 5 minutes or until cheese is melted

Christina Suter

Slow-Roasted Citrus Chicken

Take a whole chicken, remove any giblets, wash and wipe it dry.
Place the chicken breast-side down on a rack in a roasting pan.
Cut a grapefruit or lemon in half and cut off most of the rind.
Squeeze half of the fruit into the cavity of the chicken and leave it in the cavity.
Squeeze juice from the other half on the outside of the chicken.
Bake at 275 degrees for 30 minutes per pound.
This receipt is a compilation from a variety of friends

Deb Scott

Super Sweet Apple Dumpling Dessert

12 Servings   Prep: 30 min.   Bake: 35 min.

Ingredients

PASTRY:

4 cups all-purpose flour
2 teaspoons salt
1-1/3 cups shortening
8 to 9 tablespoons cold water

FILLING:
8 cups chopped peeled tart apples
1/4 cup sugar
3/4 teaspoon ground cinnamon

SYRUP:
2 cups water
1 cup packed brown sugar
Whipped topping or vanilla ice cream, optional
Mint leaves, optional

Directions
In a large bowl, combine flour and salt; cut in shortening until the mixture resembles coarse crumbs. Sprinkle with water, 1 tablespoon at a time, and toss with a fork until dough can be formed into a ball. Divide dough into four parts.

On a lightly floured surface, roll one apart to fit the bottom of an ungreased 13-in. x 9-in. baking dish. Place in dish; top with a third of the apples. Combine sugar and cinnamon; sprinkle a third over apples.

Repeat layers of pastry, apples and cinnamon-sugar twice. Roll out remaining dough to fit top of dish and place on top. Using a sharp knife, cut 2-in. slits through all layers at once.
For syrup, bring water and sugar to a boil. Cook and stir until sugar is dissolved. Pour over top crust. Bake at 400° for 35-40 minutes or until browned and bubbly.

Serve warm with whipped topping or ice cream if desired. Garnish with mint if desired. Yield: 12 servings.

Deborah Bishop

Deborah's Favorite Spaghetti Sauce
(Excellent for Entertaining)

This is a blend of pre-made and homemade and is easy to do and winner every time.

1 jar of Organic spaghetti Sauce, your choice. Deb's choice is the house brand at Whole Foods.
1 pound, or thereabouts of dark ground Turkey. Can substitute Ground Chicken, or use no meat.
12-20 organic white mushrooms, sliced.
1 can organic tomato paste.
12 - 20 pitted black olives, sliced.
1/2 organic, red or yellow pepper, sliced.
1 handful or organic cherry tomatoes halved, or 1/2 cup cubed roma tomatoes.
2 cloves of fresh garlic, pressed. (Optional)
1/4 cup organic red onion, minced. (Optional)
Organic Extra Virgin Olive Oil.
Pinch of sea salt.
Your favorite pasta seasonings. Deb's favorite is the "Italian Blend."
1/4 cup grated Parmesan.
Dash of Red Wine. (Optional)
Dash of Worcestershire sauce - to taste.

Two Sauce Pans. Grease Pans with Olive Oil.

Put Ground Turkey, a dash of sea salt and a dash of Worcestershire sauce into sauce pan on medium heat and precede to brown.

Slice and dice all ingredients such as your mushrooms, tomatoes, olives etc. About 7 mins. Place extra splash of olive oil in second sauce pan and add mushrooms, garlic and onions on med-hi heat. Sauté for several minutes.

Once Turkey is browned, ad pre-made sauce and bring to simmer.

Add Olives and Peppers mixture to the Sauté mixture for just a couple of minutes, just long enough to soften peppers and then add whole mixture to your sauce and stir.

Add can of tomato paste stirring gently. Add filtered water to dilute sauce thickness and/or use dash of wine for extra flavor.

Season to taste.
Add 1/4 parmesan and give it all a healthy stir.

Five minutes before serving, add the halved cherry or cubed roma tomatoes.

This sauce can be served right away.

Or, simmer until you are ready, careful to monitor thickness. Or, it will freeze amazingly and be perfect when you need it.

Time Tip. Put the water on for the noodles when you start the sauce and that way you can have them both ready at the same time.

JJ Frederickson

Amazing Green Smoothie

from Robyn Openshaw's Green Smoothies
Diet

Put 2-1/2 cups water in a high-powered blender

Add 1/2 tsp. stevia OR 1/4 c agave nectar

1/4 lemon with peel

2-3 tbsp. flax oil

Puree - mixture should reach 5-cup line

Add 3/4 to 1 pound washed greens (collard, chard, greens, spinach, etc.)

Puree until very smooth - mixture should reach 5-1/2 cup line

Optionally add avocado, celery or cabbage

Add fruit and puree until mixture reaches 8-cup line (bananas, frozen berries, peaches, apples, mango, etc.)

*** I add a scoop of protein and this is my favorite breakfast! I get all my fruit and veggie servings in one delicious meal. Extra smoothie can be saved for up to two days in the fridge. Shake well before drinking. ***

Jean Jones

Chicken Pot Pie A la Mississippi

Hope in Hard Times by Suzan Colon and

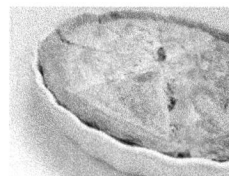

Grandmother

2 Onions diced
2 tbsp. virgin olive oil
3 chicken breasts and thighs boneless, diced
1 Cup chicken broth
½ Cup White Wine
2 Celery stalks, sliced thin
1 Bay Leaf
4 tbsp. butter
6 tbsp. Wheat Flour
3 tbsp. pepper
1 sheet frozen phyllo dough, thawed
Preheat oven to 450. In pan sauté onions in oil, add chicken, broth, wine, celery and bay leaf, simmer 10 minutes
In separate pan, melt butter then add wheat flour and pepper, whisking briskly for 5 minutes to form a roux
Place the chicken mixture in 2 – 2 qt casseroles. Add the roux and stir well.
Drape phyllo dough over casseroles and bake 20-25 minutes

397 Calories, 25 g protein, 18 g carbohydrates, 2 g fiber, 24 g fat, 100 mg cholesterol, 581 mg sodium   Excellent source of YUM!

Judy Winslow

Gazpacho Recipe (Great in the summer)

I make this with coarsely cut veggies and my hand mixer

2 cups canned plum tomatoes
1 8 oz. can tomato juice
1.5 red or yellow pepper
1 cucumber, seeds removed
1 red onion
1/4 cup olive oil
1/3 cup water
1 Serrano chili
2 cloves garlic

Red wine vinegar to taste (a couple of shakes)

Cayenne pepper

Black Pepper, coarsely ground

Salt

Top with croutons & 1/4 cup finely minced cilantro

Chopped Avocado topping optional

Add all ingredients except croutons and avocado to a blender (or bowl and use hand blender). Blend to desired texture. Chill. Add croutons and avocado. Enjoy!

Kathryn Reeves

Persian Rice & Chicken

Chicken thighs - skinned & boned

Uncle Ben's Converted Rice

Raisins

Pine nuts or slivered almonds

Yellow or red onions

Tomato sauce

Worcestershire sauce

Curry powder

Lawry's salt

Cover bottom of 9x13 baking dish with uncooked rice & raisins. Saute chicken in margarine and curry powder and place on top of rice. Slice and saute onion in pan with chicken drippings - add more marg. and/or curry if needed. When onions are limp, add one small can of tomato sauce, Worcestershire sauce, and Lawry's salt. Pour over chicken. Sprinkle generously with pine nuts or almonds. Bake @ 350 for 30 minutes or until chicken is thoroughly done.

Keiko Hsu

**Keiko's Creamy & Healthy Chilled Gazpacho
Soup** Serves 4-6

So easy to make because you toss everything in a blender, and so delicious and refreshing on a hot summer day!

3 medium-sized fresh tomatoes
1 large cucumber, preferably English seedless
1 large green bell pepper, seeds removed
½ medium Vidalia onion
1 – 12 oz. can tomato juice
1 cup plain yogurt, fat-free
1 garlic clove, chopped
3 T. extra virgin olive oil
½ tsp. dill weed
1 T. brown sugar
2 T. red wine vinegar
1 ½ tsp. salt
5 drops Tabasco sauce
Croutons (optional)

Blanch the whole tomatoes in simmering water for one minute until skin loosens. Dip in cold water, and then peel them and chop into quarters. Scoop out the seeds.

Prepare the garnish: Mince half the cucumber and place in a small bowl. Do the same with half of the green pepper and onion. Set the 3 bowls aside.

Cut the remaining cucumber, onion, and green pepper into big chunks, and place them into a blender with the tomato juice, yogurt, chopped peeled tomatoes, and chopped garlic clove. Cover the blender, and then run on high speed for one minute. Remove the lid (or the center cap of the lid) and drizzle in the olive oil, while blending on the lowest speed. Blend in the dill, brown sugar, vinegar, salt, and Tabasco.

Serve chilled in bowls, garnish with croutons and the minced vegetables. Serves 4-6

Khatira Aboulefatova

Smoothies

My favorite thing is making smoothies with my Blend Tec in the morning for myself and my kids. It is quick, easy and delicious. Here is one of Blend Tec recipes for you; Enjoy!

1 cups of grapes
3-4 strawberries, stems included
1-2 pieces of watermelon (seeds included)
1-2 pieces of cantaloupe (seeds included)
2 pieces of pineapple (core included)
1/3-1/2 piece of banana
1 cup of ice

Place ingredients in blender jar in order listed above. Secure lid on top and press Ice Crush/Milkshake on the Total Blender touchpad or button #1 on older Blend Tec blenders.

Kim L Miles

Broccoli Bacon Salad

1 package frozen broccoli (thawed)
10 strips of cooked bacon
1/2 large white onion
1/2 c mayonnaise*
1/4 c sunflower seeds (no shells)

Chop broccoli into small pieces
Chop onion into small pieces
Mix all ingredients and serve cold
* additional mayonnaise may be added to taste

Kimberley Borgens, CBC

Taco Soup Done Easy

1 lb. of ground beef or ground turkey

1 large onion chopped

1 clove of garlic

4 cans of beans (kidney, pinto, white, garbanzo, etc.)

1 can of corn

1 package of taco seasoning

1 package of ranch dressing mix

1 large can of chopped or stewed tomatoes

1 4-oz. can of chopped green chilies

1 1/2 cups of water

Brown the meat, onion and garlic together. Drain.

Add remaining ingredients to a pot and simmer for 30 minutes.

Serve with avocado, sour cream and tortilla strips.

Kristen L. Baker

Chicken, Broccoli Alfredo

This is a lower fat version

1 lb. boneless chicken, pounded and cubed (raw)

1 lb. of fettuccine pasta or pasta of your choice

1 cup of wheat flour

2 cups of broccoli florets

1 cup of promise (butter spread)

1/2 cup of corn starch

4 cups of fat free half and half

garlic chopped or minced

salt and pepper to taste

1/2 cup Parmesan Cheese

1/2 teaspoon dry mustard

Extra Virgin Olive Oil

In a bowl mix chicken, salt and pepper into flour, coat and place in pan with olive oil and garlic. Sauté and keep turning, until crispy.

In a double boiler while your chicken is cooking, melt the promise, when melted add the corn starch, after that is mixed and creates a roux, add cream, stir continuously, add dry mustard, salt and pepper and Parmesan Cheese.

Cook pasta of your choice.

Place broccoli in the microwave covered for a few minutes.

Drain pasta, add your chicken to the sauce and cover the pasta and eat!

LaTricia Smith

Shrimp Alfredo

1 box of fettuccine
1 pack of Pre-cooked shrimp
1 -2 jars of your favorite Alfredo Sauce

Cook the noodles in boiling water until done. Drain the noodles, add the shrimp and sauce. Simmer on low to medium heat until hot. Sprinkle with your favorite seasonings and serve while hot.

Leslie Cunningham

Quick, yummy & healthy
Chicken Corn Chowder:

1 Tbsp. Butter
1 8 oz. packaged pre-sliced mushrooms
3 ½ cups 2% reduced fat milk
1 cup chopped red potato
½ tsp. Thyme
½ tsp. Salt
¼ tsp. Black Pepper
1 (16 oz.) Package of frozen corn – thawed
1 ½ cup shredded, ready-to-eat roasted boned chicken breast (you can buy a roasted chicken

from your deli and use that)
3 Tablespoon chopped green onion, divided

Melt butter in Dutch oven over medium high heat. Add mushrooms and sauté for 3 minutes. Stir in flour. Gradually add milk, stirring with whisk. Add potato, thyme, salt, pepper and corn. Bring to a boil. Stir in chicken and 2 Tablespoon green onion. Cover, reduce heat, and simmer 15 minutes. Ladle soup in bowls, sprinkle with green onions

Linda Adams

Fabulous Brownies

This recipe from my daughter, Lore, is easy and inexpensive as well as yummy. She found it on the Internet and shared it with me years ago. I have it memorized!

Ingredients
1/2 cup butter, melted
1/2 cup unsweetened cocoa
1 cup sugar
2 eggs
2 teaspoons vanilla
1/2 cup flour
1/4 teaspoon salt

Directions
Preheat oven to 350 cook 30-45 minutes

Lynn Doxon

Bacon, Tomato and Cheese Open Faced Sandwiches

One of my grandmother's specialties.

4 slices bread
4 slices bacon
1 large tomato
4 slices American or Cheddar cheese

Mayonnaise or Sandwich spread
Salt and Pepper to taste

Toast the bread and cook the bacon, either by frying or in the microwave. Spread mayonnaise on the bread; place a slice of tomato on each slice.

Sprinkle with salt and pepper if desired. Break a slice of bacon in half and put it on top of the tomato. Top it all with a slice of cheese. Broil the sandwich until the cheese melts.

Lynn Hidy

Parmesan Breaded Pork Chops

4 pork chops, 3/4 inch thick
1 egg, beaten
1 tsp. salt
1/4 tsp. pepper
2/3 c. grated Parmesan cheese
1/4 c. dry bread crumbs
2 tbsp. all-purpose flour

Heat oven 350 degrees. Dip pork chops in combined egg and seasoning and then in combined cheese and bread crumbs. Bake 350 degrees 35 minutes turning chops a couple of time.

Slightly modified version of the one found on http://www.cooks.com

---

Melanie McGhee

Luscious Blueberry Smoothie

1/2 cup frozen blueberries
1/2 cup nonfat cottage cheese
1/2 cup nonfat yogurt
1/4 cup nonfat milk
1 t. peanut butter

1 T. pure maple syrup

Blend it up, pour into your most beautiful crystal goblet or glass, drop in a straw and delight in the luscious creamy taste of blueberries!

Misa Leonessa Garavaglia

Misa's Marvelous Chicken

4 boneless, skinless chicken breasts
2 Tbsp. coconut oil
1 jar artichoke antipasto (Trader Joe's)
Fresh herbs (basil, sage, rosemary, garlic chives work well, but whatever is available and you like!)
Parmesan cheese
Salt

Cook breasts in skillet in the coconut oil on medium high heat for 15 minutes per side. Add herbs and continue to cook for another 5-10 minutes until cooked through but still tender. Add artichoke antipasto and Parmesan cheese and cover for 3-5 minutes to melt. Salt to taste and enjoy!

Rayna Bergerman

Easy Parmesan Chicken

Ingredients:

4 boneless chicken breasts, pounded to 1/2 inch thickness
1 egg
1/2 cup milk
seasoned bread crumbs
2 to 3 tablespoons olive oil

8 slices mozzarella cheese, or more
1 jar (16 oz) spaghetti sauce
Parmesan cheese

Preparation:

Whisk together the egg and milk. Dip the chicken breasts in milk and egg mixture and then in bread crumbs. Heat olive oil in a large skillet over medium-high heat. Brown the chicken in the hot oil on both sides until golden, about 3 to 4 minutes on each side. Set chicken in a baking dish.

Slice 8 pieces of mozzarella cheese and put two on each chicken breast. Pour 1 jar of your favorite spaghetti sauce over all. Sprinkle with Parmesan cheese and a little more mozzarella and bake at 350° for about 25 to 30 minutes, or until bubbly. Serve with spaghetti, garlic bread and a nice green salad

---

Saskia Jennings- de Quaasteniet

Lunch favorite: Shrimp & Goat Cheese Quesadillas

Courtesy Clean Eating Magazine

Serves: 4 can easily be doubled; can be assembled up to 12 hours in advance.

Ingredients:
6 oz. frozen cooked shrimp (peeled, deveined, tail off), thawed, drained and coarsely chopped (about 1 cup)
4 oz. goat cheese, crumbled (½ cup)
½ cup jarred sliced roasted red peppers, drained
¼ cup jarred sliced green olives, drained
1 tbsp. chopped fresh basil
4 small whole-grain tortilla's (each 6-inches in diameter)
2 tsp. olive oil
¼ tsp. ground black pepper

Instructions:
1. preheat oven to 425F

2. In a medium bowl mix shrimp, cheese, roasted peppers, olives and basil. Lay tortillas out in a single layer on a flat surface. Scoop quarter of shrimp mixture into center of each tortilla. Fold tortilla into a half-moon shape, pressing gently to flatten filling evenly inside tortilla.

3. Place tortillas on a parchment-lined baking tray. Brush tops of tortilla with ½ tsp. olive oil and sprinkle with black pepper.   Bake for 6 minutes, until quesadillas are golden brown.   Remove from oven and let rest for 2 minutes.   Cut each quesadilla in half and serve immediately.

Serve with your favorite healthy green salad. Enjoy!

Sherry Prindle

Low-fat Jalapeno Poppers

Ingredients:
12 jalapeno peppers (large whole)
1 block low-fat cheddar cheese
1 block Neufatchel cheese
1 package turkey bacon
1 can bread crumbs

Important: use gloves when handling jalapenos

Halve the jalapenos, remove the seeds and soak in cold water (the longer you soak them the less spicy, so just rinse if you like the burn).

Drain and spread on paper towels to dry.

Stuff each pepper with a sliver of cheddar cheese covered with Neufatchel (the cream cheese keeps the cheddar from leaking out during baking) and dipped in bread crumbs.

Top each pepper with a half slice of turkey bacon
Bake at 350 degrees for 20 minutes

Susan Bock

Sweet Potato Chips

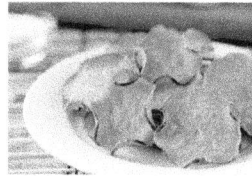

Line a cookie sheet with aluminum foil
Peel the sweet potatoes   'Shave" thin slices of the potatoes on the lined cookie sheet
Sprinkle with olive oil   Bake until crispy   Sprinkle with sea salt

---

Tanya Jones MD

EASY curried chicken

Ingredients:

One Tablespoon or more (to your taste) of a good quality curry powder
Tsp. of salt (or to your taste
Tablespoon of vinegar (white is fine)
Chicken cut up
1 Tablespoon of onion powder

1 cup cups white rice cooked in two cups of boiling water and steamed on low until done (apx. 20-25 min) (Doesn't have to be Basmati... but that is good)

Place cut up chicken in a large pot. Add one can tomato paste , onion powder, curry powder, vinegar, and salt... just cover with water barely stir it all up...

Bring to boil and then lower heat simmer until chicken is tender 40 minutes or so.

Serve the chicken over the rice... have a green salad or vegetable as a side... ENJOY

Tina Forsyth

Unbaked Chocolate Oatmeal Cookies

(a family recipe - super yum!)

5 TBSP cocoa
1/2 cup milk

1/2 cup butter

2 cups sugar

1 cup coconut

3 cups oatmeal

1 tsp. vanilla

Mix first 4 ingredients together in a pot, bring to a boil for 60 seconds. Take off heat and stir in remaining ingredients. Place on wax paper by spoonful and chill in the refrigerator. They are ready to eat once they set.

In The Kitchen With....

Wow – you have to be hungry now! **While you wait for your dish to finish – why not lay back, relax and read the articles from me and my featured contributors that follow!**

Brought to you by:

Sipping Healthy Coffee
Isn't it time you enjoy a healthy, flavorful cup of coffee?
www.sippinghealthycoffee.biz

It's simple, it's easy, its coffeelicious!

ORGANO

In The Kitchen with Kimberly Rhodes

Golden Rules on How to Start A Real Home Business

Have you ever wanted to start a home based business? Maybe you wanted some part-time additional cash flow or to transition to a fulltime career. Whatever your reason there are a few rules which can be Golden and if you apply can accelerate your success. When you discover these tips you should quickly use them to determine the business you will choose and how you will balance it with your life.

Whatever business you choose whatever goal you aspire to, there'll be Golden Rules to guide you, and you simply have to recognize them.

Listed are my 5 best Golden Rules to Starting A Real Home Business:

Golden Rule # 1: Start with the end in mind. Think about what you want your life to look like once your business has reached your definition of success. . Remember, you want your home business to work around your life not you work round your business. The only way to do that is to understand what you want your life to look like first. Think about when you want to work, how many hours, are you willing to work weekends etc... Create a schedule and plug in the times you will work your business so you are not overwhelmed with balancing your personal life with your entrepreneurial pursuits.

Golden Rule # 2: Realize you are 100% responsible for your success/. Most people want to hold circumstances or other people responsible for the lack of their success. Don't fall into that trap. Successful people know that while they can look for support, ultimately they are responsible for their results. When you practice this way of thinking you are not freaked our when something happens.

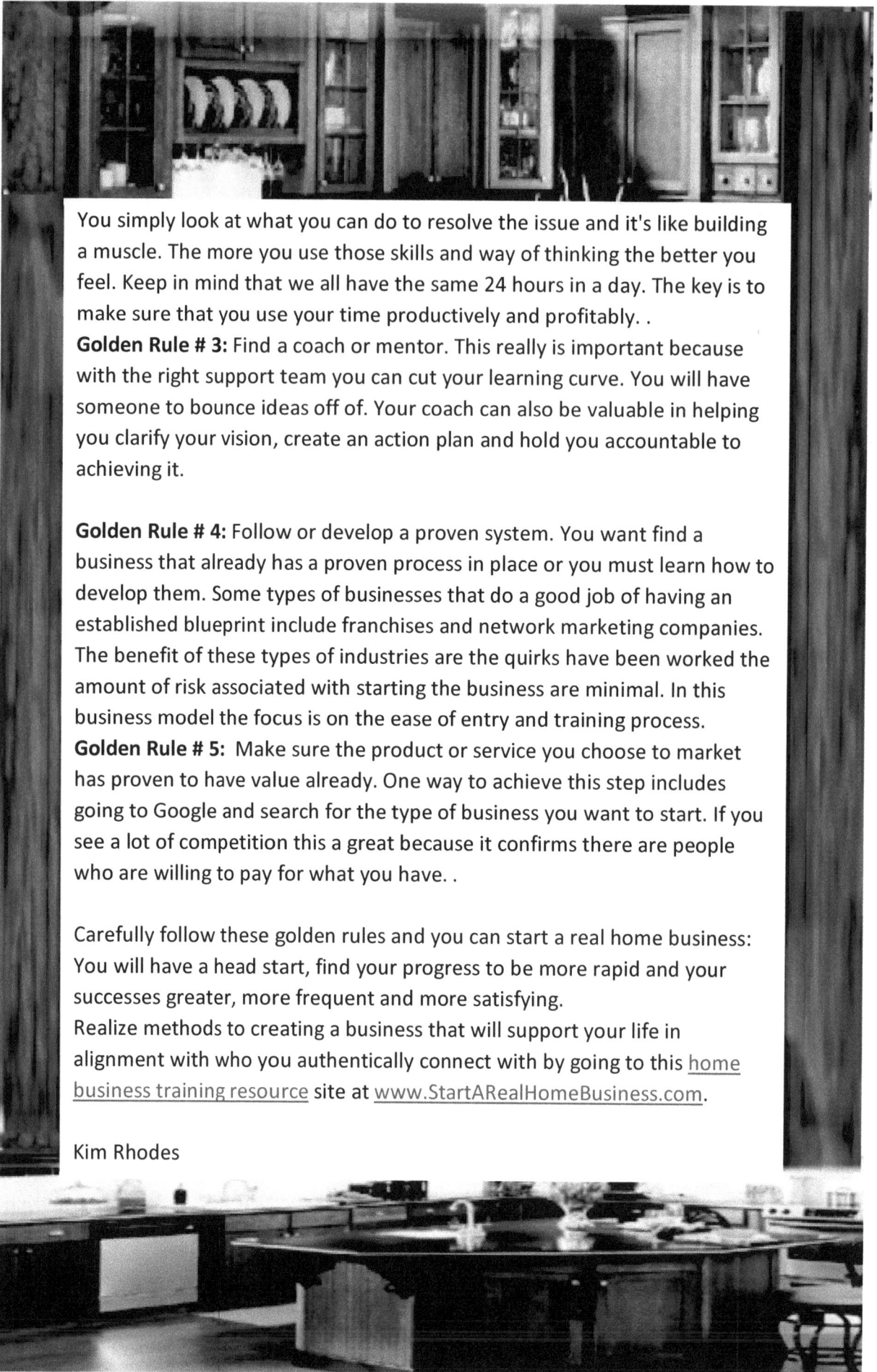

You simply look at what you can do to resolve the issue and it's like building a muscle. The more you use those skills and way of thinking the better you feel. Keep in mind that we all have the same 24 hours in a day. The key is to make sure that you use your time productively and profitably. .

Golden Rule # 3: Find a coach or mentor. This really is important because with the right support team you can cut your learning curve. You will have someone to bounce ideas off of. Your coach can also be valuable in helping you clarify your vision, create an action plan and hold you accountable to achieving it.

Golden Rule # 4: Follow or develop a proven system. You want find a business that already has a proven process in place or you must learn how to develop them. Some types of businesses that do a good job of having an established blueprint include franchises and network marketing companies. The benefit of these types of industries are the quirks have been worked the amount of risk associated with starting the business are minimal. In this business model the focus is on the ease of entry and training process.

Golden Rule # 5: Make sure the product or service you choose to market has proven to have value already. One way to achieve this step includes going to Google and search for the type of business you want to start. If you see a lot of competition this a great because it confirms there are people who are willing to pay for what you have. .

Carefully follow these golden rules and you can start a real home business: You will have a head start, find your progress to be more rapid and your successes greater, more frequent and more satisfying.

Realize methods to creating a business that will support your life in alignment with who you authentically connect with by going to this home business training resource site at www.StartARealHomeBusiness.com.

Kim Rhodes

In The Kitchen with Regina Baker

How to Say Goodbye to Your 9 to 5 to Become Your Own Boss

Leaving behind full-time employment is really never an easy decision to make. Jobs allow us to become addicted to the fact, we know for certain, "pay-day" is happening and that's one thing we know we can count on. However, with today's economy and lay-offs, job stability has lost it's loyalty and people are searching for solutions to keep the bills paid.

Some people are leaving their jobs too because they've simply outgrown the day in and day out grind and are no longer challenged mentally.

Others leave because of office politics or poor pay despite all their hard work. A few leave because they've decided that it's time to be their own boss. Maybe that's you and you're planning a new and exciting future, but you're not quite sure how to exit gracefully.

Walk Away With Dignity

Never burn bridges or close the door on additional opportunities. You and I both know that sometimes it's tempting to finally get everything you've been holding in off your chest right? But let's keep it real, you never know when you might need that former boss as a reference or as a networking opportunity, so make sure that you leave gracefully.
If at all possible, give a two-week notice and clear everything out of your to-do box to make the transition easier for the next person to take over your position. Gather contact information from colleagues and customers so that you can stay in touch so that you can form new loyalties in the future with your own business.

Remember that timing is important. While it's great to dream, dreams don't pay mortgages! So get the finances in order before you wave adios to your boss – you don't want the stress of finances nipping at your heels. Tuck away enough money in your savings to support yourself while your business is in the startup phase.

Being Your Own Boss Has Perks

Being your own boss is exciting, but it can also be trying if you've never been responsible for a business before. Do your homework and have a focused marketing plan for your business and put it to work. Understand that most businesses don't see profit overnight. But with a steady dedication, the possibilities are endless. Remember the colleagues you said goodbye to? Now is the time to network with them. Tap into their circle of contacts to spread the word about your business.

Don't buy into the myth that you have to spend a lot of money to make money. Your business budget shouldn't be spent on fancy gadgets for the office or advertising. Instead, look for all of the free resources available to help you build your business.

You should, however, understand that if you begin with a mentality that you don't have to spend money to invest in your business – there's a huge possibility that you won't succeed in business. For some reason, people tend to want everything free when it comes to their business AND at the same time, expecting potential customers to spend money with them. It just doesn't work quite that way.

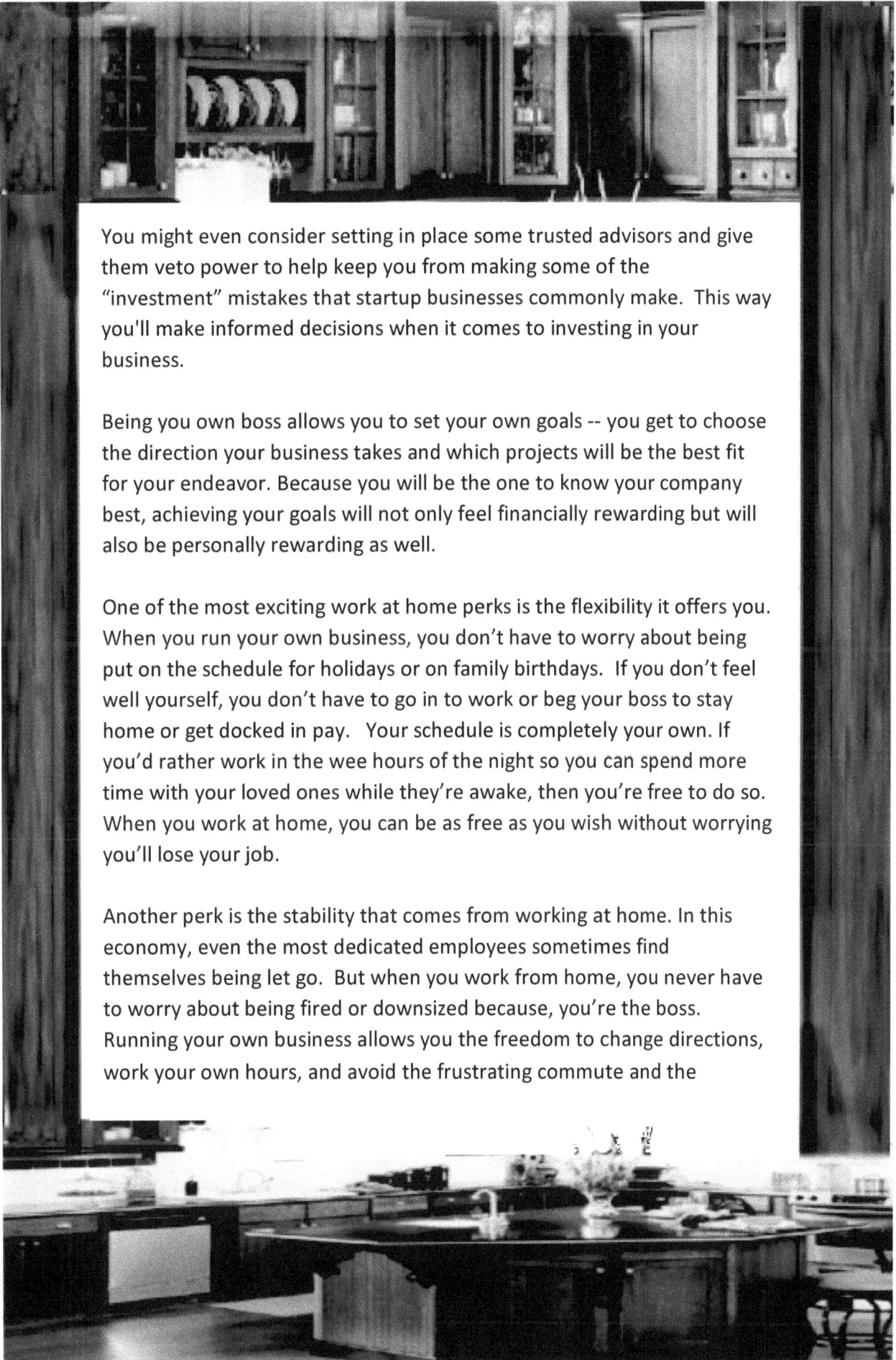

You might even consider setting in place some trusted advisors and give them veto power to help keep you from making some of the "investment" mistakes that startup businesses commonly make. This way you'll make informed decisions when it comes to investing in your business.

Being you own boss allows you to set your own goals -- you get to choose the direction your business takes and which projects will be the best fit for your endeavor. Because you will be the one to know your company best, achieving your goals will not only feel financially rewarding but will also be personally rewarding as well.

One of the most exciting work at home perks is the flexibility it offers you. When you run your own business, you don't have to worry about being put on the schedule for holidays or on family birthdays. If you don't feel well yourself, you don't have to go in to work or beg your boss to stay home or get docked in pay.   Your schedule is completely your own. If you'd rather work in the wee hours of the night so you can spend more time with your loved ones while they're awake, then you're free to do so. When you work at home, you can be as free as you wish without worrying you'll lose your job.

Another perk is the stability that comes from working at home. In this economy, even the most dedicated employees sometimes find themselves being let go. But when you work from home, you never have to worry about being fired or downsized because, you're the boss. Running your own business allows you the freedom to change directions, work your own hours, and avoid the frustrating commute and the

knowledge that you never have to worry about being laid off again. Plus, it's so much more exciting building something yourself and seeing it take off than working for someone else to build their business.

Failure Isn't an Option

People who never fail aren't trying hard enough. They're not putting themselves out there. They're playing in the sandbox when the whole yard waits to be explored. Not trying is a form of failure.
So if you've ever failed, then congratulate yourself. You had the guts to attempt something when so many other people won't even get to that first step. I love this famous quote by Jerry Rice:

"Today I will do what others won't, so tomorrow I can accomplish what others can't."
Jerry Rice

So what happens when you set out to succeed in business and you're met with failure? If you listen to negative internal dialogue, you won't get back up from that – BUT, if you see failure as one more step forward to figuring out what will work, then you'll find the success that you're seeking.

Everyone in life who has ever done anything big has failed. But they didn't let that failure determine their futures. Failure doesn't have to be the period at the end of an attempt. Instead, failure can be the teacher that shows you a way that won't work and spurs you to keep looking for a way that does.

It's All in YOUR Mindset.

While you're trying and working toward success, you have to keep your mind on the eventual outcome, not the little setbacks that are part of every business. Keep your eyes on the end goal - becoming a successful business owner - and use anything that's less than success as your helper - the thing that teaches you perseverance and a way to come up with a better solution.

I hope this hasn't dissuaded you from becoming your own boss. In fact, the intention is to inform you that being your own boss is perhaps the most rewarding career in existence. But you can't go into it thinking there's no work involved – you have to treat it just like you would your job – commitment and with a spirit of excellence. Pursuing your passion and committing to one's own passion and purpose is the best reward ever.

Regina Baker
Speaker, Consultant & Radio Personality
http://www.reginabaker.com

Regina Baker
Speaker, Consultant & Radio Personality
Boosting Visibility, Credibility and Buzz On and Offline
http://ReginaBaker.com

Careers from the Kitchen Table Home Business Directory Second Edition

In The Kitchen with Peggy Knudson

Do I need a Virtual Assistant?

Virtual assistance is not new, but I'm often asked and see small business owners and solo entrepreneurs ask "do I need a VA?"

While that answer varies from person to person, I've found that many don't understand what a VA can do for you and your business. Depending on where you are in your business, the answer differs too. Most people just getting started have the mindset that they can do it all and save money at the same time. But often, new business owners don't know what they don't know.

It's vital that business owners keep their ears open to new opportunities not only for new or more business, but to learn what they don't know! It sounds funny to say "you don't know what you don't know" to someone, and often I've been presented with a bit of defensiveness. It's not a put-down it's often a fact. No one person knows everything.

With the internet growing by leaps and bounds, no one person is really capable of keeping up with the changes, new ways to get things done, and new systems and processes that are available. No one VA can keep up either! You will find that a good VA stays on top of trends and changes and turns to others in their field to help them keep up. We network the same way you do. Getting to know other VA's makes it possible to stay abreast of changes in software, systems and processes.

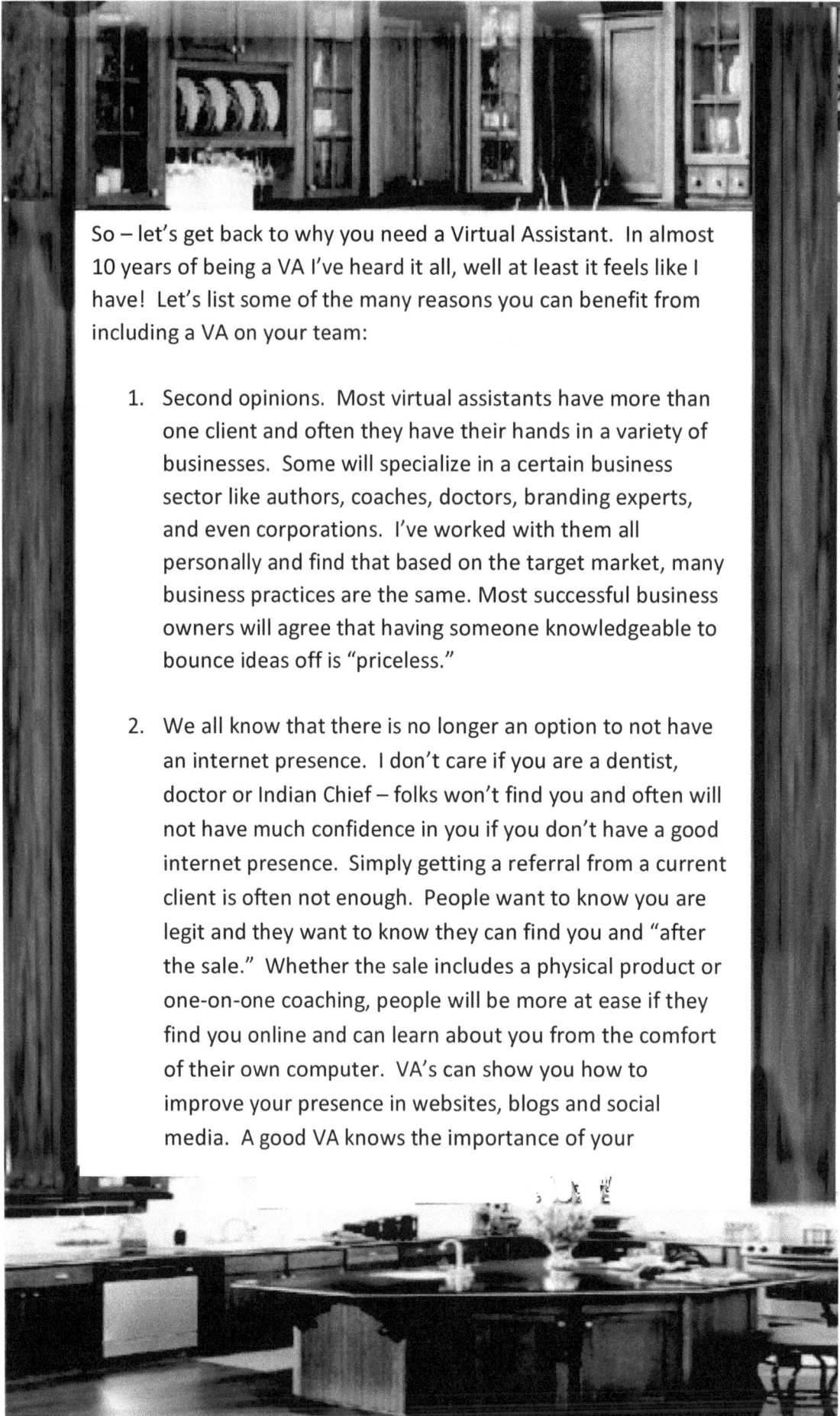

So – let's get back to why you need a Virtual Assistant. In almost 10 years of being a VA I've heard it all, well at least it feels like I have! Let's list some of the many reasons you can benefit from including a VA on your team:

1. Second opinions. Most virtual assistants have more than one client and often they have their hands in a variety of businesses. Some will specialize in a certain business sector like authors, coaches, doctors, branding experts, and even corporations. I've worked with them all personally and find that based on the target market, many business practices are the same. Most successful business owners will agree that having someone knowledgeable to bounce ideas off is "priceless."

2. We all know that there is no longer an option to not have an internet presence. I don't care if you are a dentist, doctor or Indian Chief – folks won't find you and often will not have much confidence in you if you don't have a good internet presence. Simply getting a referral from a current client is often not enough. People want to know you are legit and they want to know they can find you and "after the sale." Whether the sale includes a physical product or one-on-one coaching, people will be more at ease if they find you online and can learn about you from the comfort of their own computer. VA's can show you how to improve your presence in websites, blogs and social media. A good VA knows the importance of your

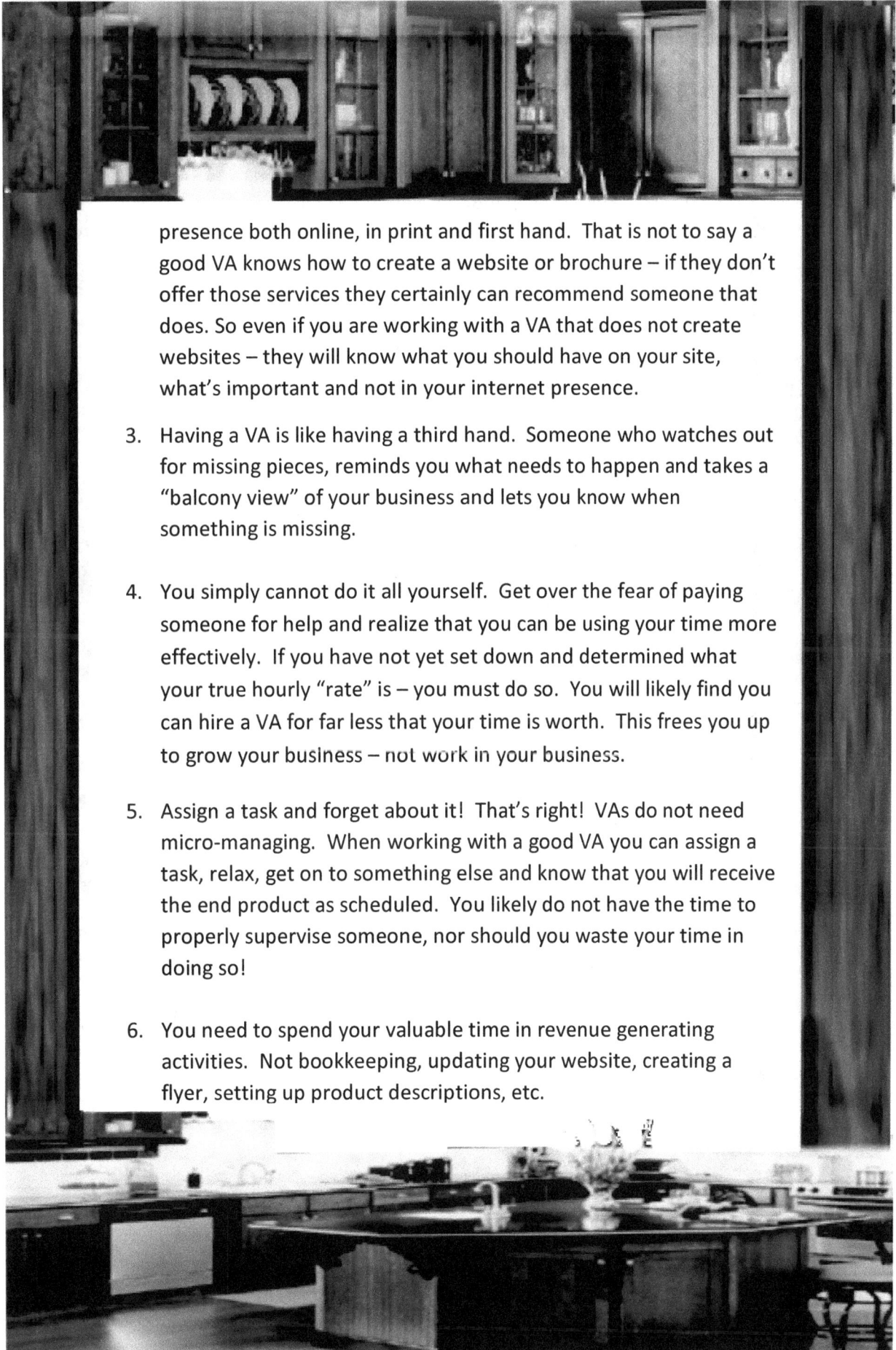

presence both online, in print and first hand. That is not to say a good VA knows how to create a website or brochure – if they don't offer those services they certainly can recommend someone that does. So even if you are working with a VA that does not create websites – they will know what you should have on your site, what's important and not in your internet presence.

3. Having a VA is like having a third hand. Someone who watches out for missing pieces, reminds you what needs to happen and takes a "balcony view" of your business and lets you know when something is missing.

4. You simply cannot do it all yourself. Get over the fear of paying someone for help and realize that you can be using your time more effectively. If you have not yet set down and determined what your true hourly "rate" is – you must do so. You will likely find you can hire a VA for far less that your time is worth. This frees you up to grow your business – not work in your business.

5. Assign a task and forget about it! That's right! VAs do not need micro-managing. When working with a good VA you can assign a task, relax, get on to something else and know that you will receive the end product as scheduled. You likely do not have the time to properly supervise someone, nor should you waste your time in doing so!

6. You need to spend your valuable time in revenue generating activities. Not bookkeeping, updating your website, creating a flyer, setting up product descriptions, etc.

7. You are hiring an independent contractor – not an employee. Virtual Assistants have businesses and run them as such. You won't be paying for "cubicle time", vacations, sick pay, insurance, taxes, etc. You pay for work done – period.

8. YOMO – Your office, movable office. Business trips are more about preparation than enjoying the flight. You can't always be where your data is. Virtual assistance is proving a cheaper alternative for traveling executives rather than utilizing emergency support available through local staffing agencies. Most importantly, it's about reassurance and knowing that someone is there to assist you – regardless of where you are.

9. Virtual assistants CAN do what you need: From web development, search engine optimization, accounting, spreadsheet and system management, telemarketing, inbound and outbound customer service, e-commerce systems, graphic design, email management, scheduling, research, double checking your work, blogs, project management, transcription, event planning, presentations, and so much more!

10. Chrissy, in a guest post on ZenHabits.net explained it perfectly: "Consider them professional organizers, time managers or simply "professional keepers." A VA manages Incoming correspondence, performs general customer care, and that's just the beginning"

11. It's no fun to work alone. I've personally worked with some of my clients for more than 8 years. We've formed great friendships! Everyone needs someone to turn to for a second set of eyes, an honest opinion, or simply to bounce new ideas or tough problems to someone for a new perspective. Plus – there's someone there, standing by to insure your business runs smoothly when you take that long vacation!

12. Last but not least – you simply cannot do it all yourself. If you are of the mindset that you don't need any help, you have enough hours in the day to get everything that needs to be addressed done – with all respect I say to you – you are kidding yourself. I really doubt your passion is bookkeeping, web design or email.

Isn't it time you take your business to the next level. One of more revenue and more fun? Freeing yourself up for revenue making opportunities and tasks, while leaving the routine to your VA will make an incredible difference in your business and your life.

Peggy Knudson
Director/Owner
Outstanding Virtual Assistance
www.outstandingvirtualassistance.com

Careers from the Kitchen Table Home Business Directory Second Edition

In The Kitchen with Raven Blair Davis

Insider Secrets to Podcasting Your Business to Success

There is power in your voice, I kid you not. Eighty percent of people remember what they hear; twenty percent remember what they read. E-Bay, Sarah Palin, CNN, Business Week, 60 Minutes, BBC, Best of Today, ESPN, Barack Obama, John McCain, all have podcasts.

Podcast is the new era. It is what's going on, it's here, it's now, and it is not going away. In fact, it's rapidly growing momentum all around the world. In Two thousand seven (2007), the market estimated that the total US total pod cast audience reached 16.5 million. In Two Thousand eight (2008), Arbitron media research released that 29 million people are listening to podcast all over the world. And the great news is the United States spending on podcast related advertising including sponsorship is expected to rise to four hundred thirty five million by 2012.

This is what every business should be doing. Every single business; big, small, just getting started, or thinking about getting started, they should all be podcasting.

Now, you're probably saying at this time, what is podcasting Raven? I am glad you asked! Podcasting, well, we're going to keep it real simple. We're not even going to get involved with the technology of it. So just think of podcasting as being an MP3 audio or video file that you can upload to different directories. You're putting your digital media files that are distributed over the internet, by syndicated download through web feed. That's all the technical stuff you need to know.

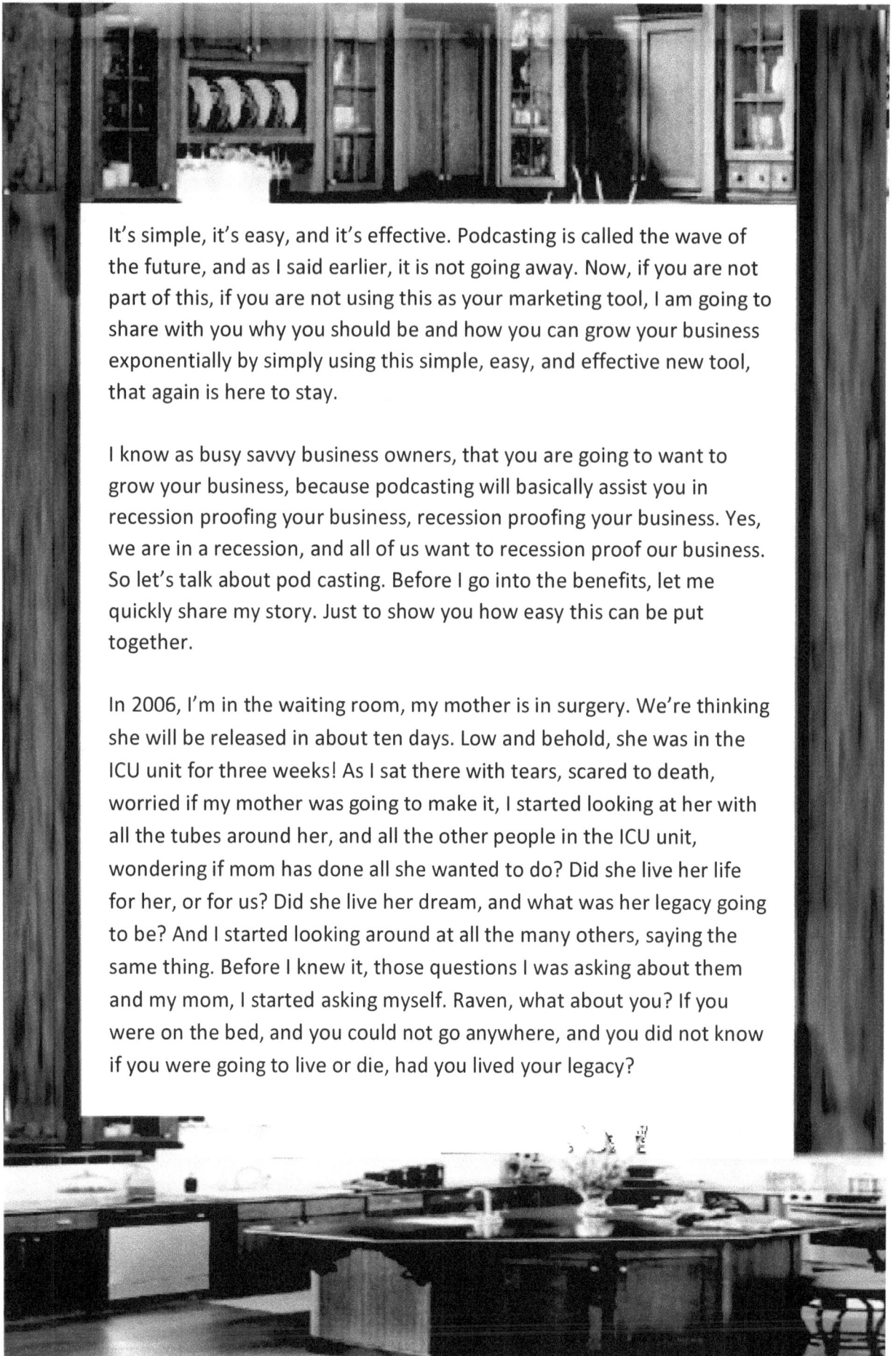

It's simple, it's easy, and it's effective. Podcasting is called the wave of the future, and as I said earlier, it is not going away. Now, if you are not part of this, if you are not using this as your marketing tool, I am going to share with you why you should be and how you can grow your business exponentially by simply using this simple, easy, and effective new tool, that again is here to stay.

I know as busy savvy business owners, that you are going to want to grow your business, because podcasting will basically assist you in recession proofing your business, recession proofing your business. Yes, we are in a recession, and all of us want to recession proof our business. So let's talk about pod casting. Before I go into the benefits, let me quickly share my story. Just to show you how easy this can be put together.

In 2006, I'm in the waiting room, my mother is in surgery. We're thinking she will be released in about ten days. Low and behold, she was in the ICU unit for three weeks! As I sat there with tears, scared to death, worried if my mother was going to make it, I started looking at her with all the tubes around her, and all the other people in the ICU unit, wondering if mom has done all she wanted to do? Did she live her life for her, or for us? Did she live her dream, and what was her legacy going to be? And I started looking around at all the many others, saying the same thing. Before I knew it, those questions I was asking about them and my mom, I started asking myself. Raven, what about you? If you were on the bed, and you could not go anywhere, and you did not know if you were going to live or die, had you lived your legacy?

Fast forwarding for time's sake, it was three months later, three months later, right there in the ICU unit of the Methodist Hospital in Houston, I began to create, format, and produce my show, right there at the hospital. From there, one show "Women Power" was born, three months later, another show mentoring from MLMB was born, and then a year later, I was asked and invited from 1320 WARL am radio to come and do an AM radio show, which I now produce; "Careers from the Kitchen Table". I shared that with you to show you that even in your darkest hour powerful things can happen. I want you to take a moment and think about what is your purpose, your real purpose, what's your passion, what's your message? Now think about how far do you want to reach with that message? How far out, do you want to touch people; locally, across the US, or like me and reach them all over the world? And see people send you emails from Africa saying "your show made a difference in my life."

That's the power of your voice ladies! That's the power of your business message and what you have to offer to the world.

Let's talk about some of the benefits, and then I am going to lay out 7 steps to producing your show. Podcasting, a lot of the benefits of it start at number one: You are perceived as the expert in your field, in fact, you've risen to celebrity status in your industry. You edge out your competition because you're looked at, and "wow, she's a talk show host," and having talk show host added to your bio will definitely open doors, and move you along, and as I said, edge out your competition . Having your radio show in podcast, you will be able to attract new customers and clients almost by default. People will find your Podcast by I Tunes, and other directories, and like me if you also place your show on your website, people will find you on the web. People will begin to hear about you from other people and want to be part of what you have. And through default, you will attract many, many, many customers and clients.

So, with one podcast, fifteen minutes, twenty minutes, thirty minutes, an hour, however long it is, you are able to reach thousands, and thousands, and tens of thousands and possible millions locally, statewide, globally, and it is viral. They are sharing you with their friends. You can podcast video or you can podcast audio. My expertise is pod casting audio. People love listening to audio. And you know what, you don't have to be a tech savvy person, because I can tell you, me sending an email, and going to your elders about it, so don't worry if you say, now wait, how am I going to do this? I don't know anything about computers. You don't have to. You don't have to know a lot to do this. It's simple. It's easy, and as I said earlier it's effective. You're going to increase your revenue for your business. You are going to develop multiple strings of income from your radio. You're going to be able to monetize in many, many different ways from your radio show. These are the benefits, just some of them, from your show, and I could go on and on. You're going to increase traffic, new subscribers, wow.

Bottom line, it is your time to shine. So, why not do it with your own radio talk show and podcast and begin to grow your business experientially. Get your message out, sell more books, get more speaking engagements, and become the star you are because there is power in your voice.

Raven Blair Davis

About Raven – aka - The Talk Show Maven!

America's Leading Authority on Leveraging the Power of Your Voice!

The Talk Show Maven Looking to the Future

Former CNN and CBS Radio host, 2011 has been a banner year for Raven as she realized a dream – launching Raven International! Raven's own broadcasting network, where she'll mentor, train and feature other podcasters and talk show hosts. It will also air replays of Raven's favorite hand-picked shows 24/7. Now you'll never miss an episode of your favorite radio show!

The New Year brings more of the same! Her new magazine **"Behind the Mic"** will launch where current and aspiring talk show hosts will find training, and tips to take your show from good to great! Topics will include how to generate income from your show, get more guests for your show and much more. **"Behind the Mic"** will be a must have for all talk show hosts; traditional radio, internet or podcasting.

Be sure to look for the new **"Boomerlicious Magazine"** too! **Boomerlicious** is for women and the men who love them! Topics will include lifestyle, health, beauty and business tips for the boomer generation.

Careers from the Kitchen Table

(www.careersfromthekitchentable.com) Airs live on CBS *(formerly CNN)* News Talk 650 Radio every Saturday at 2pm CST, CFKT targets men and women (home based businesses & enthusiasts) who are looking to spend more time at home with their children, perhaps have lost their job or have been forced into early retirement and are looking for ways to create a consistent income all from the comfort of their own home.   Be sure to stop by and sign up for your free newsletter and receive your copy of **"The Real Power of Social Networking: Profit on Facebook"** by Regina Baker

Women Power Talk Radio

(www.womenpower-radio.com) - Named one of the Best Top 100 Business Podcasts by Anita Campbell's Business Trends two years in a row, Women Power was created to help women of all ages ignite the unstoppable power that lies within them. Sign up for your free newsletter and receive the e-book **"Seven Action Steps on 'How to Ignite Your UnStoppable Power'"** http://www.womenpower-radio.com

Mentoring from MLM Divas Live (www.mentoringfrom-mlmdivaslive.com) - *Aires on AWOP Talk 247.com* Secret Home-Based Business Ingredients from MLM Women Millionaires Listeners will discover three secret ingredients needed to cook up network marketing success.

Raven's Celebrity Rave (www.ravencelebrityrave.podomatic.com) - *Aired on AWOP Talk 247.com Raven rolls out the red carpet and celebrates those who give back by spotlighting celebrities all around the world...from ALL walks of life...who are making a difference by paying it forward!*

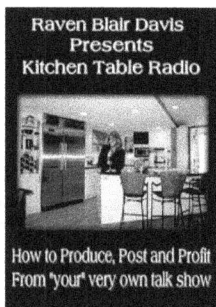

Raven's Books

Kitchen Table Radio Home Study Course (www.kitchentableradio.com) - In this course Raven shares the secrets that made her an award winning radio show host and teaches her students step-by-step how to produce and profit from their own radio show.

BONUS AUDIO: *Join Raven and many celebrities as they congratulate and celebrate Graduation with the students!*
http://www.audioacrobat.com/play/Wfrz1xSh

Broadcast Your Passion to Profits (www.broadcastpassion.com) – *In this book, Raven shares how you can attract more customers to your business with the power of your voice using radio, Internet radio, and podcasting as your platform.*

BONUS AUDIO: *Hear Raven being interviewed on the power of YOUR voice!* http://www.audioacrobat.com/play/W3HLJDhZ

How to Turn Your Telephone into a Cash Cow *(www.telephonecashcow.com)*

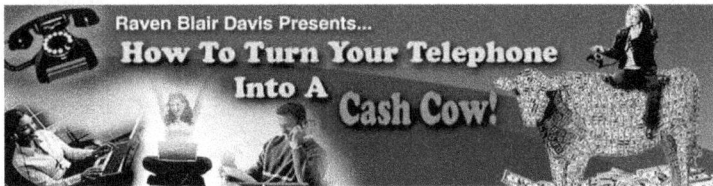

An audio eWorkbook that includes 9 innovative outlets in which Raven shares once again how effective the power of your voice can be in successfully creating or growing your business. When your potential clients hear your voice chances are they will connect with you more than through email. 20% of people remember what they read versus 80% who remember what they hear.

BONUS AUDIO: Join Raven as she explains the *Insider Secrets to Cold Calling!* http://www.audioacrobat.com/play/Wn35XKnb

---

Raven is living proof that you CAN make your dreams a reality with a bit of hard work, dedication and desire. It's up to YOU to make it happen. Every single person, even you, has the ability within to become UNSTOPPABLE!

Raven says: *"From a seed that was placed in my heart in the hospital ICU Unit to interviewing famous thought leaders and celebrities – YES dreams do come true if you follow your passion, be committed to your purpose and NEVER EVER give up on your dream! If you can dream it….you can achieve it!"*

Following are pictures of Raven hanging out with mentors and celebrities!

Raven & Alex Mandossian

Raven & Lisa Nichols

Raven & Joan Rivers

Raven & Sherri Shepherd

To hear more heart to heart celebrity interviews, be sure to visit http://www.womenpower-radio.com *and subscribe to the newsletter too!* Sign up for your free newsletter and receive the free e-book **"Seven Action Steps on 'How to Ignite Your UnStoppable Power'"**

Interested in booking Raven to speak at your next event!
You will not have anyone falling asleep!
email: raven@womenpower-radio.com or call 800-431-0842

Thanks to the Incredible Team!

Without your hard work, this book would not be in our hands today!

Certified Business Consultant, Ecommerce, and Internet Marketing Consultant
http://www.ReginaBaker.com
Reginabaker@gmail.com

Regina Baker

Darnell Brown, Graphic Artist Extraordinaire
http://www.blucanvis.com
Darnell@blucanvis.com

Peggy Knudson - Outstanding Virtual Assistance

Peggy@ovapeg.com
http://www.outstandingvirtualassistance.com

Jaemi Nicholson, Production Manager
JBN Productions   Audio Editing – Videomercials
jaemibnicholson@yahoo.com

Heartfelt THANKS to you all!

Thanks to our Sponsors

The fastest way to grow your business is by increasing the number of people you expose your business to. The more the better. There are plenty of Leads companies willing to exchange your dollars for their names. PM Marketing-NetworkLeads knows you deserve better.

The best way to grow your business is by increasing the numbers of people you expose your business to, as well as increase the quality of what you do, what you say, what and how you present, and how you duplicate this with your downline.

When you work with PM Marketing, you have access to Leads, Tools, Systems and Training. The owner is Peter Mingils. Peter's taught with Dr. Charles King at the University of Illinois in Chicago at the UIC Network Marketing Certification Course. He was a corporate sponsor and on the Board of Advisors for the Direct Selling Women's Alliance (DSWA). He is also the President of The Association of Network Marketing Professionals (The ANMP).

PM Marketing offers 27 Weekly Webinars and Conference Calls for Training and Support, 20 Educational Movies, Several On Line Training Courses, 400+ Archived Audio recordings, and much more for free for their customers and their down lines.

Without exception, you have never seen anything like this before.

Please go to http://www.networkleads.com/bookspecial for a glimpse.
Call and ask for a personal presentation. Mention this book for special offers.

Contact
Peter Mingils
peter@networkleads.com
(386) 445-3585

Great Cleaning Products

Better Business Opportunity

www.enjoUS.com

Michael Rodriquez, President

Creating Liquidity for the Equipment Finance Industry

michelle.rodriguez@hswfinancial.com www.hswfinancial.com

Trini Rocha
956-343-8111

To find direction, first look inside yourself. A life of meaning and passion flows from within; it is not assembled by others.

Beth Dennard, Ed.D
www.brightfuturesllc.com
218-486-0023
bdennard@brightfuturesllc.com

Brad Carran, MBA
Vice President, Sales & Training
"Get Paid to Advertise Your Business!"
www.friendsbuy.net
281-748-9237

The Heartbeat of America!

Raven's Recommended Businesses

Business Listings are In Alphabetical Order

A.K. A COACH AND COMPANY
Annie Kirschenmann
6844 35th St. SE
Windsor, ND 58424
Email: annie@akacoachandcompany.com
Phone: 701-763-6406
Website: www.akacoachandcompany.com
Facebook: www.facebook.com/pages/AK-A-Coach-and-Company/26696788139?sk
LinkedIn: http://www.linkedin.com/in/anniekirschenmann
Twitter: www.twitter.com/#!/AnnieKCoach

Visit http://www.CreativityMatrix.com for your free "right brain – left brain" business tips delivered directly to your email inbox once a month. Just signup for the newsletter!

A STRONGER BOND
LaTricia Smith
PO Box 48522
Cumberland, NC 28331
Email: info@astrongerbond.com
Phone: 910-816-9270
Toll free: 888-568-9619
Website: www.astrongerbond.com
Facebook: www.facebook.com/astrongerbond
LinkedIn: www.linkedin.com/in/latriciasmith
Twitter: www.twitter.com/LaTriciaSmith

Be sure to get your free resources that will improve your relationships at http://www.astrongerbond.com/resources

ADONAI BUSINESS SOLUTIONS, LLC
Kristi Pavlik
332 Stoll
Lansing, MI 48917
Email: kristi@adonai-llc.com
Phone: 517-507-5939
Website: http://www.adonai-llc.com
Facebook: https://www.facebook.com/#!/TeamAdonai
LinkedIn: http://www.linkedin.com/in/kristipavlik
Twitter: http://twitter.com/KristiPavlik

Do you begin each day overwhelmed and not sure where to start? Do you find yourself over-tasked or forgetting things that need to be done? Download a complimentary copy of How to Find Your Ideal VA System as my gift to you.   http://www.adonai-llc.com

AMBIT ENERGY
Ken and Gretchen Umbdenstock
Email: gretchenumbdenstock@yahoo.com
Phone: 847-417-2229
Website: www.umby.energy526.com
Website: www.umbyljoinambit.com

AMERIPLAN®
Joelle Niedecken
Email: jniedecken@ameriplan.net
Website: http://www.deliveringonthepromise.com/dreamsrock

ANNOINTED ASSISTANT
Christine Davis
PO Box 720154
Byram, MS 39272-1054
Email: Christine@AnnointedAssistant.com
Website: www.AnnointedAssistant.com
Facebook: http://www.facebook.com/AnnointedAssistant
LinkedIn: http://www.linkedin.com/in/annointedassistant
Twitter: http://twitter.com/A2Assist

ANOTHER 8 HOURS, INC.

Kelly Poelker

106A East Fourth St.

O'Fallon, IL 62269

Email: kp@another8hours.com

Phone: 618-624-3080

Website: http://www.another8hours.com

Facebook: http://www.facebook.com/kellypoelker

LinkedIn: http://www.linkedin/in/kellypoelker

Twitter: http://www.twitter.com/kellypoelker

If you're a business owner who is in complete overwhelm and struggling to get it all done, you need to put Another 8 Hours in your day. Call me for a free 30-minute consultation. If you're interested in pursuing a career as a Virtual Assistant, take advantage of our free Virtual Assistant Self-Assessment Tool at http://www.academyvp.com/virtual-assistant-self-assessment

AUNT K'S PLACE

Lea Rutherford-Williams

Phone: 877-257-3721

Website: www.auntksplace.org

Website: www.auntksplace.com

Website: www.etenterprises.us

Website: www.LeaSpeaks.com

AUSTIN PROPERTIES UNLIMITED MULTIPLE LISTING SERVICE

Realtor - Alvernad Austin

Website: www.har.com/LadyAustin

REGINA BAKER

Speaker, Consultant and Program Director, AWOP Radio Network

PO Box 24813

Houston, TX 77229-4813

Email: email@reginabaker.com

Phone: 800-294-1461

Website: http://ReginaBaker.com

Please be sure to subscribe to Regina's offer and get your free report "Sales Funnel Marketing" http://reginabaker.com/sales-funnel-process/

BE A LEGACY – QUEEN OF ACCOUNTABILITY
Kimberley Borgens, CBC
PO Box 8633
Stockton, CA 95208
Email: dreamteam@bealegacy.com
Phone: 209-993-7632
Website: http://www.bealegacy.com
Facebook: http://www.facebook.com/QueenofAccountability
LinkedIn: http://linkedin.com/in/kimberleyborgens
Twitter: http://twitter.com/BeALegacy

When you are tired of doing business alone! Get "20 Ways to Increase Your Confidence" free report and more tools on accountability at www.bealegacy.com. Get the E-book Partner Up for Success and begin creating your ideal accountability partner.

BLESS-D
Joan Day-Gilbert
6454 Park Central Way #D
Indianapolis, IN 46260
Email: Bless-d1@sbcglobal.net
Phone: 317-989-8601
Website: http://www.bless-d.com

BONNIE TERRY LEARNING
Bonnie Terry, M. Ed., BCET
Phone: 530-888-7160
Website: http://www.bonnieterry.com
Twitter: http://twitter.com/#!/bonnieterry_btl
Blog: http://bonnieterry.com/blog

All individuals who want to improve their learning skills for themselves or their children whether they have dyslexia, a learning disability, ADHD, are falling through the cracks, or are

even gifted but take too long to do their homework.   Get 10 FREE Homework Tips at
http://www.BonnieTerryLearning.com

BEVERLY BOSTON

Master Coach-For BIG Thinkers
Email: info@BeverlyBoston.com
Phone: 604-727-4363
Website: www.BeverlyBoston.com

For the next generation Big Thinkers get 3 FREE reports on client attraction and solid business building principles for your small businesses go here: www.BeverlyBoston.com

BRIGHT FUTURES CONSULTING

BETH DENNARD, ED D
Email: bdennard@brightfuturesllc.com
Phone: 281-486-0023
Website: www.brightfuturesllc.com

DR. LINNE BOURGET, MA, MBA PH.D.

Website: www.whatyousayiswhatyouget.com

Every woman must know her best to have the most success with the least stress! For help from the national leader in strengths-based business growth, visit www.whatyousayiswhatyouget.com and sign up for our free monthly positive leadership newsletter with practical tips to strengthen your success! Free articles, Dr. Bourget's full bio, and client list, testimonials PLUS 40 products to help you with more gain and less pain! Email us for small business consulting offerings.

BREAKTHROUGH RESULTS, LLC

Cathy A. Hansell, CCSR, MS, JD
Executive Producer and Host, Safety Breakthrough Talk Radio
Email: chansell@breakthroughresults.org
Phone: 888-609-6723; 908-652-1366

Website: www.breakthroughresults.org

CARMEN CHANDLER
Jewelry Designer
Email: chandler.creations@ymail.com
Phone: 281-380-2022

CHRIS CARTER – ATTORNEY
Email: Cris@CrisCarterLaw.com
Website: www.CrisCarterLaw.com
Website: www.CrisCarterMVP.com
The legal and business advice your business needs at a price you can afford. Visit today and receive the audio "Your Guide on Hiring an Attorney"

TRACI CAMPBELL
Website: http://www.traciscampbell.com
Go to the contact page on www.traciscampbell.com and send us your email address and enter in code RAVEN10 in the subject line to receive a FREE audio and transcript as well as 20% discount on The C.H.A.M.P Within program!! (book and workbook)

CREATION CONSULTING PRACTICE
Dr. Venus Opal Reese
10220 Nantucket Dr.
Providence, TX 76227
Email: dr.vor@drvenusopalreese.com
Phone: 214-551-9233
Website: http://www.drvenusopalreese.com or www.defyimpossible.com
Facebook: http://www.facebook.com/drvenusopalreese
LinkedIn: http://www.linkedin.com/in/drvenusoreese
Twitter: www.twitter.com/dr_venusoreese

For executives, entrepreneurs, CEOs and heart-centered agents of change who want to make BIG money, make a difference, be FULFILLED, and be PROUD of yourself—all at the same time! Visit http://www.defyimpossible.com

TOM 2 TALL CUNNINGHAM

34 Arizona Dr.
Brampton, ON, Canada L6Y 0R6
Email: tom@tom2tall.com
Phone: 416-414-9620
Website: http://www.tom2tall.com
Facebook: http://www.facebook.com/pages/Tom2Tall/121083711291696
LinkedIn: http://www.linkedin.com/company/tom2tall
Twitter: www.twitter.com/#!/tom2tall

I would love to work with you to encourage and support you in reaching your definite chief aim and goals in life in whatever way I can. Organo Gold is the official and the only Partner of the Napoleon Hill Foundation. They sell the world's healthiest coffee, infused with 100% organic ganoderma. To request free samples, fill in your address and telephone number at the link http://tom2tall.coffeemillions.com/tour/products/

COUCH TALK LIFE COACHING

Ashley Dais
326 Kingsport Drive, NE
Concord, NC 28025
Email: couchtalklifecoaching@gmail.com
Phone: 704-619-7028
Website: www.ashleydais.com
Facebook: http://www.facebook.com/#!/CouchTalkLifeCoaching
Twitter: http://twitter.com/#!/AshleyDias

I am a counselor and life coach and I work with men and women who struggle with mental, emotional, and social roadblocks to help them become unstuck and break negative cycles. Do you or someone you know struggles with being stuck? I provide a FREE Planning Guide Session for those who are ready to get started to becoming free of their "stuck Syndrome!" Sign up at http://www.ashleydais.com

CONFIDENCE CONNECTIONS

Kathleen B Schulweis, CPCC, PCC
Strategic Coaching for Success
Phone: 323-935-6477
Website: http://www.linkedin.com/in/confidenceconnections

Need a Confidence Boost? http://www.confidenceconnections.com for help and support!

MARIANA COOPER

Website: www.trustyourahamoments.com

Website: www.ahamoments.tv

Facebook: www.facebook.com/ahamomentsinc

To get your free gifts to include the full audio of my sold out Teleseminar "God Won't Deliver a Million Dollars Into Chaos" , including a powerful guided meditation and the free transcript plus a subscription to the Aha! Moments Ezine with free tips, articles and info for Enlightened Entrepreneurs go to: www.trustyourahamoments.com

CREATING BEING WELL

Saskia Jennings-de Quaasteniet

37 Silver Point Drive

Parry Sound, ON, Canada P2A 2W8

Email: Saskia@creatingbeingwell.com

Phone: 705-773-8411

Website: www.creatingbeingwell.com

Saskia is the one for heart-centered support & guidance when YOU are ready to move forward in life: to feel better, happy, more balanced and open for inspiration, so you can easily manage your life's challenges. We will be Creating Being Well together! www.creatingbeingwell.com

DR. SARAH DAVID, PH.D.

Email: sdavid@consultant.com

Visit www.empoweredwomensinstitute.com for a free report on the 7 Characteristics of Successful Entrepreneurs and an opportunity to take a free personal brand assessment, subscribe to the Empowered Women's Institute Newsletter for exciting upcoming announcements on pre-launch activities, training, networking and an opportunity to be a *Charter Member* as we launch our new online community to help you lead, learn and connect with other empowered women!

BILL DAVIS

Lifestyle Coach

Website: www.mydailydirector.com

DISCOVER THE AMAZING YOU! COACHING
Deb Scott
PO Box 551
Newburyport, MA 01950
Email: deb@greenskyandbluegrass.com
Phone: 978-462-2215
Website: http://www.greenskyandbluegrass.com
Facebook: http://www.facebook.com/authorandmotivationalspeaker
LinkedIn: http://www.linkedin.com/in/debscottauthorspeaker
Twitter: @greenskydeb

If you want to be your best in Business or the business of Living - I can help you! Click here to get your FREE GIFT of three 30 minute Coaching sessions - http://www.greenskyandbluegrass.com/free-professional-coaching

DREAMS ROCK
JOELLE NIEDECKEN
Email: jniedecken@ameriplan.com
Phone: 877-303-4065 432-689-9447
Website: http://www.dreamsrock.com

Visit http://www.deliveringonthepromise.com/dreamsrock TODAY to receive your FREE prescription card valued at $100

EDWARDS & ASSOCIATES
Linda Howell Edwards
PO Box 724051
Atlanta, GA 31139
Email: LEdwards@theedwardsgroup.org
Phone: 678-239-4479
Website: www.theedwardsgroup.org

FRANKLIN QUEST EDUCATION AND LEADERSHIP FOUNDATION, INC.
Tyra Franklin, MBA/PA
"Your destiny is hiden among your fears"
 Website: http://franklinquest.pbworks.com

FYNTOON SOLUTIONS

Sheila McClain

2000 W. Kettleman Lane Ste 201A

Lodi, CA 95242

Email: fyntoon@yahoo.com

Phone: 209-712-2073

Website: www.fyntoonsolutions.com

Facebook: http://facebook.com/Sheila.McClain.CertifiedLifeCoach

ELLEN GAVER

Email: EcoMomTeam@charter.net

Phone: 805.474.822

Website: http://www.EcoMomTeam.com

LOU GILES

Independent Associate

Phone: 832-513-5916

Website: www.smartchoicelegal.com

GLOW LIFE COACHING

Anne Gordon

2521 NW Coe Ct.

Bend, OR 97701

Email: anne@glowlifecoaching.com

Phone: 541-306-4445

Website: www.glowlifecoaching.com

Facebook: www.fcebook.com/annegordonor

LinkedIn: www.linkedin.com/pub/anne-gordon/23/848/7a5

Visit www.glowlifecoaching.com to sign up for her newsletter and blog. You will be the first to hear about events, products and free stuff. Plus, you will receive inspiring stores and tools to help you on your journey.

GREAT SMALL BUSINESS ADVICE

Allison Babb

Small Business Coach

Email: info@greatsmallbusinessadvice.com

Phone: 678-401-7948

Website: www.GreatSmallBusinessAdvice.com

For a 1-hour audio on How to Attract More Clients, you can go to
www.greatsmallbusinessadvice.com/audio

GROUND LEVEL CONSULTING

Christina Suter

3579 E Foothill Blvd #320

Pasadena, CA 91107

Email: Christina@groundlevel-consulting.com

Phone: 310-463-5942

Website: www.grourndlevel-consulting.com

LinkedIn: http://www.linkedin.com/in/christinalsmith

Let me help clarify what your business needs in a free initial consultation: Fill in the Contact form on my website, mention "Kitchen Table" in your message, and Opt In for the newsletter and access to the audio archives from Christina talk show "Ask Christina First" on the Amazing Woman Of Power Network

HAIR DREAMS BY CHRISTAL, INC.

Christal Mercier

514 Texas Parkway, Suite A

Missouri City, Texas 77489

Email: HairDreamsByChristalInc@yahoo.com

Phone: 877-499-9433

Website: www.HairDreamsbyChristal.org

LinkedIn: http://www.linkedin.com/pub/christal-mercier/20/238/8a5

Twitter: HairDreamsInc

We focus on women and children who suffer from various types of hair loss, due to cancer, alopecia, medication side-effects, etc. For a more detailed list of our services or to inquire about donating to our organization, please visit: http://www.hairdreamsbychristal.org

MONICA HANCOCK

Window Fashions Designer

Email: mhancock@creationsbymonica.net

Phone: (281) 820-1977

Website: www.creationsbymonica.net

For ideas on window treatment designs, you can go to www.creationsbymonica.net

HARMONY HARBOR HYPNOSIS

Angie Monko

2476 Pheasant Run Drive

Maryland Heights, MO 63043

Email: 4monko@att.net

Phone: 314-422-6520

Website: www.harmonyharbor.com

Facebook: www.facebook.com/HarmonyHarborHypnosis

LinkedIn: www.linkedin.com/in/harmonyharbor

Twitter: www.twitter.com/angiemonko4monko@att.net

Visit http://www.harmonyharbor.com and get access to my free newsletter, Create Your Destiny, and free report on how to release weight forever without willpower. You can also apply for a complementary coaching session!

ROBERTA HARRIS

Motivational Life Coaching

Motivational Speaking

Email: rdhartist@att.net

Phone: 713-256-9037

Website: www.robertaharris.com

HEIR TO LIFE, LLC

Arris Charles

11601 Shadow Creek Pkwy #317

Pearland, TX 77584

Email: Arris@HeirToLife.com

Phone: 832-729-6317

Website: www.HeirToLife.com
LinkedIn: http://www.linkedin.com/in/heirtolife
Twitter: CoachArris

Tired of just going through the motions? Ready to empower your mind, body and spirit to fulfill God's extraordinary calling for your life? Wondering how to balance your life on the inside and out? Visit http://www.InnerLifeFitness.com to download a free report to help you live with Authentic Life Balance.

HELP 2 GROW LIFE COACHING

MARTHA JOHNSON

Phone: 678-949-9195
Website: www.Help2GrowLifeCoaching.com
Help2GrowTalkRadio: www.help2grow.podomatic.com

VICTOR HOLMAN

Business Performance Coach
Email: victor.holman@lifecycle-performance-pros.com
Phone: 202-415-5363
Website: www.Lifecycle-Performance-Pros.com

To get a FREE BUSINESS MANAGEMENT KIT and jumpstart your business, go to www.Lifecycle-Performance-Pros.com

DR. RENEE HORNBUCKLE

Email: reneehornbuckle@sbcglobal.net
Website: www.reneehornbuckle.com

If you're already a Coach or you would like to become a client, you can learn more about the benefits of being a Compass Client/Coach. Visit www.mylifecompass.com/womenofinfluence to find out more and join my team as a client or become a Certified Compass Coach!

I LOVE MY LIFE! COACHING

Alanna Levenson

13547 Ventura Blvd., #242,

Sherman Oaks, CA 91423

Email: Alanna@i-love-my-life.com

Phone: 213-400-7970

Website: http://i-love-my-life.com

Facebook: https://www.facebook.com/pages/I-Love-My-Life-Coaching/192310894122167

LinkedIn: http://www.linkedin.com/pub/alanna-levenson/0/3a0/7a0

ILLUMINATED LIFE, LLC

Melanie McGhee

718 Hickory Lane

Maryville, TN 37801

Email: Melanie@peacefruit.com

Phone: 865-384-4104

Website: http://www.peacefruit.com

Facebook: http://www.facebook.com/peacefruit

Twitter: http://www.twitter.com/melaniemcghee

I provide small group retreats, private retreats, coaching and psychotherapy. Visit my site - http://www.peacefruit.com - when you opt-in, I will send you a free meditation recording along with regular encouragement and insights about how to create a more peace-filled life.

IMPACT COACHING LLC

Susan Brown, Ed.S.

Certified Leadership and Success Coach

Email: susanbrown.impactcoaching@gmail.com

Phone: 678-787-2406

Website: www.impactcoach.wordpress.com

Internet Radio Show: http://thewinonline.com/shows/awaken-the-leader

Take the first step in getting your personal leadership development plan by Contacting Susan for a free consultation at 678-787-2406 or log on to her website at www.impactcoach.wordpress.com.

Listen to Susan on *Awaken the Leader Within* found at: http://thewinonline.com/shows/awaken-the-leader

INSPIRED LEARNING CENTERS CANADA INC
Rayna Bergerman
56 Deermoss Cres. SE
Calgary, AB, Canada T2J 6P4
Email: Rayna@inspiremorestudents.com
Phone: 403-863-1939
Website: www.inspiremorestudents.com
Facebook: www.facebook.com/rayna.bergerman
LinkedIn: http://ca.linkedin.com/pub/rayna-bergerman/30/b7b/965
Twitter: www.twitter.com/raynabergerman

To grow a confident and capable learner download your FREE 7 Part Mini-Course focusing on action steps you can take right now to improve your child's academic and personal growth. Go to www.InspireMoreStudents.com

INTERNATIONAL GIFT EXPRESS
Carol Newman
A Gift of Excellence
Phone: 415-381-5252
Website: www.vernoncompany.com/newman.htm

LIBERATED LIFE COACHING
CRISS ITTERMANN
Life & Small Business Coach
Email: info@liberatedlifecoaching.com
Phone: 866-993-8932
Website: LiberatedLifeCoaching.com

For an exclusive 60 minute free audio called "SURRENDER™ to Passion" please visit www.revx.me/table

JJ THE LIFE COACH
JJ Frederickson
PO Box 113
Honey Creek, WI 53138
Email: JJ@JJthelifecoach.com

Phone: 414-732-3320
Website: http://www.jjthelifecoach.com
Facebook: http://www.facebook.com/jjthelifecoach
LinkedIn: http://www.linkedin.com/in/jjthelifecoach
Twitter: http://twitter.com/jjthelifecoach

The first half of life you're on the treadmill, maybe managing a household, forging a career, or both. As a mid-lifer, things should be easier. You worked hard to get where you are, and now you're ready for some fun. But you're still on the treadmill and can't seem to get off. Why? For years, stress and fear did a tango in your brain -- a tango that's created mental patterns and habits that hold you back and keep joy at arm's length.   JJ the Life Coach can help you take back your brain and take back your life! JJ takes people from midlife stress to their midlife best. She coaches and teaches mid-lifers how to tackle stress in their jobs, relationships, blended families, finances, and retirement. She is the creator of Live Life Easy Stress Solution DVD and Workbook, and as WTMJ's original Life Coaching Expert, her weekly TV segment gave viewer tips on how to get out of their heads and start living life easy! Want less stress, right now? Sign up for the free 90-Second Trick to Stop Stress in its Tracks at www.JJtheLifeCoach.com

JEAN JONES
2601 Cartwright Rd Suite D259
Missouri City, TX 77459
Email: jaepolk4@aol.com
Phone: 281-702-220

Email Jean for more on free products for you as an Arbonne pamper hostess, free spa day and new consultant training as well as Holiday Specials and free gift wrapping!

JSYI A DIVISION OF RIGHT ON ENTERPRISES
Deborah Bishop
414 Munn Rd.
Nashville, TN 37214
Email: livealimitlesslife@gmail.com
Phone: 615-376-9905 / 800-582-8772
Website: http://www.deborahbishop.com
Facebook: http://www.facebook.com/deborahbishop

Your Personal Solution to Professional Success.
Whether you are starting up or starting over, discover how you can stop struggling and start

thriving today. Schedule your FREE one-on-one Consultation now at
http://www.deborabishop.com

KIM L. MILES, LLC

Kim L. Miles
3931 S Jebel Way
Aurora, CO 80013
Email: kim@kimlmiles.com
Phone: 303-690-7661
Website: http://www.kimlmiles.com
Facebook:http://www.facebook.com/media/set/?set=a.2256864113100.118499.1593278215&saved#!/CoachKimMiles
LinkedIn: Kim Miles (ACC)
Twitter: Kim_Miles

Sign up for my newsletter and a 30 minute complimentary phone coaching session via
http://www.kimlmiles.com

KIMBER KING

Email: Kimber_king@msn.com
Phone: 801-923-8744
Website: www.kimberking.com

Kimber King is an expert in Social Networking and what it takes to make money from home using the internet. Visit www.kimberking.com for a FREE 30 minute recording that you will learn 4 simple steps you can start using right now to turn your "play-time" on Social Networking sites like FaceBook and Twitter into profits!

LDRA PERFORMANCE CONSULTANTS, INC.

Linda Adams
PO Box 12119
Baltimore, MD 21281
Email: linda@letschataboutcredit.com
Phone: 888-592-4512
Website: www.letschataboutcredit.com
Twitter: credittweet

Our 52 week online Personal Credit Builder Program is designed to guide you through the conflicting information out there on how to improve your credit. We help you create a strong foundation so that you will be able to build and maintain your good credit. Credit education is for everyone. Because Identity Theft is a rising threat to everyone's good credit you can e-mail me for a free special report on Identity Theft and a short training video on how to get your free credit report from www.AnnualCreditReport.com.

DIANE LAMPE
Entrepreneur and mentor, best-selling author
Email: diane@lampeteam.com
Phone: 972-670-7691
Website: www.lampeteam.com

For how to create a business helping protect families or to view our services, you can go to www.lampeteam.com

LEARNING RX
Clara M. Samuelson
Phone: 832.886.5878
Website: www.learningrx.com/sugerland

DIAMOND LEONE
Creative Coach
Email: diamondleone@gmail.com
Phone: 703-209-9012
Website: www.DiamondLeone.com

To get a free guide to help you discover what you're passionate about, go to www.diamondleone.com/passion

ANNE-MARIE LERCH
Business Strategist & Mindset Coach
Email: info@CoachMeNow.com
Phone: 1-877-83-SMILE (76453)
Website: www.CoachMeNow.com
For a free Audio Summary of "Think and Grow Rich" go to www.CoachMeNow.com

HONEY LEVEEN, LUTCF, CLTC

Your LTC Insurance Specialist LLC

Phone: 713-988-4671

Website: www.honeyleveen.com

LIFE ARENA COACHING

Lynn Doxon

4005 Tara NE

Albuquerque, NM 87111

Email: lynn@lifearenacoaching.com

Phone: 505-459-3597

Website: www.lifearenacoach.com

Facebook: http://www.facebook.com/home.php#!/pages/Life-Arena-Retirement-Coaching/231602116866331

LinkedIn: https://www.linkedin.com/e/fpf/37456703

Twitter: @lynndoxon

I am eager to work with anyone who is retired or will soon retire to create a vision and plan for the next 5 to 30 years. Bring vision, energy and direction to your retirement years. To discover the best second career to support your retirement goals go to www.lifearenacoach.com

LIFE BY DESIGN COACHING/RESULTS CONSULTING

Dr. Lisabeth Saunders Medlock

4420 Mimosa Rd

Columbia, SC 29205

Email: lbdcoaching@aol.com

Phone: 803-960-1844

Website: www.lifebydesigncoaching.org

Facebook: http://www.facebook.com/#!/pages/Life-By-Design-Coaching/181753829028

LinkedIn: http://www.linkedin.com/pub/lisbeth-saunders-medlock/8/bb7/7b6

Twitter: http://twitter.com/#!/lbdcoaching

At Life By Design Coaching I offer individual coaching, workshops, group and individual assessments and a range of consulting services. I focus on personal accountability-the belief that you are in control of your life and the decisions you make that shape your life and create your path. You design your life!

Our coaching company, located in Columbia, SC, focuses on assisting you to redesign, revitalize and redirect your life to achieve your goals and dreams. We address the gap between what is and what can be. Having a life coach is like having a personal trainer to help you reach your life goals.

We specialize in helping clients who seek coaching during a period of transition. You may be feeling stuck, facing difficult decisions, wanting to improve your health and wellness, changing careers, or going through relationship issues.

Life coaching can help you turn life's challenges into a springboard for new beginnings. Instead of just coping and "getting through it", you will begin to see new options and new opportunities to actively live by design, not default.   I offer a FREE half hour coaching session and am often running special packages. Check out www.lifebydesigncoaching.org to sign up for a free session and to learn more about the services. The website also includes free life coaching tip of the week videos.

LIFE CAREER BUSINESS COACH

Dr. Fred (Coach Doc Fred) Simkovsky

3076 Paige Ave.

Simi Valley, CA 93063

Email: fredsimkovsky@yahoo.com

Phone: 510-506-8281

Website: http://www.lifecareerbusinesscoach.com

Facebook: http://www.facebook.com/fsimkovsky

LinkedIn: http://www.linkedin.com/in/fredsimkovsky

Self-employed people, Under-employed people, Unemployed people who want to become successful in their lives and careers. I provide individualized coaching, simple conversation, an action plan, and support. Group coaching and mentoring. Training and Development. Sign up for my monthly free newsletter for on-going encouragement and advice at my website; http://www.lifecareerbusinesscoach.com

LIFE COACHING WORLD WIDE

Kristen L. Baker

2 Waterview Circle

Litchfield, NH 03052

Email: lifecoachbaker@aol.com

Phone: 603-204-9728

Website: http://www.lifecoachingworldwide.com
Facebook: http://www.facebook.com/pages/Life-Coaching-World-Wide-Where-Your-Dreams-Become-A-Reality/169934022691

My services include: Life Coaching and Wellness Coaching. I coach in all areas of life, anxiety disorders, fears, phobias, and self-esteem, confidence building, career, chronic pain and WHOLE Life Coaching. Visit www.lifecoachingworldwide.com opt in to receive 6 modules to unstoppable confidence.

LIVE AND LOVE RICHLY, LLC

Leslie Cunningham

7781 Nez Pierce Drive

Bozeman, MT 59715

Email: leslie@financialdating.com

Phone: 406-586-5561

Website: www.financialdating.com

Visit Leslie's web site, http://www.FinancialDating.com for free articles, free resources and to get her free report, "15 Financial Mistakes Most Couples Make and how YOU can successfully avoid them (written especially for married women entrepreneurs). And take the next steps to create more time and money in your business, marriage and life

LAURA LOPEZ

Email: Laura@Laura-Lopez.com

Phone: 713.828.8829

Website: http://womenspeakerswhorock.com/

Website: www.Laura-Lopez.com

Twitter: www.twitter.com/connectedleader

Blog: www.LauraLopezBlog.com

Become a better leader and achieve stronger results through others! Download your free e-workbook by Laura Lopez to help you assess and plan your approach to becoming a connected and committed leader. http://www.laura-lopez.com/Assets/Free_CCL_Eworkbook.pdf

DEBORAH MADISON
Phone: 713.208.9622   888.298.1888
Website: www.prepaidlegal.com/hub/dmadison and www.greatworkplan.com

MARCIA MERRILL,
AKA, The Transition Chick
Marketing Coach-Guerrilla Marketing, Career/ Life Transitions Coach
Website: www.eCareerCorner.com

Please visit my web site & sign up for your FREE Transition Triumph Toolkit! And get my newsletter as a Bonus! Contains valuable information, resources & special discounts!

MARTHA LASK CONSULTING
Martha Lask
120 West Mt. Airy Avenue
Philadelphia, PA 19119
Email: Martha@marthalask.com
Phone: 215-247-1740
Website: www.marthalask.com
Blog: http://www.marthalask-blog.com

Martha Lask Consulting provides customized consulting and coaching services to leaders, sole proprietors, management teams and staff in the non-profit and corporate sectors.   She encourages thoughtful, compassionate communication as she helps her clients shape possibilities and transform challenges into desired outcomes. Click here for free pdf resources about compassionate communication and a story about a "creative journey."

To see Martha's Blog: http://www.marthalask-blog.com/

To see Martha's Artwork:
http://www.marthalask.com/about/MarthaLask.html#holidaycardarchive

PAUL McCORMICK
"The Millionaire Mentor"
Phone: 866.333.0852
Website: theauthenticmillionaire.com

MISA LEONESSA LIFE COACHING

Misa Leonessa Garavaglia

6350 Wright St.

Felton, CA 95018

Email: inspire@misacoach.com

Phone: 831-335-1265

Website: http://www.misacoach.com

Facebook: http://www.facebook.com/pages/Misa-Leonessa-Life_coaching/196486313059

LinkedIn: http://www.linkedin.com/pub/misa-garavaglia/b/582/259

Twitter: http://twitter.com/#!/misaleonessa

Are you ready to move from survival into a thriving life? Then it could be time to work with Misa to leave that forest of mediocrity and become the person you KNOW you were meant to be. Misa can help you to have healthier, more intimate relationships, live from your authentic self, be inspired by your future instead of driven by your past, and grow a deeper spiritual life. As a Life Coach and Spiritual Director, Misa has superb listening skills, creates a safe environment for honest reflection, offers strong support and encouragement, draws out solutions from her clients, and is a creative option generator. In addition to one on one and group coaching and spiritual direction, Misa also offers classes, workshops, and seminars and is a 5 star rated speaker. Selecting the right coach or spiritual director is important. Sign up for her newsletter and Misa will give you 2 free sessions to jump start your journey into the authentic you and makes a FULL guarantee of her services or your money back! Visit her website to learn more about coaching, spiritual direction, and classes being offered. www.misacoach.com

MOTIVATIONAL MASTERMIND

Sherry Prindle

601 E Highland Ave

St. Joseph, MO 64505

Email: sherry@motivationalmastermind.com

Phone: 817-657-5301

Website: www.motivationalmastermind.com

Facebook: http://www.facebook.com/MotivationalMastermind

LinkedIn: www.linkedin.com/in/SherryPrindle

Twitter: www.twitter.com/sherryprindle

Have you always wanted to help people? Do you have an idea for making the world a better place? What if you could earn a living following your dream changing lives? Go to www.MotivationalMastermind.com and click "How Can I Make Money Changing Lives" for a free profitability analysis and mini-marketing plan with starter steps for your idea.

MONA-VIE

Ruth Van Buren

Phone: 702.437.4900 cell 702.354.4900

Website: mymonavie.com/ruth

"Drink it! Feel it! Share it!"

MY KICK ASS COACH

Vicki Garcia

1726 Hogar Dr.

San Jose, CA 95124

Email: Vicki@mykickasscoach.com

Phone: 408-723-5290

Website: http://www.mykickasscoach.com

Facebook: http://www.facebook.com/mykickasscoach

LinkedIn: http://www.linkedin.com/profile/view?id=18437827&trk=tab_pro

Twitter: www.twitter.com/mykickasscoach

If you are a professional who wants to do away with self-sabotaging thoughts and behaviors, download Success Killers, my free e-book or sign up for your Daily Kick in the Ass at http://mykickasscoach.com

MYANDA SOLUTIONS

Shaun Stephenson

Community Wealth Building

Speaking Engagements

Special Events & Programs

Inspiration and Collaboration

Life/Self-Empowerment Coaching

The Circle of Ten Movement

Email: Shaun6@comcast.net

Phone: 609-560-8370

Website: www.shaunstephenson.com

Website: http://thecircleoften.com

MY HEART TIES & APPLE CREATIVE GROUP

Leah Humphries

Entrepreneur & President

Email: leah@applecreativegroup.com

Phone: 814-833-1950 / 814-746-6325

Website: www.applecreativegroup.com

Website: www.myheartties.com

NANCY ALERT & ASSOCIATES, LLC

Nancy Alert

6226 Old Dominion Dr.

McLean, VA 22101

Email: nancy@nancyalert.com

Phone: 703-861-7355

Website: http://www.nancyalert.com

Facebook: www.facebook.com/AllAboutArlington

LinkedIn: www.linkedin.com/in/NancyAlert

Twitter: www.Twitter.com/NancyAlert

Nancy is licensed in Virginia, Washington DC and Maryland in addition to selling new construction nationally and internationally. Nancy is one of the few agents in the area who literally lists your home in the specific city, state and or countries where the buyers for your home are. We live and do business in a global economy; it's NOW time for you to hire a global agent with the personal touch, NOT just a local agent! Nancy teaches classes on how to invest in real estate, how to purchase or sale your home as a short sales, business development and social media. Nancy has had featured articles in March 2010 issue of Black Enterprise Magazine, July 2010 issue of Commonwealth Magazine (a real estate magazine) and she has written an article for DocuSign.com.

If you are selling your condo or house, downsizing, or looking for a home call Nancy Alert, Nancy specializes in Condos and single family homes in Arlington, Alexandria, McLean, Great Falls, Washington DC, Bethesda, Potomac and National Harbor. Nancy Alert can get you the condo or home you desire or sell yours fast, Nancy Alert knows how to write a winning contract in the market. With an Arlington, McLean, Washington DC life style you are close to metro, close to shopping and close to the action call Nancy Alert at 703-861-7355 or visit Nancy online at www.NancyAlert.com because you need a specialist in this Real Estate Market!

All buyers or sellers who register online for my Weekend Events Calendar and enrolled in My Customer Sweepstakes promotion will receive a chance to in a $250.00 Visa Gift Card once a month. Buyers and sellers who mention Careers from the Kitchen Table and use me as their agent will receive a $1000 credit at settlement towards closing cost and credit.

NJ HOME STAGING AND REDESIGN
Angela Gagauf
Email: a@njhomestagingandredesign.com
Phone: 201-317-9072

To learn more about NJ Home Staging and Redesign and to receive our free report, "The Top 10 Mistakes to Avoid When Showing Your Home", visit our website at www.njhomestagingandredesign.com

NUMIS NETWORK
Mark Perkett
Email: marekperk@cox.net
Phone: 949-212-2682
Website: http://www.perksprofits.com

SHEILA PEARL
Life Coach & Speaker
Email: info@LifeCoachSheila.com
Phone: 201-303-5990
Website: www.SheilaPearl.com

For "3 Magic Tips for Feeling Good NOW", go to www.LifeCoachSheila.com/3tips
For a 30-min. Discovery Conversation, call Sheila

ELIZABETH GILMOUR
Master Pilates Practitioner
Email: 281-890-3777
Phone: lissa@pilatesofchampions.com
Website: www.PilatesofChampions.com

Call or write today for an appointment to discuss how the *Pilates of Champions Experience* can work for you.

NEW WORLD VISIONS INTERNATIONAL

Tanya Jones
5 Ariel Court
Placitas, New Mexico
Email: drtanyaheals@gmail.com
Phone: 404-895-9552 or 505-895-9552
Website: www.tanyajonesmd.com
Facebook: https://www.facebook.com/#!/profile.php?id=690708895
LinkedIn: http://www.linkedin.com/pub/tanya-jones-md/3/114/549
Twitter: www.twitter.com/#!/DrTanya

ONLINEBUSINESSMANAGER.COM

Tina Forsyth
Box 29016
2515 Highlands Rd W.
Lethbridge, AB, Canada T1J 4Y2
Email: tina@onlinebusinessmanager.com
Phone: 877-576-2229
Website: www.onlinebusinessmanager.com
Facebook: www.facebook.com/tinaobm
LinkedIn: http://www.linkedin.com/in/tinaforsyth
Twitter: www.twitter.com/tinaforsyth

If you are an entrepreneur ready to take your business to the next level I invite you to get your copy of the Free Report: 100+ Ways that an Online Business Manager can Help Boost Business at www.OnlineBusinessManager.com

OUTSTANDING VIRTUAL ASSISTANCE

Peggy Knudson
Phone: 907-731-5758
Website: http://www.outstandingvirtualassistance.com
Facebook: http://www.facebook.com/#!/ovapeggy
LinkedIn: http://www.linkedin.com/in/ovapeg
Twitter: @ovapeg

Isn't it time you take your business to the next level?
Call for your free, no obligation consultation today!

OXYFRESH WORLDWIDE, INC.

Anne M. Duffy

12233 Pine Valley Club Dr.

Charlotte, NC 28277

Email: Aduff2@aol.com

Phone: 704-953-0261

Website: www.oxyfresh.com/anneduffy

Facebook: Anne Linesch Duffy

LinkedIn: http://linkdin/AnneDuffy

PRACTICAL ASSISTIVE TECHNOLOGY SOLUTIONS

Phyl T. Macomber {and Rob}

Phone: 802.484.3537

Website: www.practicalatsolutions.com

RIMI AND COMPANY

Michelle Peavy

7251 Topping Rd

Mississauga, Ontario, Canada L4T 2Y6

Email: michelle@rimipv.com

Phone: 877-643-6254

Website: www.michellepeavy.com

Facebook: http://www.facebook.com/reqs.php?type=1#!/michelle.peavy

LinkedIn: http://www.linkedin.com/pub/michelle-peavy/0/23a/3b4

Twitter: @michellepeavy

CATERINA RANDO, MA, MCC

Business strategist, master coach, speaker & publisher

Author of *Learn to Power Think*

Phone: 415 668-4535
Email: cat@attractclientswithease.com
Website: http://www.attractclientswithease.com
Website: http://www.powerdynamicspub.com
Website: http://www.caterinaspeaks.com

Call or email Caterina and mention this book to receive a $200.00 discount on any coaching course or book publication project.

HELEN RACZ

Teacher of Vibrational Law, Speaker, Energy Healer and CieAura Founding Master Retailer.
Phone: 281-578-7949
Email: helenracz@comcast.net
Website: www.HelenRacz.com

For free resources to support entrepreneurs with releasing limiting beliefs and energetic blocks to prosperity, go to www.HelenRacz.com/cieaura

RAPID BUSINESS BUILDING

Christina Scheiner, the Massive Income Mentor
Email: info@rapidbusinessbuilding.com
Phone: (415) 897-7001
For the free Ebook, Rapid Building Building NOW !!!, go to:
www.RapidBusinessBuildingNOW.com

DAWN RICKABAUGH, BROKER

Owner Financing Coach
Note Queen / Rickabaugh Realty
Phone: 626.292.1875
Fax: 626.451.0454
Website: www.NoteQueen.com

Download your free copy of my book, "Seller Financing on Steroids"

MARY RIVES

Energetics of Health and Wellness

Website: www.energeticsofhealthandwellness.com

RM CREATIONS

Renee and Major Jones

Phone: 713.443.3748 281.880.8668

Website: www.rmcreations.com

ROBERT "ROSIE" AND VIKKI "TAYLOR" ROSENKRANZ

Vikki Cummings-Rosenkranz, Internationally Certified Energy Wellness Consultant

Email: Rosenkranz@EarthPatriot.net

Phone: 713.298.5808 281.770.7092

Website: www.EarthPatriot.Net

Website: www.EarthPatriot.Info (catalog and income opportunity page)

SBS

Susan Bock

8201 Newman Ave. Ste 102

Huntington Beach, CA 92647

Email: susan@susanbock.com

Phone: 714-847-1566

Website: www.susanbock.com

Facebook: http://www.facebook.com/susanbock

LinkedIn: www.linkedin.com/in/susanbockcoachandspeaker

Twitter: www.twitter.com/susanbockspeaks

Susan Bock Transformational Speaker and Coach.   Visit her website and download free resources - such a Learn to Build Your Self-Muscles or Are YOU Stuck in a Rut?

SC HEALTH SOLUTIONS

Sharon Cadle, CEO/Founder

Website: www.LeSharonbeautiboutique.com

SECOND TIME AROUND

Lorraine Edey, PhD, LCSW, ACC

PO Box 1779

Jasper, GA 30143

Email: loridey@aol.com

Phone: 678-454-1272

Website: www.secondtimearoundlove.com

Facebook: http://www.facebook.com/lorraine.edey

LinkedIn: http://www.linkedin.com/in/lorraineedey

Second Time Around Love believes that couples who are married for the second time can escape the pain of yet another divorce by learning to thrive and enjoy passionate, intimate, loving lives together.

You bring history, knowledge and the joy of your new love – and we provide guidance, inspiration and passionate recipes for extraordinary relationships and the marriage of your dreams.

Dr. Lorraine Edey is a Certified Imago Therapist and Relationship Coach whose experience in psychology, social work and relationship building spans more than 30 years. Her innovative 10 step process is a full proof method that helped couples in their 40's and 50's attain the next level of marriage mastery and enjoy a new love mindset.

You can contact Dr. Edey for a no cost strategy session. Secxaroundlove@aol.com

SYNERGY BREAKTHROUGHS

Sandra Tucker Jones

1660 Liege Dr.

Henderson, NV 89012

Email: synergybreakthroughs@gmail.com

Phone: 303-400-8875

Website: www.synergybreakthroughs.com

Facebook: http://www.facebook.com/sandytjones

LinkedIn: http://www.linkedin.com/pubs/sandy-jones/4/231/206

Go to www.SynergyBreakthroughs.com to discover more about life coaching and hypnotherapy, and to receive your free Vision Board Screensaver!

THE TOP PRODUCER GROUP, LLC
Carol Mazur
8722 New Forest Drive
Wilmington, NC 28411
Email: coachcarolmazur@gmail.com
Phone: 910-681-1110
Website: www.thetopprotraining.com
Facebook: http://www.facebook.com/RECoaching
LinkedIn: http://www.linkedin.com/in/carolmazur

The Top Producer Group, LLC offers affordable real estate coaching membership options, giving EVERY agent access to personalized one on one real estate coaching and training. Our Integrity Rule ensures that everything we share has been tested and proven to work by current top producers. Visit http://www.TheTopProducerGroup.com for FREE Coaching Tips.

A SOUTHERN VOICE FOR BOLD SELF-EXPRESSION
Tuck Self, The Rebel Belle
Email: Tuck@TheRebelBelle.com
Phone: (803)736-9240
Website: www.therebelbelle.com
Grab a copy of my free e-guide!
If you are ready to liberate yourself from past conditioning, contact Tuck at (803) 736-9240 or Tuck@therebelbelle.com

LORI SNYDER
Phone: 516-708-9261
Website: www.coachlorisnyder.com

Would you like to get a fresh start towards empowering yourself? During this six week e-course, you will discover, explore and create a whole new outlook to start building your best life. You will also learn powerful new tools that you can use to make the best decisions and choices to become truly happy and successful in every area of your life.
GO to www.Coachlorisnyder.com and go to the products page and sign -up for free e-course.

TAKE CHARGE! WITH DR. KATHRYN

Kathryn Reeves

102 Lifton Ct.

Roseville, CA 95747

Email: drkathryn@drkathrynonline.com

Phone: 916-663-8266

Website: http://www.drkathrynonline.com

Facebook: http://www.facebook.com/TakeChargeCoach

Twitter: drkathryn1

I provide spiritual guidance to those called to step onto the spiritual path. I require commitment and a willingness to let go of old, negative thought patterns and beliefs and to hold an open mind. Join my list on my website and receive a F*R*E*E* "Spiritual Journey Starter Kit" as well as an opportunity to schedule a F*R*E*E* Discovery phone call! Visit http://www.drkathrynonline.com

TAXMAMA®

Eva Rosenberg, MBA, EA

Phone: 800-594-9829   818-993-1565

Website: www.TaxMama.com Where taxes are fun!

Website: www.TaxMama.com/TaxQuips   And Answers are free

Website: www.IRSExams.com Become an Enrolled Agent

Website: www.MarketWatch.com   the TaxWatch column

Twitter: www.twitter.com/taxmama

THE ENCHANTED SELF

Dr. Barbara Becker Holstein, Founder

Phone: 732.571.1200

Website: www.enchantedself.com

THE NATURAL EXECUTIVE

Timi Gleason

Email: timi.gleason@gmail.com

Phone: 619-333-6945 (google voice)

Website: www.fatandthirstyradio.com   www.thenaturalexecutive.com

Senior Health & Leadership Coach

- Company: The Natural Executive
  "Specializing in quick weight loss & reducing the need for prescription drugs"
- http://TNE.tsfl.com (stands for: The Natural Executive - Take Shape for Life)
- www.RX-FreeZone.com (Timi's blog about water and hydration)
- National client base
- Call to discuss your goals at 619-333-6945 (Pacific Time)
- Timi.Gleason@gmail.com
- Email me with your name and address for my two free articles:
  "Slender Body; Young Body"
  "My Doctor Said I Can Stop My Meds"

THE SHATTERED CEILING CORP

Yvonne Silver

24 Evansdale Landing NW

Calgary, Alb, Canada

Email: Yvonne@theshatteredceiling.com

Phone: 403-999-4749

Website: www.theshatteredceiling.com

LinkedIn: http://ca.linkedin.com/in/yvonnesilver

Twitter: www.twitter.com/shatteredsilver

LIVING ROYALTY NATION – "COACHING FOR WOMEN THAT LITERALLY PAYS"

Debora D. Jenkins

Email: Admin@DeboraDJenkins.com

Phone: 718-644-0951

Website: http://www.deboradjenkins.com

Facebook: http://www.facebook.com/LivingRoyalty

THE VISION BOARD TRAINING

Bonnie Bruderer

Website: VisionBoardParties.com

Facebook: www.facebook.com/VisionBoards

Will you be the next business to have a Vision Board Kit? We make the product, you make $$$! $500 of the private label fee www.TheVisionBoardTraining.com

THE VOICE OF THERMOGRAPHY
Dr. Robert L. Kane
Phone: 650.868.0353
website: www.thermographyexpert.com

THERAPURE.COM HEALTH ESSENTIALS
Jeff Tollefson
30776 Mirage Circle
Menifee, CA 92584
Email: jeff@therapure.com
Phone: 877-846-8669   951-679-3519
Website: http://www.therapure.com
Facebook: www.facebook.com/therapure
YouTube: www.youtube.com/therapure

KALIN THOMAS
Email: kalinthomas@yahoo.com
Phone: 404-863-8182
Website: www.seetheworldproductions.com

For more on how Kalin got into the TV industry and travel writing, listen to her 1-hour interview with Raven at http://www.womenpower-radio.com/archives.html.

KAREN TOMPKINS
Classical Feng Shui Consultant
Email: karen@fengshuibeyondthemyth.com
Phone: 214-774-9019
Website: www.FengShuiBeyondtheMyth.com

For *The 8 Myths of Feng Shui* and *From Hitler to Haiti, 56 Years of Feng Shui Influences on Global Events,* go to www.FengShuiBeyondtheMyth.com

UNFORGETTABLE BRANDS
Judy Winslow
5592 Eastwind Dr
Sarasota, FL 34233
Email: jw@unforgettablebrands.com
Phone: 941-921-7440
Website: http://www.unforgettablebrands.com
Facebook: https://www.facebook.com/judywins
LinkedIn: http://www.linkedin.com/in/judywins
Twitter: http://twitter.com/#!/judywin

We all want to be seen, heard and remembered. A sustainable business can change the lives of many. Touch more people -- Leave a lasting impression. For entrepreneurs and game-changers interested in accelerating results, start with my F.REE gift to you – the 'Being Unforgettable Starter Kit', which can be found at http://www.UnforgettableBrands.com

UPYOURTELESALES
Lynn Hidy
PO Box 42
Paul Smiths, NY 12970
Email: lynn@upyourtelesales.com
Phone: 315-751-0146
Website: http://www.upyourtelesales.com
Facebook: https://www.facebook.com/pages/UpYourTeleSalescom/94567576544
LinkedIn: https://www.linkedin.com/in/lynnhidy
Twitter: http://twitter.com/#!/upyourtelesales

Sign up and receive our easy 3 step objection handling technique, never be surprised by the objections you hear the most again at http://tiny.cc/SignUpYourTeleSales

VISION IN PURPOSE COACHING AND TRAINING
Anita Kirkman
254 Wedgewood Terrace Rd,
Madison, AL 35757
Email: anita@visioininpurpose.com
Phone: 256.721.4553
Website: www.visioninpurpose.com

Facebook: http://bit.ly/visioninpurposefb
LinkedIn: http://linkd.in/coachanitak

ENLIGHTEN - EMPOWER – TRANSFORM. We empower home office business women to prosper by transforming their beliefs around time, money, self, and leadership. Get your "Success Building" Virtual Gift Bag including 3 powerful products that will reveal key money making mindsets that empower you to:

1. Conquer the five common mistakes that kill your revenue and keep you stuck.

2. Learn all about ideas that sales superstars use to become who they are today and how you can become like them too!

3. Master the mindsets behind the marketing that help you and your business grow healthily and smoothly.

DR. TAFFY WAGNER, D.MIN

Certified Educator in Personal Finances and Consultant www.WifeCFO.com
Email: drtaffy@wifecfo.com
Phone: 303-576-0670

For a no-cost report on how to settle debt, you can go to www.wifecfo.com/products

WELLNESS BEYOND BELIEF
Khatira Aboulfatova
230 Westcott St. Suite 215
Houston, TX 77007
Email: Khatira_a@wellnessbeyondbelief.com
Phone: 832-876-9147
Website: http://www.wellnessbeyondbelief.com
Facebook: http://www.facebook.com/khatira.aboulfatova
LinkedIn: http://www.linkedin.com/pub/khatira-aboulfatova-m-d/1/255/921

Being healthy is a lifestyle by design. Love working with people, who is looking for better ways to transform their health physically, mentally and financially. You can change the way you age naturally from inside and out; you will look and feel 10-20 years younger, vibrant and energetic like you were in your youth. Visit http://www.wellnessbeyondbelief.com for more information.

WESTCHASE SPECIALTY PHARMACY

Christina Barnett, Pharm.D.

11301 Richmond Ave, St K-101

Houston, TX 77082

Email: CBarnett@WestchaseRx.com

Phone: 281-497-5214

Fax: 281-497-5215

Website: www.WestchaseRx.com

Facebook: www.Facebook.com/WestchaseRx

People aren't made from cookie cutters; their medicine shouldn't be, either. Westchase Specialty Pharmacy provides customized medications to match individual patients' needs. Medicine can be made to address personal medical dilemmas like hormone and thyroid balance and pain management. Medicine can be made to suit you better by combining multiple meds into fewer (smaller) capsules, making them into liquids or lozenges or lollipops, or making them sustained-release for fewer doses each day. Medicines that are on back-order or have been discontinued by manufacturers can be provided by our team of specially trained compounders. Even your pets – from fluffy to furry to feathery – can be medicated more easily and accurately with our help. Visit the pharmacy for a tour of our amazing facility, to meet our outstanding Patient Care Team, and receive a special "Welcome Gift" of 50% your first Private Consultation or Personalized Nutritional Supplement Regimen.

WESTERN & SOUTHERN LIFE

Craig Anthony Nicholas

Sales Representative

Phone: 800-289-0849

Website: www.wslife.com

WINGS FOR WOMEN

Keiko Hsu

152 Lombard St #704

San Francisco, CA 94111

Email: keiko@wingsforwomen.net

Phone: 415-738-2313

Website: http://www.wingsforwomen.net

Facebook: http://www.facebook.com/pages/Wings-for-women/197249213658076

LinkedIn: http://www.linkedin.com/in/keikohsu
Twitter: wingsforwomen

Live a Joyful Life After Divorce ... Attain new heights in your life, career, relationships! www.WingsForWomen.net. If you're a busy, career-focused woman who is recently divorced and ready to move on to reinvent your life, visit our website www.WingsForWomen.net and get our free gifts: - A special report "Three Myths that Keep Women Trapped After Divorce ... and How to Break Free"- "Your Passions Discovery Tool" ... A Guide To Identify Your Top 5 Passions

WINNING AT LIFE INTERNATIONAL, LLC

LAWRENCE COLE

The Xtreme Marketing Guy
Email: lcole@xtrememarketingguy.com
Phone: 888.474.2161
Website: http://www.xtrememarketingguy.com
Facebook: http://www.facebook.com/xtrememarketingguy

To get your FREE report on "The 7 Deadly Sins of Small Business Marketing", Visit http://www.xtrememarketingdoneforyou.com

WOMAN'S WELLNESS CENTER

Terry Tribble, MBA, CMF

Email: info@houstonlacebrow.com
Phone: 713.522.PINK (7465)
Website: www.HoustonLaceBrows.com

WORLDSPEAK LANGUAGE PRESCHOOLS AND IN-HOME CHILD CARE SYSTEM

Angelika Putintseva

Director and Founder
Email: info@WorldSpeakSchool.com
Phone: 310-441-5222
Website: www.WorldSpeakSchool.com

YOUR ANGEL GUIDE FOR SUCCESS

Tami Gulland, ATP, CM

5133 Caton Lane

Waunakee, WI 53597

Email: tami@angelsforsuccess.com

Phone: 608-850-6437

Website: www.angelsforsuccess.com

Facebook: http://www.facebook.com/tamigulland

LinkedIn: www.linkedin.com/in/tamigulland

Twitter: www.twitter.com/tamigulland

Reduce stress, struggle and overwhelm now! Increase your connection with your Angels and intuition. Get your free report "5 Surefire Steps to Get the Life and Career Answers You Need from Your Angels" at: www.AngelsForSuccess.com

YOUR EVERYDAY EMOTIONAL INTELLIGENCE COACH

Patricia Clason, RCC

2437 N Booth St.

Milwaukee, WI 53212

Email: patricia@patriciaclason.com

Phone: 414-374-5433 / 800-236-4692

Website: http://www.patriciaclason.com

Facebook: www.facebook.com/patricia.clason

Linkedin: http://www.linkedin.com/in/patriciaclason

Twitter: http://twitter.com/EQCoachClason

Emotional Intelligence Coaching is inner strength training for success. Learn more with free resources at www.accountabilitycoachingassociates.comand a free e-book at www.lightly.com/faith.   Since you are reading this book, you are my perfect client!!

"The future belongs to those who believe in their dreams"

Eleanor Roosevelt

"You can be whatever you want to be. There is inside you all of the potential to be whatever you want to be.

All of the Energy to do whatever you want to do.

Imagine yourself as you would like to be doing what you want to do and then each day take one step toward your dream. And though at times it may seem TOO difficult to continue, hold on to your dream.

One morning you are going to awake to find that you are the person you dreamed of and that you are truly doing what you wanted to do.   Yes, for you your vision has come true simply because you had the courage to believe in your potential and the strength, despite your challenge, to hold on to your dream."

Donna Levine

Get the First Edition of Careers From the Kitchen Table Home Business Directory!

Learn more business secrets from the experts, explore more than 60 stories from those who have made the move and enjoy more great recipes for the busy entrepreneur!

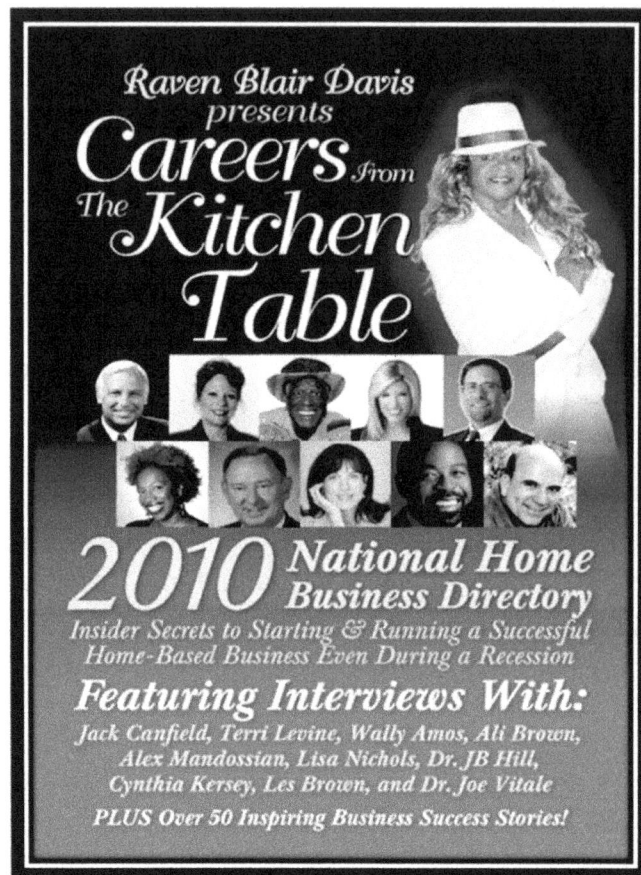

Order Your Copy Today!

http://www.2010homebizdirectory.com

Careers from the Kitchen Table Home Business Directory Second Edition